THE AMERICAN REPUBLIC

ORESTES A. BROWNSON:
WORKS IN POLITICAL PHILOSOPHY

SERIES EDITOR: Gregory S. Butler

VOLUME I
The American Republic
Its Constitution, Tendencies and Destiny

The American Republic

Its Constitution, Tendencies and Destiny

ORESTES A. BROWNSON

with a new introduction by Peter Augustine Lawler

ISI Books

2003

The American Republic *was first published in 1865 by*
P. O'Shea, 27 Barclay Street, New York, New York.

Cataloging-in-Publication Data

Brownson, Orestes Augustus (1803-1876)
  The American republic : its constitution, tendencies and destiny /
  Orestes A. Brownson — Wilmington, DE : ISI Books, 2002,
  [c1865].

  p. / cm.

  ISBN 1-882926-86-2
  1. Political science. 2. United States — Politics and government.
  I. Title.

  JK216 .B76 2002   2002108427
  320.4/73--dc21   0211

Printed in Canada

Cover design by Glenn Pierce
Interior design by Kara Björklund

ISI Books
the imprint of the Intercollegiate Studies Institute
3901 Centerville Road
Wilmington, Del. 19807
www.isibooks.org

*T*o the Hon. George Bancroft,
the erudite, philosophical, and eloquent Historian of the United States, this feeble attempt to set forth the principles of Government, and to explain and defend the Constitution of the American Republic, is respectfully dedicated, in memory of old friendship, and as a slight homage to genius, ability, patriotism, private worth, and public service, by the Author.

Contents

Editor's Preface to the ISI Edition

*T*his edition of *The American Republic* represents the first release in ISI Books's projected five-volume serial collection titled *Orestes Brownson: Works in Political Philosophy*. As the first comprehensive reprinting of Brownson's political writings in over a century, the series is intended to be of use to the growing body of students and academicians interested in the scholarly exploration of one of the most significant Catholic political thinkers in American history.

Orestes Brownson was well known among his contemporaries as an influential, and at times controversial, member of the New England Transcendentalist movement. This early influence would be short lived, for upon his conversion to Catholicism in 1844 Brownson's literary career gradually faded into near oblivion among the American intellectual elite, save for the occasional spirited encounter with the American church hierarchy. In our own day, however, his work has attracted an unprecedented level of attention. Since the resurrection of Brownson marked by the 1939 publication of Arthur M. Schlesinger Jr.'s *Orestes A. Brownson: A Pilgrim's Progress*, several highly informative biographies have appeared, including works by Doren Whalen (*Granite for God's House*, 1941), Theodore Maynard

(*Orestes Brownson: Yankee, Radical Catholic,* 1943), Americo D. Lapati (*Orestes A. Brownson,* 1965), and Thomas R. Ryan (*Orestes A. Brownson: A Definitive Biography,* 1976). In addition, a number of important monographs, collections of essays, and doctoral dissertations have added significantly to the literature. Important works include Thomas R. Ryan's *The Sailor's Snug Harbor: Studies in Brownson's Thought,* 1952; Lawrence Roemer's *Brownson on Democracy and the Trend Toward Socialism,* 1953; Per Sveino's *Orestes A. Brownson's Road to Catholicism,* 1970; Hugh T. Marshall's *Orestes Brownson and the American Republic,* 1971; Leonard Gilhooley's *Contradiction and Dilemma,* 1972; Russell Kirk's *Orestes Brownson: Selected Political Essays,* 1955 and 1990; Gregory S. Butler's *In Search of the American Spirit: The Political Thought of Orestes Brownson,* 1992; and R. A. Herrera's *Orestes Brownson: Sign of Contradiction,* 1999.

To what do we owe this revival of perhaps the most significant Catholic apologist in American history? One may argue that the sobering impact of the World Wars and the dismal failure of utopian optimism have compelled scholars to re-examine thinkers such as Brownson. His call for a return to the traditional wisdom of classical and Christian civilization is now viewed by some as a welcome change from the secularized socialist culture that has been building throughout the modern age. Moreover, the substance of what Brownson had to say in the mid-nineteenth century about the essential compatibility between American constitutionalism and Catholic moral and social teaching has attracted a great deal of attention from contemporary scholars who fancy themselves on the cusp of a "catholic moment" in the postmodern West.

The particular essays and books to be included in this series have been carefully selected as highly representative of major themes across the full historical spectrum of Brownson's career as a political philosopher. The primary aim of the series is to make available a comprehensive array of materials dealing broadly with theoretical, philosophical, and theological considerations as they have a bearing upon questions of political order, particularly in the American context. (Of less concern are essays, book reviews, and other sources that focus exclusively on contemporary and immediate political issues of Brownson's day, that is, pieces that are of only antiquarian interest.) With this in mind, the series will, of course, include the widely studied works on political theory and philosophy, such as *The American Republic* and the critical essays on socialism. Also included will be many of the little known early writings dealing with Brownson's views on religion and humanitarian socialism, most of which were not included in the original collected works published in the 1880s (*Brownson's Works*, ed. Henry F. Brownson, 20 vols. [Detroit: Thorndike Nourse, 1882–87]). In addition, the series will feature a representative selection of the dozens of mid- to late-career analyses of religion, theology, and civilization that best illuminate the distinctive elements of Brownson's mature political thought. As series editor it is my hope a collection of this type will be of use to the contemporary student of American politics and culture by bringing the original "catholic moment" thinker back into the discussion.

> — *Gregory S. Butler*
> *New Mexico State University*
> *September 2002*

PETER AUGUSTINE LAWLER

Introduction to the ISI Edition

Orestes Brownson (1803–76) was born in Vermont and into poverty. At a young age he moved with his family to Saratoga County,
New York.[1] There he was largely self-educated, but he still managed
to memorize almost all of the Scriptures by the age of fourteen. Following the example set by his family, for most of his life he was an
ardent religious seeker, never attaching himself for long to any one
church. (His brother Oren eventually became a Mormon, and Orestes
eventually became a Catholic.) Brownson was in the first half of the
1820s a Presbyterian, but he left that church because of its harsh and
rigid discipline and its extreme rejection of reason in favor of revelation. He then joined the Universalist ministry and stayed there until
he concluded that the Bible did not really teach universal salvation.
For a while he was a devotee of the form of secular, utopian socialism
taught by Robert Owen and Fanny Wright. He was then a humanitarian political activist, belonging to the New York Workingman's
Party and denouncing laissez-faire capitalism as worse than medieval

*This introduction depended at every turn on the careful, capable, and exceedingly patient
work of Diane Land. Many Berry College students also contributed, particularly Elizabeth Amato and Kelly Walsh. Thanks once again to the Earhart Foundation for its generous support.*

serfdom. When he became an atheist, he was the only kind of atheist he could be: a militant atheist.

In the 1830s, Brownson became a Unitarian minister and friend of William Ellery Channing. He began to read contemporary, progressivist French and German philosophy, particularly the French thinker Benjamin Constant. Brownson was an advocate of the progressive church of the future, one that would synthesize the partial truths embodied in Catholicism and Protestantism. And in 1838, with the intention of getting Americans to think more carefully and synthetically about religious and political issues, he founded a quarterly review. He wrote an enormous number of essays and reviews for quarterlies over the years, and they were and are the source of his controversial reputation and influence. Brownson's second and far more enduring periodical, *Brownson's Quarterly Review*, contained almost nothing but his own essays and reviews and was published from 1844 to 1864 and again from 1873 to 1875.

Brownson from 1836 to 1841 was an important spokesperson for the Transcendentalist movement in American thought, generally sharing the views of Thoreau and Emerson. His Unitarianism was at one with his Transcendentalism. He was, in other words, a pantheist and a Gnostic. He taught that Jesus Christ was merely a model man, that Christ's human perfection is within the reach of us all and somehow both merely natural and divine. During his Transcendentalist phase, Brownson rejected orthodox Christianity because it teaches man's alienation from God. He identified the voice of humanity with the voice of God, and he taught that the kingdom of God—which was perfectly just and free of all oppression—could be established on earth.[2] He also predicted the inevitability of a class war almost a decade before *The Communist Manifesto*.

The socialist-Transcendentalist Brownson considered himself a radical but not a revolutionary. He understood his writing, as Gregory

Butler explains, to be an "outgrowth of the American tradition, and he thought he saw in the American Constitution the germ of the new, perfected organization of mankind."[3] Brownson saw in the Jacksonian Democratic party a vehicle for realizing his ideals on an American foundation, and he made an active effort to direct that party's thought. He became "President Martin Van Buren's man in Massachusetts," and he accepted a patronage job from the government.[4]

Butler astutely notes that Brownson's new American religion really was not incompatible "with some of the major philosophical presuppositions present at the founding of American liberalism," particularly Jefferson's "modern ersatz religion." Butler's view is that "Brownson saw his political thought as merely a step toward the fulfillment of the secret wishes of his countrymen," which were, and are, to find, as Brownson himself remarked, "an easier way to get to heaven than by penance, mortification, self-denial, and detachment from the world."[5] It is very likely that had Brownson remained a Transcendentalist, he would be widely and admiringly studied as part of the mainstream development of American thought.

The presidential election of 1840 was a political disaster for Brownson. Thousands of copies of his article "The Laboring Classes" were distributed by the Whig party as evidence that the Democratic party secretly intended to abolish wage slavery, and that article really did contribute to Van Buren's defeat. Brownson's uncritical, progressive faith in democracy was destroyed, and he subsequently became "a conservative in politics." That political conversion was a prelude to his rapid advance toward "religious conservatism."[6]

No doubt also contributing to Brownson's new political moderation was the fact that soon after the election he read Aristotle's *Politics* for the first time and "studied the histories and constitutions after ancient Greece and Rome."[7] He began to read and think like a statesman. By 1844, Arthur Schlesinger Jr. complains, Brownson had "swung to the far right," favoring John C. Calhoun for president. The Democratic historian rightly notices a significant change in Brownson's politics, but he mistakes moderate conservatism for fanatical extremism.[8]

In the early 1840s, Brownson moved toward orthodox Christian theology. He learned from Pierre Leroux that any progress man might make cannot depend on himself alone, but rather on his communion with, and the continuous action of, a Creator. He also concluded that belief in supernatural revelation and creation is not incompatible with reason. More than that, he now saw that "the Transcendentalists exalt impulse and feelings above the very rational nature which is constitutive of the human personality."[9] Brownson was baptized in the Roman Catholic Church in 1844. Bishop John B. Fitzpatrick of Boston received him into the Church, urging him to forget about philosophical speculation and to adhere to textbook scholasticism. Brownson tried to follow the bishop's advice but failed; the consistently orthodox but also relentlessly philosophical Brownson was more often than not at odds with the American Church hierarchy.

In 1857 Brownson wrote *The Convert,* a quite singular and philosophic interpretation of his conversion. In this book, he makes clear the thought that led him to the Church and away from the humanitarian and sometimes Gnostic forms of thought that had guided his earlier devotion to radical social reform. *The Convert* also shows his mastery of the best European Catholic thought of his time, and of the Thomistic and Augustinian components of the great Catholic tradition. Brownson was a genuine scholar who read difficult books closely in the languages in which they were written. But he was not primarily a scholar. As Russell Kirk puts it, "Orestes Brownson knew practically everybody and wrote about practically everything in the nineteenth century."[10] According to Schlesinger, Brownson's most famous biographer, "In the course of a long and stormy life, Brownson took almost every side of every hot question and was a sledgehammer controversialist at every step along his tempestuous path."[11]

Brownson was known and greatly respected by many of the best European Catholic thinkers. The most extravagant judgment came from the French theologian Alphonse Gratry: "I firmly believe that America is not proud enough of her Brownson. He is the keenest critic of the nineteenth century, an indomitable logician, a disinterested lover of the truth, more than a philosopher, a sage, as sharp as Aristotle, as lofty as Plato, the Newman of America."[12] Lord Acton's high judgment concerning Brownson's thought is well known. He was also admired by John Henry Newman, despite Brownson's rather extreme attack on Newman's work concerning the development of Christian doctrine. More impressive than this disagreement are the similarities between the two converts. Newman certainly thought so: He offered Brownson the first professorship at his proposed Catholic University of Ireland. But opposition from the Irish in America forced Brownson to decline the honor. The erudite Yankee and the Irish immigrants, in fact, never did warm up to each other. The immigrant interest was in securing ethnic and religious enclaves in America; Brownson wanted to convert all Americans to the true faith.

Brownson prided himself on being the first American who was not an abolitionist to favor the emancipation of slaves as a measure to win the Civil War. He thought that Divine Providence had given the "general" or national government the power to abolish slavery in the name of natural justice without assuming unconstitutional powers.[13] His belligerence on the matter, including his demand that all Catholics, especially priests and bishops, be loyal to the nation's cause and opposed to slavery, put him at odds with the archbishop of New York. It also led to his nomination by the Republicans as a candidate for Congress from his district in New Jersey. The thought was that some Democrats would vote for Brownson because he was a Catholic. That did not happen, and his religion lost him a considerable portion of the Republican vote. He did not come close to getting elected.

After discontinuing his quarterly, Brownson had no source of income, and he had no savings. Seeing his plight, his friends in New York, including Father Isaac Hecker, arranged an annuity for him, one that would pay him $1,000 a year for life. This gift, which might be regarded as providential, gave Brownson the leisure to write *The American Republic*, which was published in 1866. But now that Brownson had the leisure to write, he was without an audience, "completely forgotten by all my countrymen, except a small number of personal friends & without the slightest influence on public affairs."[14] That isolation may too have been providential, insofar as it allowed him to write less polemically and be more detached than usual from partisan strife. Most of *The American Republic* may have been written before Brownson was given the annuity, and most of the ideas had been expressed in earlier articles. But the book's final form is still more measured, more directed to the whole human good, and more edifying and philosophical in its view of his nation's distinctive and unprecedented future, than any of his particular articles.

In the essay that follows, my purpose is simply to clarify and assess the significance of Brownson's purpose and argument in this fine—and unjustly neglected—American, Catholic book. I refer to Brownson's other writings when I judge them helpful, but I do not consider the fascinating and complex issue of the development of Brownson's thought at all. My modest and relatively unhistorical goal is to consider what he was thinking when he was writing this particular work. To make Brownson's often rather strange observations accessible to students of American politics and philosophy today, I illuminate them with comparisons to the thought of Alexis de Tocqueville, whose *Democracy in America* is often viewed as the best book on America and the best book on democracy. Brownson and Tocqueville often make the same friendly but tough criticisms of American democracy. Evidence of that fact, I hope, will prompt readers to spend some time with Brownson so that they can come to appreciate his deep and distinctive contribution to American thought.

Reason and Revelation:

Brownson's Devotion to the Truth

The American Republic is Brownson's comprehensive political work. For Brownson, that means it must be much more than a book about politics. He says that he "endeavored throughout" this book "to refer my particular political views to their general principle, and to show that the general principles asserted have their origin and ground in the great, universal, and unchanging principles of the universe itself" (cviii).[15] Political life cannot be understood simply on its own terms. All that exists is created through the Creator's rational will and can be understood as a whole that incorporates all aspects of human being.

There is no other place to begin but with Brownson's striking and singular devotion to the truth, the whole truth. Love of truth, his friend Isaac Hecker wrote, was his predominant passion.[16] More than, say, the author of the Declaration of Independence, Brownson is concerned with the truth—and much less with the rhetorical effectiveness—of what he says about nature and God. Rarely is there indirection or equivocation in his writing. When he writes rhetorically or for edification, he aims to elevate his audience. *The American Republic* has many rhetorical moments, but their intention is to increase the devotion of his nation and his fellow citizens to the truth about God and man.

One sign of Brownson's devotion to the truth is that never has a thinker been so willing to admit that he has simply changed his mind. Brownson calls *The American Republic* "not only the latest, but . . . my last [statement] on politics or government," and he asserts that the book "must be taken as the authentic, and the only authentic statement of my political views and convictions." Anything he said before that conflicts with that statement he now retracts; he boasts, "I have never been the slave of my own past." He now, as always, regards truth as "dearer to me than my own opinions" (cv–cvi). And he is particularly hard on those who prefer opinions or theories to a candid analysis of the facts.

Brownson adds that he "honor[s] virtue wherever I see it, and accept[s] truth wherever I find it" (cx); the first chapter of this book begins with the ancient maxim about "the whole of human wisdom . . . , 'Know Thyself'" (1). He was, in a most Socratic way, relentless in his examination of opinion, and he was never so partisan as not to acknowledge that almost all opinion, even that of his political enemies, embodies part of the truth. Even the opinions of political adversaries must be integrated dialectically into a more comprehensive view, one that transcends the partisanship of a particular time and place. The truth, properly understood, is the friend of virtue. There is no need to lie to support virtue. The truth is that there is natural, political, and divine support for acting morally, and the man who knows *that* is, in fact, furthest from despair.

Brownson had a Socratic love of wisdom, but his love was informed by a Christian premise. Plato and Aristotle distinguished between the love of wisdom that animates the few and the lies or conventions that characterize political life. They were not opposed to deception when writing for a political audience, and they wondered inconclusively about whether the gods or nature really support moral aspirations. Modern thinkers, insofar as they are informed by Machiavelli, connect truth to effectiveness. They are pragmatists. What is true is what works in changing the world. The truth is not to be discovered, but made. As Marx said, the point of philosophy is not to understand the world, but to transform it, because the truth is that we can only understand what we have made and can control.

Later modern thinkers, those influenced by Pascal and Nietzsche, are existentialists. They are convinced that Machiavellian will cannot succeed in completely remaking the world. The pragmatic project is, finally, an ineffective diversion from the terrible truth, which is that our deepest longings for knowing and loving cannot be satisfied. Only our courage, not our knowledge, can keep us from despair. Christian teaching, however, says that human beings have been made to know the truth, and that what they can know is fundamentally Good News. Brownson should grab our attention, then, because he so clearly affirms philosophic views that are neither pragmatic nor existentialist. And he does not point back to Greece in an effort to bypass the Christians. As a philosopher especially, he is a dissenter from the dominant trends in the American tradition. By thinking about Brownson as a dissident, we can connect him to the struggle on behalf of the truth, and against ideological lies, that was undertaken by the anticommunist dissidents Aleksandr Solzhenitsyn and Václav Havel.[17]

Brownson became a Catholic because he thought that the realism associated with St. Thomas Aquinas was true. He was a boldly intellectual Catholic convert. For Brownson, true religion *must* be catholic, that is, universal. It must express the true solidarity of the whole human race, of all rational and finite beings, under the Creator of all that exists. According to Brownson, the truth is that "all real principles are catholic," because "there is nothing sectarian either in nature or revelation" (cix). Reason and revelation are the two ways human beings have of knowing the truth, and Brownson affirms "the catholicity of truth under all its aspects."[18] But he does not fail to distinguish between reason and revelation, between what we can know through our natural capabilities and what we can only know through supernatural authority. Brownson contends that "in philosophy, reason, which is the same in all men, and in each man, is the only authority recognizable."[19] Intellectual freedom is indispensable not only for those who

XXII   *The American Republic*

engage in philosophical inquiry—in principle, all of us—but also for the Church. The true Church aims to show the agreement between philosophy, or science, and faith. This can be done not by subordinating science to dogma, but by allowing the dogmas of faith to be challenged by free minds. Brownson is adamant that there can be no "official" Catholic philosophy, not even that of St. Thomas.

Brownson finds that "[t]he principal cause of the deplorable state of philosophy" in Catholic colleges is "the lack of free independent thinkers—in the fact that we philosophize not for the sake of the truth, but for the sake of some philosophic theory, ancient or modern, and always more or less under the weight of authority."[20] He does affirm authorities to which it is necessary and reasonable to submit: revelation, tradition, and natural and historical facts. But in philosophy he opposes "traditionalism" because "if it means any thing, [it] denies to philosophy to hold from reason as its principle, and seeks to place it on the same line with supernatural theology, as a discipline to be received on authority."[21] He reports that he learned from his study of Catholic theologians that the Fall did not destroy nor essentially distort human reason: "The human mind cannot have all science, but it has real science as far as it goes, and real science is the knowledge of things as they are, not as they are not" (58). The "traditionalism" Brownson opposed at the time was the largely French movement led by Bonald, Maistre, Lamennais, Bonnetty, and others. But his argument that "[t]raditional philosophy is a misnomer" has, of course, a much wider application.[22]

Brownson emphatically does not view natural reason and supernatural theology as antagonistic human goods; he does not view their relationship as that of Athens versus Jerusalem, rational self-sufficiency versus humble submission to authority. "It is *certainly* true," he writes, "that science does not and cannot conflict with the revelation of God."[23] Human beings who reason well in pursuit of the truth eventually discover the limits of reason. We can know that there are mysteries, parts of reality that elude comprehension by our intellects. Most importantly, perhaps, "Let philosophy go as far as it can, but let the philosopher never for a moment imagine that human reason will ever be able to understand itself."[24] The philosopher will never know, through reason alone, why rational, finite beings came into being.

Given our need to understand what we cannot explain with reason alone, "Revelation is not the basis of philosophy, but no philosophy of any value can be constructed without it."[25] Human reason can affirm the human need for, and the possibility of, revelation's truth. More than that, "There may be truths of philosophy, that is, of the natural order, distinct from the truths of the supernatural order . . . which we could never by our natural intellect find out, but which when revealed to us we may discover to be evident to our natural reason."[26]

Brownson's example of such a self-evident truth is the creation of the world by God. It is clear to him that "[n]othing in man, in nature, in the universe, is explicable without the creative act of God, for nothing exists without that act. That God 'in the beginning created heaven and earth,' is the first principle of all science." And creation must be active and continuous. "It is as bad philosophy as theology, to suppose that God created the universe, endowed it with certain laws of development or activity, wound it up, gave it a jog, set it a going, and then left it to go of itself. It cannot go of itself, because it does not exist of itself" (82). So both the ancient Epicureans and the modern Deists are bad philosophers. (Brownson actually goes further: "Old Epicurus was a sorry philosopher, or rather, no philosopher at all" [82].) Something like Deism, or belief in the God of the Declaration of Independence who "endowed" but does not actively endow, cannot possibly be true.

So we must, in the name of reason, abandon all pretensions to self-sufficiency or autonomy: "All created things are dependent, have not their being in themselves, and are real only as they participate, through the creative act, of the Divine being" (61). The real world and our apprehension of it are only possible because of Providence, or God's inexplicable gifts to us: "Creation itself is a miracle, and our personal existence is a standing miracle, for we exist at any moment only by virtue of the continuous creative act of God."[27]

We could not have figured out simply by using reason to analyze the natural facts available to us that the world was and continues to be created by a providential God. But once we are told of that fact through revelation, argues Brownson, we know that it is the most reasonable account of the origin and perpetuation of all things. Theology aids human reason in making sense of the facts it perceives about nature: "In this sense, tradition, both as to the natural and as to the supernatural, renders an important service in the development of reason, and in conducting us to philosophic truth."[28] Biblical revelation and Christianity in particular are indispensable for philosophy's development. The dogmatic denial of the possibility of the truth of revelation, as articulated in tradition and in theology, leads to philosophical regression. So Brownson distinguishes between "philosophy in the sense of unbelief and irreligion" and "philosophy in the sense of the rational exercise of the faculty of the human mind on the divine and human things, aided by the light of revelation."[29] That is why Brownson did not think Thomas Jefferson was much of a thinker. It is also why he thought that only a Catholic could see and defend the proper basis for freedom of thought.

Brownson thought the Jeffersonian doctrine of the Declaration of Independence was true, but not in the way Jefferson did. It is true that "under the law of nature, all men are equal, or have equal rights as men." Therefore, "one man . . . can have in himself no right to govern another" because a "man is never absolutely his own, but always and everywhere belongs to his Creator." We can affirm that the natural law originates with a Creator, and that we are dependent on Him and not on ourselves. It is that affirmation, the very opposite of the Lockean principle of self-ownership, that is the foundation of human equality or the doctrine that we have "equal rights as men." All governments that truly protect rights depend on the assumption that man is not God, and all despotism originates in the "sophism," "error," and "sin" that in some sense he is (76). Only the Catholic or Thomistic understanding of the relation between reason and revelation, or nature and the Creator, can make sense of America's founding principles. Brownson consistently displays ambivalence toward the Declaration: He affirms its political conclusions but not the Jeffersonian or Lockean way of reaching them.

Brownson affirms St. Thomas's view that what human beings can know through natural reason is largely available only to "the *elite* of the race." So for "the bulk of mankind a revelation is necessary to give them an adequate knowledge even of the precepts of natural law," although "in some men it can be known through reason alone." That is, some men need revelation more than others. But Brownson does not agree with the classical philosophers that a few men do not need revelation at all. The wisest of men, in fact, should see its necessity the most, because they are most aware of the limits of human reason. Those who know the natural law best should also know best that its origin and legal character are not really explicable without what we know about the Creator through revelation.[30] They know, in particular, that God Himself could not possibly be bound by natural law: "To pretend, as some do, that God is tied up by the so-called laws of nature, or is bound in his free action by them, is to mistake entirely the relation of Creator and creature."[31]

Brownson, despite his acknowledgment of the inequality of human minds, was convinced that the Catholic Church's defense of the truth in America should proceed mainly by argument. He opposed the Church when it distrusted reason or disparaged science, and he was a critic of the American Catholic education of his time, insofar as it did not make a place for both philosophy and theology. He complained that "we have found no epoch in which the directors of the Catholic world seem to have so great a dread of intellect as our own." His Church seemed animated by "the conviction expressed by Rousseau that 'the man who thinks is a depraved animal.'"[32] The thought is that a man is either smart and thoughtful or pious and orthodox, and in Brownson's own experience nothing is further from truth: "The true policy, in our judgment, would be not to yield up thought and intelligence to Satan, but to redouble our efforts to bring them back to the side of the Church, so as to restore her to her rightful spiritual and intellectual supremacy."[33]

Brownson genuinely believed that Americans were particularly ready for Catholic instruction precisely because they were "freemen" who distrusted "blind obedience" and demanded reasons: "Blind obedience even to the authority of the church cannot be expected of the people reared under the American system . . . because they insist that obedience shall be . . . an act of the understanding, not of the will or the affections alone." Far from being "uncatholic," "the obedience of a free man, not of a slave . . . is far more consonant to the spirit of the church, and far more acceptable to God, than simple, blind obedience" (264).

Christopher Lasch has observed with admiration the extent to which Brownson aimed to provoke argument in America over the truth of religious doctrine. His concern with that truth led him to attack the insipid idea that an American civil religion which suppressed doctrinal differences should be promulgated. Teaching a vague, general faith that denies the importance of human differences regarding fundamental questions, thought Brownson, is really a form of tyranny. Brownson saw in the work of Horace Mann—and would have seen in the pragmatism of John Dewey and Richard Rorty—a thoughtless form of conformism that privileges comfort and control over truth. He rejected the deeper Hobbesian doctrine behind pragmatism which holds that peace is more important than truth and justice. Because he preferred truth to comfort, Brownson's thought is nobly anti-bourgeois; the people can and should be better than hedonistic middle-class materialists.[34] Like Tocqueville, Brownson understood that metaphysics and theology tend to lose ground in democracies, and he wrote to fend off that degradation in America.[35] He rejected the theoretical view that undergirds American decadence: There is no such thing as theological or metaphysical truth, but if there is, people are better off not knowing it.

Because Brownson advocated a genuinely liberal education for all Americans, he tended to be against public education. He thought that children need to be raised in a particular religious tradition, one that embodies a comprehensive view of fundamental truth. They ought to be prepared to engage in public arguments over the two great human concerns, politics and religion.[36] In America, disputes over religion need not lead to war or violence. Here, even the true Church has authority only to persuade, not coerce, human beings. America, Brownson contended, is closer than any other nation to embodying the true view of the relationship between church and state; from America, "the church has all she needs or can receive" (271). The Catholic Church's mission of evangelization is neither supported nor impeded by the American government, and the Church has full freedom to wield political influence through persuasion. "It is true," Brownson admits, "the church is not formally established as the civil law of the land." But "nor is it necessary that she should be; because there is nothing in the state that conflicts with her freedom and independence, with her dogmas or her irreformable canons." In one sense, "The American state recognizes only the catholic religion," because its Constitution and laws are free from the peculiarities of "sectarianism" (262–63).

The authentically American understanding of liberty reflects, in part, an openness to the one truth about God and being, so there can finally be "no antagonism" between the state and the church (262). Thomas Jefferson worried mainly about "religious tyranny," the use of political authority to impose religious conformity.[37] But his solution to that form of tyranny was another form of intellectual tyranny, the imposition of the thoughtless indifferentism of Unitarianism.[38] Brownson opposed both forms of religious tyranny because he genuinely believed that reason led the mind in the direction of religious truth, the truth about human liberty and destiny under God, and that God makes that truth available to all human beings.

Brownson also criticized American Catholic education insofar as it did not prepare Catholics to be active citizens of their nation. Catholic schools, he complained, "do not educate their pupils to be at home and at ease in their own age and country"; they are not "prepared for the work that actually awaits them in either church or state."[39] Catholic citizens, in fact, can be not only good, but the best, American citizens. Only the Catholic view of the relationship between political order and religious truth can form the basis of a true and complete understanding of the American Constitution. Brownson even claims to be convinced that the American people are already Catholic in spirit. They are, he observes, "not at heart sectarian," and the present "nothingarianism" should not be understood as a prelude to an embrace of pantheistic humanitarianism or easygoing nihilism. It is, instead, "their state of transition from sectarian opinions to positive Catholic faith," to the realization that true religion must be catholic (cix). This description was clearly meant to be inspiring. It was not necessarily untrue, but such an outcome was not the only possibility.

Brownson's considered judgment mirrors Tocqueville's: The American Protestant sects are too infused with the spirit of individualism to have much of a genuinely religious future. Americans might become pantheists or secularists, or they might abandon their individualism and accept the authority of the Catholic Church. The fact that the Church is progressing in democratic America, Brownson and Tocqueville agree, is at first glance surprising. But the mind longs for a rational account of all that exists, for unity and harmony. One such account is offered by pantheistic humanitarianism, another by the Church's assertion that reason and revelation are compatible.[40] (Brownson appears to have learned the connections among modern humanitarianism, socialism, and pantheism from the conservative Spanish thinker Donoso Cortes. Cortes, Brownson writes, is "intent on showing the errors, absurdities, and fatal tendencies of humanitarian or pantheistic socialism.")[41]

The pantheists obliterate human individuality; the Catholics preserve a place for that individuality as a divinely given and inextinguishable mystery that can be affirmed as a necessary premise of all science and all human thought. Pantheism is more consistent or unified than Christianity; in its view reason can readily comprehend everything without the assistance of revelation. But pantheism cannot account for the being who reasons and longs for the truth. On the one hand, Catholic doctrine, especially in its Thomist form, actually accounts for the facts about human nature and history as we experience them. The premise of pantheism, on the other hand, is that there is a contradiction between truth and the distinctively human experiences of truth and liberty: As most of our scientists now say, human beings are no different from the other animals and have no special place in nature. If we think or feel differently, we are wrong. In affirming this scientific abolition of difference, pantheism is indistinguishable from materialism. As Brownson and Tocqueville saw, pantheism completes in theory the leveling tendency of democracy.

According to Tocqueville, pantheism is the most seductive philosophical system in a democratic age. He asserts that "all who remain enamored with the genuine greatness of man should unite and do combat against it."[42] Brownson, after becoming a Catholic, wrote mainly to engage in that combat. He was repulsed both by pantheism's intellectual laziness—its preference for systematic thought over careful attention to the distinctions that constitute human reality—and its aversion to human greatness or individuality. Pantheism opposes truth to virtue. The truth, pantheists believe, is that the human liberty required to make sense of virtue does not exist. But Brownson is certain of the compatibility of truth and virtue: The truth is that free beings can live well in light of the truth. I have to add that since Brownson's time many Protestants have become fundamentalists. Like pantheists, fundamentalists believe that the truth allegedly revealed by modern science cannot be reconciled with Christian virtue, and so they have moved their denominations some distance away from both individualism and Unitarianism in the name of biblical morality. Even Southern Baptists, for example, are centralizing and issuing official statements of doctrine. But unfortunately, fundamentalists have affirmed the authority of revelation at the expense of the good of human reason and human science. They could benefit from Brownson's confident and well-defended view that the comprehensive claims of Darwinism, for example, are not truly scientific (60–61), and that Christians should attack these claims not because they undermine morality or the Bible but because they do not square with the facts. Our scientists shy away from the hard work of thinking about what distinguishes human being from other forms of being. Maybe the best service Brownson can perform for us is to remind Americans of the Catholic third way between what we today call secular humanism and fundamentalism.

At one point in *The American Republic*, Brownson explains that "[t]he rationalism and humanitarianism of the last century and the present are only the reaction of human nature against the exaggerated supernaturalism of the Reformers and their descendants, the Jansenists, who labored to demolish nature to make way for grace, and to annihilate man in order to assert God." The humanitarians and the Reformers each possess part of the truth, and the war between the partisans is based on the premise that one or the other view must be completely true. That is, the modern rebellion on behalf of reason and nature was based on the insight that to deny their goodness is misanthropic, but in denying the supernatural Creator, the humanitarians went too far. They imprisoned man in nature. And the denial of God is finally as misanthropic as the denial of human nature. Both secular humanists and Calvinists need to "listen to the church who accepts the truth and rejects the exclusivity of each" by restoring the harmony between reason and revelation, while clearly distinguishing between the natural and the supernatural, nature and grace, God and man.[43]

Political Life: The American Republic

Brownson considers the American republic—its Constitution and its government—in light of these philosophical concerns. Although he focuses on the political life of a particular people in light of universal truth, he does not mean there is one best constitution appropriate for all people everywhere and at all times. He also does not mean that all human beings can or should organize themselves as a single whole politically. Politically, Brownson's concern is only for his people, the people of the United States, or the American republic. Philosophically and theologically Brownson is a Catholic, a member of a community that, in principle at least, includes all human beings. But politically he is an American, a member of a particular people that has sovereignty

over a particular part of the earth. In characteristic fashion, he inte-
grates—or denies that there is a real tension between—these two loyalties.

All political order, in Brownson's view, depends on the authority
of God. He contends that "if there were no God, there could be no
politics" (cix). The foundation of government cannot be rooted in nature alone, as Jefferson, and even Aristotle, thought. "An imperative
will, the will of a superior who has the right to command what reason
dictates or approves," Brownson explains, "is essential to government;
and that will is not developed from nature, because it has no germ in
nature" (59). It makes no sense to say that nature has the right to tell
human beings what to do: "Nature is not God, has not created us,
therefore has not the right of property in us" (63). What God wills is,
if properly understood, in accord with natural reason, but His will is
not itself natural. Brownson says that "natural law is called natural
because it is promulgated by the Supreme Lawgiver, through natural
reason, instead of supernatural revelation."[44]

We do not know of the existence of God-as-Supreme-Lawgiver
through natural reason. Still, we can know, once we are told by revelation of the Creator, that the foundation of all law is "the eternal will
or reason of God," and that "all acts of a state that contravene it are,
as St. Augustine maintains, violences rather than laws" (60). Brownson
agrees with certain critics of St. Thomas's understanding of natural
law. We do not know through natural reason alone that what we call
natural law is promulgated by a lawgiver and somehow enforced;
that is, we do not know that it is law in the strict sense. In order to be
law, natural law has to be promulgated by a supernatural Creator. All
nations that take seriously the rule of law, that are not merely bands
of robbers, must understand themselves as existing under God. That
is why political or republican life, properly speaking, is impossible
without knowledge of the Creator. Brownson believes that nations

must seek to know what God's providential will is for them as groups of rational and moral beings organized in a particular time and place, and Americans have erred in not pursuing such knowledge.

That is why Brownson asserts that the United States in 1865 "has more need of full knowledge of itself" than any other nation (1). The nation's self-ignorance was the cause of the Civil War, and self-knowledge is now needed to bring that war to an end intellectually, to end the sectional conflict over the Constitution's meaning. "The work now to be done by American statesmen is even more difficult and more delicate than that which has been accomplished by our brave armies" (4). Only this intellectual work can discern the true providential mission of the American people, which is "the realization of the true idea of the state, which secures at once the authority of the public and the freedom of the individual" (3).

It is "not simply national pride" that causes Brownson to say that the establishment of America is "the beginning of a new and more advanced order of civilization" (173). Brownson's echo of *Federalist* 14 is striking. There Madison asks, "Is it not the glory of the people of America, that, whilst they have paid a decent regard to the opinions of former times and other nations, they have not suffered a blind veneration for antiquity, for custom, or for names to overrule the suggestions of their own good sense, the knowledge of their own situation, and the lessons of their own experience?" But while Brownson admired the unprecedented political accomplishment celebrated by Madison, he rejected the American self-understanding by which Madison defended it. Madison, Brownson thought, did not understand the true idea of the state or the true constitution of the American republic. Brownson wrote as a loyal patriot with true veneration for what our country's fathers accomplished ("The country is above party, and all those who love their country, and wish to save the noble institutions left us by our fathers, should fall into the ranks of one and the same party");[45] he also agreed with Lincoln that the perpetuation of our political institutions required a better intellectual defense than our fathers had given.

The true idea of the state, its authority and its limits, is determined by reflection on the truth about the whole human being. "Religion, society, property," Brownson observes, "are the three terms that embrace the whole of man's life" (11). Public authority (which is concerned with man as a social and political being) must be reconciled with economic liberty (man as a material being) and religious liberty (man as a spiritual being). Insofar as human beings exist distinctively between beast and God as natural and social beings, Brownson agrees with Aristotle that they are political animals. But they also share some qualities in common with the other animals and with God's supernatural existence, and so they are in certain respects free from political domination.

Brownson rejects views of human life that are too democratic or that consider human beings as simply animals with material needs, and he sees the irony of calling such views humanitarianism. He also rejects Christian—Jansenist or Calvinist—views that are too ethereal or otherworldly, that do not do justice to the goodness and fullness of man's natural existence. And he also rejects the ancient view that the human being is simply a political animal, a denizen of the "cave" who is completely dependent on his political community. More generally, Brownson emphatically rejects all theoretical conceptions of human life. Theory necessarily proceeds through abstraction, and as such is prone to confusing part of human being with the whole of human being. Brownson's rejection of theory is really a rejection of modern philosophy, which is "a method of reasoning instead of presenting principles to intellectual contemplation." Modern thought is really "a philosophy of abstractions," which Brownson contrasts with philosophy as "it should be, a doctrine of reality, of things divine and human." The abstractness of modern philosophy is mirrored by the abstractness of much of modern life—"cold, lifeless . . . satisfy[ing] neither mind nor heart."[46]

Brownson opposes, above all, the abstract universalism that animated the French Revolution, a universalism that collapsed the real distinctions separating the economic, political, and spiritual conditions that constitute human existence. Tocqueville, in his *The Old Regime and the Revolution*, said the French revolutionary thinkers aimed to uproot "man-in-himself" from the constraints of tradition and law. Thus, their revolution was carried out not in the name of France or Frenchmen but in the name of all human beings. Its goal was to erase artificial national distinctions from the map in the name of nature.

The revolutionaries' model was, in a sense, the Christian religion, which is essentially catholic—that is, universal. It includes all human beings, and it transcends the limitations of political life. Christianity, rightly understood, is not connected with any specific government or social order. Tocqueville contrasts the universality of Christianity with the pagan religions of the pre-Christian world, in which religion functioned within the confines of a particular society and was directed toward members of that society, not mankind generally. What the revolutionaries did was to apply the universal and missionary spirit of Christianity to political life, obliterating the distinction between political and spiritual existence that Christianity itself presupposes.[47]

The revolutionary attempts to overcome human alienation by using revolutionary or political means to abolish political life in pursuit of satisfying Christian longings in this world. But as Tocqueville explains, such efforts are doomed to fail, because there is no political way to satisfy the longing for immortality tormenting every human heart. The only way to succeed would be to somehow destroy a part of human nature itself, a possibility only now available through biotechnology.[48] The revolution of 1989, then, which marked the end of the revolution that began in 1789, was a victory for the Thomistic or realistic view that human nature is strong enough to resist revolution.

Brownson also resisted another modern temptation, which is to blame Christianity for the revolution. Some modern thinkers, including Rousseau in *The Social Contract*, tried to restore pagan or civil theology in the name of the integrity of political life. But for Brownson, the problem with civil theology is that it is not true; the Creator does not *really* have a special concern for Americans in particular, and human beings are not only citizens. The Americans' care for Americans in particular is political or strictly natural, and it is not to be confused with the spiritual or supernatural solidarity they have with all human beings. Brownson's goal is to perpetuate both spiritual and political life by properly separating them. The political liberty and authority of the citizen and the state are not incompatible with Christian liberty and the authority of the church. The confusion of the political and spiritual dimensions of the individual is the result of modern philosophy's abstraction of part of the person from the whole. Brownson's antidote for abstraction is dialectic.

The American union of authority and liberty, Brownson says, is dialectical, doing justice to both "the natural rights of man and those of society." The American dialectic brings together what is true, and rejects what is false, about both "Greek and Roman" and "modern" republics. The ancient republics allowed the state to dominate absolutely the individual; the modern ones "assert[ed] individual freedom to the detriment of the state" (3). The modern doctrine of rights is corrected with the ancient view of man as a social and political animal. The ancient view of man's comprehensive duties to the state is corrected with the Christian view of liberty.

Only through the influence of Christianity did human beings discover the rights of man in the precise sense. Ancient republics recognized citizens, not all men, as beings with rights "held independently of society" (54). But Christianity teaches that the human being is more than a citizen, and so holds that "the grand defect of the ancient

Graeco-Roman civilization" was to have "no space for individual rights" (53). Christians, in other words, accept St. Augustine's criticism of Greco-Roman civil theology and natural theology. The premise of civil society is that the human being is really a citizen and nothing more, and natural theology, the theology of the philosophers, was based on the premise that the human being is merely a part of nature.

Brownson is aware that philosophers, wherever they exist, teach the unity of the human race according to nature. But that "unity asserted by the old Eleatics, the Neo-Platonists, or the modern Unitarians" is "dead or abstract." Not just modern philosophy but all philosophy uninfluenced by Christianity roots transpolitical liberty in the abstract unity of reason, not in the real solidarity or "living unity" of all human beings discovered through revelation. The philosophic view of human unity taught by the ancient philosophers did not challenge the tyranny of the *polis* over individuals, because only the minds of the few—not whole human persons—were regarded as free. The truth about human unity becomes a political constraint only when it is rooted in recognition of the common existence of all human beings under the living God, the active and continuous Creator (224).

For Brownson, the human being is free by nature to perform his duties to his supernatural Creator. Natural rights, from this view, are only ambiguously natural rights. The heart of the Christian view of natural rights is that "God is to be obeyed rather than man," and through that claim the Church, both theoretically and practically, opposed "the absolutism of the state." But for Catholics especially, natural rights are still *natural* rights. Brownson says that "Catholicity asserts the natural equality of all men, by asserting that all have equal rights, and denies that any natural rights were forfeited or lost by the transgression of our first parents. . . . Hence Catholicity recognizes in nature something sacred and inviolable, which even the church must respect."[49] The Christian view of natural rights is quite different from those held by the leading founders, which were based largely on the thought of Thomas Hobbes and John Locke. The view of Hobbes and Locke is based, unrealistically, on the consideration of an abstract being who is neither social nor religious by nature, and who exists in freedom to negate his natural existence. Brownson's is based on a realistic idea of what a whole human being is.

Brownson and James Madison do seem to agree that conscience, or the capacity of the individual to have communion with God independently of political society, is the indispensable foundation of natural rights. The biggest difference between Brownson and Madison is that Brownson's justification of this right does not rest on the authority of personal or individualistic views of the Creator, but on the authority of the Church, which is not to say that the Church has a political right to compel religious obedience. Freedom from political authority is asserted with a corporate religious authority in mind. The right of conscience is the right to pursue what is genuinely true about God and what is good for all human beings, and so it points in the direction of a catholic church or spiritual community. Religious liberty, for Brownson, is most fundamentally freedom of the church. The right of conscience is accorded to natural reason, but only in confidence that natural reason should be free to discover its natural limitations. The right of conscience, for Brownson, makes no sense without the Christian premise that all human beings can and should discover the truth about their duties to the Creator. Madison's defense of that right is compromised by our suspicion that he does not believe in the Creator, and that he certainly does not believe in God's active and continuous creation or Providence.[50] For Madison, freedom of conscience does not point the individual in the direction of the true and universal or catholic church.

Human beings, Brownson explains, have both natural rights and civil rights, and they have corresponding duties, those of the creature

and those of the citizen. Catholics, while rejecting political absolutism, recognize that "[i]ndividuals, to a certain extent, derive their life
from God through society, and insofar as they depend on her [soci-
ety], and they are hers, she owns them, and has the right to do as she
will of them." In other words, the duties the citizen owes the state are
not a necessary evil, but a positive good. For Madison, government
exists primarily to protect property, but Brownson's view of government is more positive and expansive. "Next after religion" government "is man's greatest good"; it ranks higher than the private enjoyment of property (13). On this point, Brownson is more Greek and
Roman than modern; he knows that human flourishing always occurs
in a political context. The Church could certainly not do its work if
the political community did not exist. Brownson goes even further:
"The Romans held Rome to be a divinity, gave her statues and altars,
and offered her divine worship. This was superstition, no doubt, but it
had in it an element of truth. To every true philosopher there is something divine in the state" (50). As Aristotle says, what the state can
accomplish is divine in comparison to what the individual can do on
his own, and the "true philosopher" acknowledges that fact.[51]

Brownson does not say that Christianity discovered individual or
personal freedom. Barbarians had a lively sense of it, "but for themselves only." They were incapable of generalizing their experience of
personal independence "into the doctrine of the rights of man, any
more than the freedom of the master has been generalized into the
rights of slaves to be free." Barbarian liberty, as Tocqueville also sees,
was unreasonably and unjustly assertive, but it could not have been corrected by natural reason alone. Tocqueville claims that "it was necessary that Jesus Christ come to earth to make it understood that all members of the human species are naturally alike and equal."[52] The Greeks
and Romans were only admirable despite the fact that they had slaves.
Slavery exists in a civilized nation only as a remnant of barbarism.

In a nation where Christianity is dominant, the remnants of barbarism tend to gradually disappear. One reason that Brownson, a Christian anti-slavery man, was not an abolitionist is that he was convinced that American slavery did not have much of a future.

The theory of the leading founders was that government originates in the free consent of sovereign individuals. Brownson explains
that this theory, which derives from the social compact theory of
Hobbes, Locke, and Rousseau, is not that of the "true philosopher"; it
does not correspond to what human beings can see with their own
eyes. In a letter, he wrote that "[m]y aim in my book was, in opposition to Hobbes and Rousseau, to maintain that the state originates in
man's social nature."[53] And he begins his chapter on government with
the observation that "[m]an is a dependent being, and neither does
nor can suffice for himself" (11). For that reason, "He is born and lives
in society, and can be born and live nowhere else. It is one of the
necessities of his nature" (12). Without government, human beings
cannot "render effective the solidarity of the individuals of a nation,
and to render the nation an organism, . . . to combine men in one
living body" (13).

National solidarity is a natural human potential rooted in necessary human dependence. It is also in accord with the real but limited
human powers of knowing and loving one another. The universality
of reason and even religion, given our natural possibilities and limitations, cannot be the model for political order. The proper political
form, for Brownson, is the nation, the modern equivalent to the *polis*.
Brownson, a Catholic religiously and a nationalist politically, thought
national solidarity perfectly compatible with the solidarity of the human race through reason and faith, as long as the state was properly
understood. He disagrees with those who say that the American political order is rooted in the universal principles of the Declaration of
Independence. The American Revolution, he says, was waged on be-

half of the rights of Englishmen, that is, the rights of the citizens of
Great Britain (135). But the Declaration's assertion of the universality of certain natural rights is, properly understood, true, and our
particular nation exists, in part, to protect those rights.

Given our need to flourish as social but limited beings, government deserves our love, loyalty, and obedience. "Loyalty," Brownson
says, "is the highest, noblest, and most generous of human virtues,
and is the human element of that sublime love or charity which the
inspired Apostle tells us is the fulfillment of the law" (15). Loyalty is
more specifically human or particular than the supernatural virtue of
charity. And charity cannot replace loyalty as a political or national
passion. So Christianity elevates "civic virtues to the rank of religious
virtues [by] making loyalty a matter of conscience" (83). Brownson
even asserts that "[h]e who dies on the battle-field fighting for his
country ranks with him who dies at the stake for his faith." More
precisely, "Civic virtues are themselves religious virtues, or at least
virtues without which there are no religious virtues, since no man
who does not love his brother does or can love God" (84). Human
beings approach the universal through the particular, and love of the
personal Creator cannot be separated from love of other particular
human beings. Human love is never for human beings in general. All
men are brothers, but men will not know what brotherly love is unless they really experience political solidarity with their fellow citizens.

It would be the height of ingratitude for Catholic Americans to
ridicule their nation's founders, and so any correction they offer to the
founders' thought must be as loyal Americans and with the magnifi-
cence of the founders' accomplishment in view. When Brownson writes
of the *Federalist*, he calls those essays "masterly and profound."[54] Catholic statesmen throughout the world, in fact, ought to be chastened by
the fact that what the Protestant and politically atheistic American

founders built was more in accord with Catholic principles than anything they themselves have ever accomplished.[55] Because of this accomplishment, Brownson writes that he is not of the "political school"
of Donoso Cortes and other European Catholic conservatives; he has
"more confidence in constitutionalism or parliamentary government"
because he realizes that "it affords the only political guaranty of liberty, civil or religious . . . now practicable."[56]

The Republic

The brotherly love that is the foundation of the civic virtues is distinctively political. It is not the more immediately natural love of
those who share one's "blood," race, or lineage. Brownson, following
Aristotle, portrays political life as emerging out of, but as different in
kind from, patriarchal or tribal authority. His fundamental political
distinction is between republican or civilized and despotic or barbarian authority. "The characteristic of barbarism is, that it makes all
authority a private or personal right; and the characteristic of civilization is, that it makes it a public trust" (26). A despotic society serves
the personal aims of the ruler or ruler group and is organized eco-
nomically, not politically. Brownson believes that human authority
originates with the father, on whose authority that of tribal elders or
chiefs is modeled. But the genesis of authority cannot explain its even-
tual transformation into political or republican authority. Thus,
Brownson agrees with Locke that political authority cannot be derived from parental authority; the loyalty of citizens is different in
kind from the obedience of children (26).

The difference between the republic, or the "state," and barbarian
despotism is that the state is *territorial*, not *personal*. Territorial authority is rooted in a people's attachment to the soil (189). In a state, the
people are connected by their common occupation of a particular part
of the earth, not genealogically. The more "mixed" a nation is in terms

of race and genealogy, the more "civilized" it is, because authority becomes more political and less personal (132). A common misinterpretation of Brownson's thought is to identify this notion of America as a "territorial democracy" with the idea that American political power and authority is supposed to be diffuse or local. But in truth, Brownson uses the term "territorial democracy" to refer to a particular kind of nation; the territorial principle is the foundation of all distinctively political authority. As Brownson puts it, "American democracy . . . is not territorial because the majority of the people are agriculturalists or landowners, but because all political rights, powers, or franchises are territorial" (190).

The idea of territorial democracy is not incompatible with the division of power within the nation into particular territorial units, such as the American states. Brownson notes that Athens "introduced the principle of territorial democracy"; the Athenians divided their city "into demes or wards, whence comes the term *democracy*." This "was a real territorial division, not personal nor genealogical." But it is not this division of power within Athens that made it a territorial democracy, but the territorial—as opposed to personal—basis of power. The loyalty of all citizens was to the city or state of Athens, not to any particular ruler or ruling group (249).

The idea of the republic, Brownson explains, originates with the Greek *polis*.[57] Republican authority is the civilized kind that emerged with the Greeks and Romans. "Every people that has a real civil order, or a fully developed state or polity, is a republican people," and all true or legitimate political authority is republican. The state that is republican is constituted by public, not private, wealth, and that wealth is held as a public trust, not a private right, unlike in despotism, where wealth "is the private estate of the sovereign" (189). Despotic sovereignty can be nomadic: It can follow the sovereign wherever he goes. But republican sovereignty is limited to a specific territory.

"The sovereign people of the United States are sovereign only within the territory of the United States" (190), writes Brownson. They are an "organic people, fixed to the soil, and politically independent of every other people." They are "in the modern sense, an independent sovereign nation," and so they determine their own political destiny independently of other peoples but under God (125). The idea that there is one best form of constitution or government for people everywhere is destructive of all legitimate government, because human beings are so constituted that republican or public life must be territorial or particular. The people of the United States often make the mistake of judging other nations too severely according to their own principles. The result is that they tend to support revolution everywhere and political life as it really exists nowhere.

Brownson even criticizes "[t]houghtful Americans" who hold that the "American system" is the best. His view is more nuanced: The American system is the best, but other nations are not less enlightened because they do not choose it. The choice of our system, in fact, is not open to them at all. It is not compatible with their providential constitutions, and so "an attempt to introduce it in any of them would prove a failure and a grave evil" (120). That does not mean that statesmen from other nations cannot learn from the American system, but what they can use would have to be compatible with and adapted to their historical situations.

Republican government is not always or even usually democratic. Monarchies and empires, such as the Roman and even Napoleonic empires, can be republican. The king who says, "I am the state" is a despot; a republican king acknowledges that his power is delegated to him by the people and is under God (115). Furthermore, democracy founded on the individualistic, revolutionary principles of the seventeenth and eighteenth centuries is often barbaric. If the rights of men are based on the natural selfishness of apolitical individuals, then government exists not to pursue the public good but to protect private rights. For every man to view himself as irresponsibly and personally sovereign is as despotic as it is for a king or emperor to view himself in that way. The theory of Hobbes and Locke denies that the loyalty and duties of citizens are either natural or really in accord with the will of a providential Creator. Together with their theoretical successor Rousseau, they attempted to destroy the properly republican influence of Christianity (33). Brownson believes that "[i]t is not monarchy or aristocracy against which the modern spirit fights, but *loyalty*."[58]

The facts that a people are "organic" and that loyalty is the fundamental civic virtue point away from the personal assertiveness that leads to revolution. Brownson is characteristically hostile to the revolutionary tendency of his age, because there is something undeniably barbaric about almost all revolution—even, he hints, the American Revolution. But he adds that the real tendency of revolutions has been to eliminate "barbaric elements" (103); this was the real result of the Civil War. The republican results of revolution have often been better than what the revolutionaries themselves intended. Brownson paradoxically affirms revolutionary results but not revolutionary means, though he also opposes the doctrine of "passive obedience," favoring resistance to despotism when such resistance is prudent (16, 69).

Properly understood, political life is limited by both the extent of a nation's territory and the nature of political life. Properly republican government cannot, for instance, subsume the authority of the Church or the individual's natural right to religious liberty. To do so would be characteristic of despotism, which is always absolutist, in that it denies the distinctions among the economic, political, and religious realms of human existence. By working to preserve those civilized distinctions, Brownson contends, Christianity perfected or corrected Roman republicanism: "Christianity in the secular order is re-

publican, and continues and completes the work of Greece and Rome"
(27). Christianity was not, as some say, the cause of Rome's fall; the
Christians understood and affirmed Roman republicanism better than
the pagan Romans did.

Feudalism, Brownson explains, was a regression from Roman republicanism into barbarism. In feudal despotism, power was held as a
personal right by the aristocrats, while the king was just a "shadow."
So it fell to the Church to protect the people from the despots and keep
civilization alive. The monks were the "chief agents in delivering European society from feudal barbarism," which was the consequence of
Rome's fall (106). Brownson aims to convince us that Christianity
cannot flourish "in any patriarchal or despotic nation," and its influence is always to turn barbarism into civilization (27). Hence, it tends
to undermine the premise of hereditary aristocracy: "In the Christian
order nothing is by hereditary descent, but every thing is by election
of grace" (98).

Brownson rejects the tendency of some Catholics to idealize the
Middle Ages because it was a time when Catholicism dominated Europe. Martin Luther, he knew, was less the initiator than the spokes-
man for heresies that had flourished for centuries. The fact that Catholic
princes had often protected heretics was perhaps the Reformation's
main cause. The Catholic Brownson boldly writes, "We agree with the
Protestant historians that society in the sixteenth century was in a
most wretched state," and that Catholic leaders dealt poorly with the
challenge posed by the Reformation.[59] He writes in a rather Machiavellian way about the efforts of Pope Adrian VI, "which, if we were to
judge the policy of the vicar of Jesus Christ after human modes of
judging, which we do not allow ourselves to do, proved so disastrous."[60]

Like Tocqueville, Brownson opposes those who discredit the Catholic Church by identifying it with the despotism of the *ancien régime*.
Not only are the Church and republican government or territorial

democracy compatible, the Church is as politically republican as she is theologically authoritarian. Tocqueville worked to make the Church and democracy compatible by correcting the opinions of both priests and democratic statesmen. Brownson is much more convinced that they really are compatible, because the personal rather than territorial loyalty characteristic of feudal barbarism was really anti-Christian. Because genuinely republican government is possible, the city or republic or nation need not be seen as a band of robbers undeserving of our loyalty. The Church makes it clear how republican political life really is a human good, just not a comprehensive good.

The Constitution

Brownson aimed to make clear that non-democratic forms of government are perfectly legitimate as the choices of sovereign peoples occupying various parts of the world. He also was critical of democratic despotism, or the tyranny of the majority, which is the consequence of the selfish and irresponsible individualism of Hobbes and Locke. Democracy is not a good in itself; Brownson, Tocqueville, and the *Federalist* all agree that it must be judged by its ability to produce good government and protect minority rights. But Brownson's positive purpose is still to defend American democracy rightly understood. He is emphatic that the political forms of aristocracy and monarchy are neither possible nor desirable for his nation. His goal is to get America to understand itself as a territorial democracy, that is, as a nation of public-spirited citizens under God occupying a particular part of the world. He emphatically understands America *politically*: Both despotic and vaguely humanitarian understandings of our nation reduce human beings from political and religious to merely economic beings. Brownson explains what is possible for the American nation.

Every nation or people constituted politically has at its origin, thought Brownson, a providential constitution "given by God himself, operating through historical events or natural causes" (91). Providence, from this view, *is* "God operating through historical facts" (157). A providential constitution is "[t]he law of all possible developments" for the nation (112), which are present at the nation's beginning. They must be understood to have been given by God, because they certainly were not created by human beings. No nation can create itself, or give itself a government or written constitution out of nothing: "The nation must exist, and exist as a political community, before it can give itself a constitution" (91). The movement Hobbes describes from a chaotic, asocial individualism to government never has and never could happen.

Even without revelation we can see the need for Providence in the limits of man's nature. Contrary to what the revolutionaries say, man cannot free himself from the constraints and direction given him by historical facts. Brownson contrasts the true statesman who lets himself be governed by those facts with "the mad theorists" who attempt to establish a wholly new government uprooted from "national traditions, the national character, or the national life" (122). Such theorists foolishly deny the fact that the "constitutions conceived by philosophers in their closets are constitutions only of Utopia or Dreamland" (99).

Brownson distinguishes between the providential, or unwritten, constitution and the written Constitution of the United States (141). The former is properly constitutive or "organic," while the latter is legislative (99). The law is laid down by a people already constituted. An unwritten constitution is always the precondition for a written constitution, and political stability and progress both depend on the congruence of the written with the unwritten constitution. The idea of the providential constitution is what guided "wise and able statesmen, who understood their age and country, who knew how to discern between normal developments and barbaric corruptions." The providential constitution articulates the way effective statesmen must be guided by human nature, historical facts, and their responsibility to the Creator. If Rome had been guided by such men, they might have "preserved Rome as a Christian and republican empire to this day." But regrettably, Brownson sighs with *Federalist* 10, "real statesmen" only rarely hold political power (112).

Brownson employs the idea of the providential constitution partly to show citizens their proper loyalty to an order worthy of their devotion and beyond their manipulation. He shows that the constitution of "the people" in the political sense is not merely conventional or even natural. Its mysterious givenness, like that of language, must be divine in origin. That the providential constitution is *real*—and not merely some founding myth—is the foundation of American loyalty not merely as practical judgment or vague sentiment, but as "virtue," a matter of "conscience." The truth is that neither selfish calculation nor public opinion can provide an adequate foundation for political virtue.[61] Even Jefferson, once at least, acknowledged that we must view our liberty as a gift from God before we will make sacrifices as citizens on its behalf.[62] From this perspective, the doctrine of the providential constitution "is unquestionably conservative; for it makes the constitution sacred."[63]

Brownson's doctrine of the providential constitution is opposed to the naïve view of the philosophers and statesmen of the eighteenth century that the tyranny of the majority could be restrained by a written constitution. Even the addition of checks and balances, although useful, is far from enough. The use of checks and balances and other devices to compel compromise is based on the fact that "government is a practical affair, and cannot be carried on without an adjustment of opposing interests, which more or less offend theoretic unity." Although "[t]he aim of the real statesman is to organize all the interests and forces of the state dialectically" (107), most decisions of government are not the result of the dialectical resolution of opposites with the common good in mind. The error comes in believing that checks and balances or an institutional solution "can alone suffice for the maintenance of authority on the one hand and individual freedom on the other." They cannot be substitutes for religion.[64]

Even Calhoun's complicated solution of the "concurrent majority," although perhaps an improvement on the *Federalist* in fending off majority tyranny, could not really, by itself, have avoided the clash of interests that produced the Civil War. Perhaps this policy "could have staved off the crisis for a few years, but could not have prevented it or its final results." In any case, postwar America would soon become too homogeneous for such a sectional solution to have any relevance. Brownson notes that like the authors of the *Federalist*, Calhoun—whom he calls "the most sagacious and accomplished statesman our nation has ever produced"—attempted to secure liberty without reference to divine authority.[65] Calhoun's differences with the *Federalist* were merely over institutional details; both agreed that the problem was the tyranny of the majority and that the solution was some sort of balance of power. Even the best of American thinkers, then, with the exception of Brownson himself, have not been radical enough in their critiques of the framers' constitutionalism.

Brownson criticizes the American people and statesmen of his time for forgetting their constitution's providential origin and "treat[ing] it as their own creature" to be manipulated at will.[66] But, in fact, they do not appear to have been conscious of the providential, unwritten constitution until Brownson wrote his instructive book. Even Brownson admits that the state-of-nature doctrine of Hobbes and Locke "is the political tradition of the country" (34). And the framers of the Constitution understood their work in light of the doctrine of the Declaration of Independence. That is precisely the problem.

Brownson is an unambiguous critic of the author of the Declaration of Independence. By making consent the foundation of government, Jefferson "declared that governments originate in convention, and that law derives its force as law from the will of those it is to bind." Jefferson declared, in other words, "the purely human origins of government,"[67] and the foundation of obedience is nothing but enlightened self-interest. Brownson attacks "the so-called Jeffersonian democracy, in which government has no powers but such as it derives from the consent of the governed, and is personal democracy or pure individualism—philosophically considered, pure egoism, which says, 'I am God'" (222). Government needs more than unfettered egoism to sustain loyal, dutiful citizens, and democracy needs more to remain a true republic.[68]

Brownson's efforts are aimed at replacing the Declaration's false and pernicious view of the foundation of American government. He does not hesitate to write that "the theory held by our fathers" is "unsound and incompatible with the essential nature of government" (154). There is no other way, in fact, to defend their practical accomplishments but to boldly reject their theory. He adds that the age of the American founding "whatever its practical belief, embraced a purely atheistic philosophy," and that contradiction between practice and theory explains why its conventional theory cannot defend its constitutional practice.[69] Brownson asserts that "the doctrine of the origin of government in compact, in the sense asserted in the eighteenth century, is now . . . maintained by no statesman worthy of his name."[70] Once compact theory reached its extreme and misanthropic conclusion in Rousseau, no real political leader could take seriously either its truth or its utility.

Brownson's criticism of our political fathers is part of his criticism of "modern liberalism" generally for its political atheism. Certain elements of liberalism, such as the doctrine of natural rights, "are taken from Christian civilization, and are, in themselves, true, noble, just, and holy." But liberalism also "assumes an independence of religion, of conscience, of God, which is alike incompatible with the salvation of souls and the progress of society." The indispensability of the idea of the providential constitution shows liberals that "if they would study the question, . . . religion offers no obstacle to any thing true and good they wish to effect, and even offers them that very assistance without which they cannot effect or preserve it."[71] Liberal ends, and the effective means for securing them, are really incompatible with atheism. Calhoun and the authors of the *Federalist* were excellent but characteristically modern liberals. In a way, Brownson is a postliberal or postmodern thinker. He sees, as Tocqueville did, that modern liberal democracy—popular government devoted to the protection of human liberty—must be understood on a new and more realistic foundation, given the loss in credibility and the practical weakness of the theory of Hobbes and Locke. But unlike most postmodernists, Brownson is not inventing a new founding myth. He criticizes political atheism not only because it does not work, but also because it is not true.

Brownson's idea of the providential constitution is just as much for statesmen as it is for citizens. He makes it clear that God's Providence leaves ample room for free will and human error. It is to guide, not replace, statesmanship. The idea of Providence is not to be confused with "fatalism" (111). Brownson adds that Providence should not be expected "to work miracles to counteract the natural effects" of human ignorance and stupidity. We should not even think that God will act politically on behalf of bad rulers who are "irreproachable and saintly in their private characters and relations." When it comes to achieving what is possible for a nation and saving her from ruin, what counts is "true statesmanship" and a people's "patriotism." Private virtues are important to the fate of the individual, but they never

saved a nation: "Edward the Confessor was a saint, and yet he prepared the way for the Norman conquest of England" (113).

Brownson borrowed the idea of the providential constitution from
the French conservative thinker Joseph de Maistre, for whom he had
great admiration. Maistre wrote, Brownson recognized, against revolutionary Jacobinism and so on behalf of the requirements of political stability. While acknowledging that Maistre was a monarchist,
Brownson claims that monarchism "is by no means a necessary conclusion from the great generative principles of political constitutions
that he insists upon."[72] He sees that Maistre is right to say that constitutions are generated, not made. But Maistre unreasonably "excludes
all human agency from their formation and growth." In saying that
constitutional development "must be wholly divine, and contain no
human element," Maistre leaves no room for "reason and free-will" in
statesmanship (91–92). Maistre's unwritten constitution, in
Brownson's eyes, could not properly be called republican, because it
leaves no room for political life. And that presents a problem for Americans because, for them, to be guided by their providential constitution
is to be republican.

Certain providential facts made America republican; "[i]t was
not the foresight, wisdom, conviction, or will" of the people. The people
"established no monarchy or nobility at the close of the War of Independence, for the simple reason that neither was in our constitution."
Only the "commons," not the royalty and nobility, of England emigrated to America, and so our constitution recognizes only democracy, not monarchy or aristocracy. Brownson holds that "[t]he constitution was determined for us by the Providence of God, which so
ordered it that only the commons emigrated, and so created and arranged circumstances to compel us from sheer necessity to live under
a government from which royalty and nobility are excluded."[73]

Providence here is identified with necessity, as is American democracy. Monarchy and aristocracy are not possible for us, and so republicanism understood as a form of democracy is what is best *for us*. Here Brownson again approaches Tocqueville, who said that both the Americans and Europeans of his time ought to regard democracy as providential, as what they have been given and cannot change. The American question, determined by our unwritten constitution, is to decide what sort of democracy we will have, and statesmen who do not confine themselves to that question futilely fight against the historical facts and against God.[74] Brownson himself assures Americans: "I am not warring against the political constitution of my country, nor am I seeking in any respect to change it; for I am no revolutionist, no monarchist, no aristocrat." He merely wants the constitution interpreted according to principles of "law and justice," and not by the arbitrary rule of an unprincipled majority.[75]

Other parts of our unwritten constitution include the science and art of Greece and the republicanism of Rome. Still another is Christianity, which compels us, in a way, to understand republicanism as compatible with both the rights of citizens and the rights of man, whatever modern theorists say. Finally, our unwritten constitution incorporates certain British political institutions, including the common law, which we have democratized, not rejected, and which keep alive "[s]omething of the Christian tradition."[76] On occasion, Brownson even calls attention to the Christian resonance of the words of the Declaration of Independence about truth, liberty, inalienable rights, and the Creator. Hence, contrary to the opinion of our leading founders, "The American constitution is not founded on political atheism, but recognizes the rights of man, and, therefore, the rights of God."[77] In thinking about Brownson's seemingly contradictory remarks on the Declaration, we can blame them either on his incoherence or that of the Declaration itself.

That the Declaration is incoherent is consistent with Brownson's view of American decline; the founding generation was "still influenced by anterevolutionary traditions." But since Jackson's presidency, the founding theoretical atheism has passed "into the practical life of the people."[78] Ironically, when the theory seemed credible it did not completely dominate political thought or practice, but as the theory becomes incredible its dominance grows. So democracy has lost its moral restraints over time by conforming itself ever more completely to obsolete Lockeanism. (Maybe this really is the history of America!) Brownson suggests that the providential constitution, in the absence of statesmanship, gives Americans progressively less real guidance. But actually to say that in *The American Republic* would have been out of keeping with his postwar celebration of that constitution's victory over secession. Brownson is inconsistent in his tale of American progress and American decline, but he might well say that the inconsistency will be dialectically resolved when Americans reflect properly on the lessons of the Civil War.

That Brownson does to some extent include the universal, natural rights of the Declaration as part of our providential constitution and as part of the true Christian contribution to republican but properly limited government separates him from Maistre in another way. Maistre famously declared that he knew Frenchmen, Italians, Persians, and so forth, but not Man himself. And so he condemned the French and other revolutions for proceeding in the name of abstract Man, not real or particular men. But Frenchmen, Brownson would answer, are men. Politically their existence and loyalty is particular or territorial, and that is the truth of Maistre's anti-revolutionary criticism. All men have some national or political identification, and that does and should separate them. But all men also share both religious solidarity and natural rights with all other men, and that fact was a Christian discovery.

The republic or state does not encompass the whole human being. Men are more than citizens, and so the French*man* is more than a French citizen. That fact demands political recognition through the doctrine of rights. Although Brownson argues for the harmony between our duties as citizens and our rights as men, he acknowledges, "I am a man before I am a citizen, and my rights as a man can never be subordinated to my duties as a citizen."[79] More than that, the influence of Christianity points away from the barbarism of hereditary privilege and toward the equality of all citizens under the law. The idea that a particular person has a divine right to rule is, in fact, antirepublican. All genuinely republican rulers, including monarchs, rule on behalf of a people constituted politically under God, and the doctrine of natural rights, properly understood, is a reflection of the Christian addition to republican thought that all men—not just citizens—are equally under God.[80]

The United States

Brownson understands the United States as an unprecedented form of a nation or state. He actually sometimes prefers to say "the American State" rather than "the United States."[81] In doing so he emphasizes that a Lockean understanding of the American Constitution as based on the consent of "sovereign individuals" is incompatible with the idea of the state: If individuals are sovereign, then all obedience to government is voluntary. A Lockean union would not consist of citizens but of confederates, people who use each other to advance their private interests. A union among sovereigns is only an "alliance." And what is true of sovereign individuals is also true of sovereign states.

If the states were sovereign at the time of the Constitutional Convention, then they could have formed only a confederacy or alliance, not a state or nation to which they have a duty to be loyal. Sovereign states and sovereign individuals can withdraw from alliances voluntarily at any time. If this statement of the historical facts is accurate, then Calhoun was right to say that America is not really a single nation or political community, and secession from the confederation would be indeed an "incontestable right." Likewise, opponents of secession could not appeal to "the language or provisions of the Federal constitution" to support their case. If the constitution itself is a compact, or a merely conventional arrangement among sovereigns, then its provisions do not have any effect on those confederates who withdraw their allegiance to it (129).

The theory of "the framers of the constitution," Brownson writes, was "the almost universal belief of the time among political philosophers" that all government has a conventional origin. The framers thought they "were constituting a real government," but they also thought they had produced "a treaty, compact, or agreement among sovereigns" (153). "The right of secession certainly was never contemplated by the framers of the constitution," Brownson admits, but that does not mean they gave a coherent argument against it.[82] This theoretical confusion is fatal for a government the framers believed they had, in effect, constituted out of nothing. For Brownson, it is clear that no real government can originate in a merely conventional compact. Under Hobbesian-Lockean compact theory, the United States would have no right to treat secession as rebellion and "to suppress it by employing all the physical force at its command" (138).

It is true that many leading framers who held the compact theory did not think that obedience to government was voluntary for sovereign individuals. Sovereignty would have to be surrendered to fend off anarchy; individuals who think clearly about their interests consent to be governed. But Brownson asks whether an individual can surrender what he has been given by nature to a simply conventional authority on the basis of interest. If his interests, or his *opinions* about his interests, change, who is to say that he cannot reclaim what is his by nature from an arbitrary authority that he constructed for his own benefit? The key question remains whether we have a nation or a confederation, whether we have the duties of citizens or the interests of confederates, whether sovereignty is territorial or personal. The framers' confused but ultimately confederate—and quite mistaken—answer to this question can be blamed on "the little account which they made of the historical facts that prove that the people of the United States were always one people" (154).

According to Brownson, the question of whether America is a nation can be determined "not by the theories of American statesmen, the opinions of the justices, or even by the constitution itself." The historical facts trump all these methods of constitutional interpretation. America was a nation at the time of the writing of the written Constitution—a nation *de facto* and so a nation *de jure* (131). It was and remains *one* nation, one sovereign people, under God. The common opinion, shared by Jefferson and Madison, is that each American is somehow loyal not to one nation, but two. Both sovereignty and allegiance are divided between the individual's particular state and the United States, "as if there was a United States distinguishable from the States." But there can be (and here Brownson echoes Hobbes) only one political sovereign; to say otherwise is to institute civil war, a war that begins in the division within each citizen's soul. Brownson writes, "There is no divided sovereignty, no divided allegiance." The truth, rooted in the providential constitution, as interpreted through national history, is that "[t]he sovereign is neither the General government nor the States severally, but the United States in convention. The United States are the one indivisible sovereign, and this sovereign governs alike general matters in the General government and particular matters in the several State governments" (205).

From the beginning, the Americans were one people, one nation, but they were never such a people without being politically organized into and by the states. The states cannot exist without the general government, nor the general government without the states. The expression of this indivisible and distinctive form of national authority is the convention. The people acting in convention authorized the written Constitution, and the people in convention can alter the written Constitution if they view it as somehow destructive of the unwritten constitution (206). "This constitution," Brownson explains, "is not conventional, for it existed before the people met or could meet in convention." The unwritten constitution is what made the convention possible. America is held together not by a merely conventional compact, but by "a real and living bond of unity" (144). And the expression of that national unity is "the sovereign convention" (160).

Because American government is not conventional, it can be altered by convention. It is the providential constitution, not the written one, that citizens should regard as sacred. *Federalist* 49 hoped that the written Constitution would eventually acquire the "veneration time bestows on everything," since it would be so hard to change. But it would not, in fact, be impossible for the people to change it. And how can the people venerate something they created for themselves and might alter at will? The people, in fact, cannot change the providential constitution; it is genuinely beyond their deliberation. It can and should be venerated. On this point, Brownson thought Jefferson was more consistent than the authors of the *Federalist*, for unlike them he knew that veneration was incompatible with the consent of sovereigns. Jefferson did not *want* veneration, but rather a revolution every generation. Brownson also argues that rooting government wholly in consent is incompatible with a nation's political responsibilities over time: "The doctrine that one generation has no power to bind its successor is not only a logical conclusion from the theory that governments derive their just powers from the consent of the governed . . . but is very convenient for a nation that has contracted a large national debt" (43–44).

Because the unwritten constitution is a matter of fact, Brownson must defend with facts his assertion that "[c]ertain it is that the States in the American Union have never existed and acted as severally sovereign states" (135). Before their independence, they were colonies and their people were "British subjects." The Declaration of Independence and the war for independence were exertions not of several independent sovereign states but of "states united, or the United States, that is, states sovereign in their union, but not in their separation." For Brownson, "This is of itself decisive of the whole question" (136). But he goes on to add more evidence anyway: "No one of the states of the Union has ever been known or recognized by any foreign power as an independent sovereign nation."[83] The only one of "our prominent statesmen" to affirm the unity of the colonial Americans was John Quincy Adams, and he, an extreme nationalist, alone was right. Consider the evidence: the colonies' submission to the same sovereign authority, the same community of origin, the same "language, manners, customs, and law." And they were united to England in the same way through the common law. Their union with England "was national, not personal"; it was with the nation, not the king. And with independence the sovereignty the colonies shared under the English nation became the national sovereignty they shared as Americans (136).

The evidence concerning the original American union, the Articles of Confederation, also supports this conclusion. "The Confederation was an acknowledged failure, and was rejected by the American people, precisely because it was not in harmony with the unwritten or Providential constitution of the nation." Its failure was in recognizing the states as sovereign and in substituting "confederation for union." The Articles did not recognize the existing American reality, but were rather a failed attempt to impose something new. The nation's "instinct of unity" resisted confederation twice—in 1787 and in 1861 (140). The principle of confederation shows its weakness most clearly in war. As a "disintegrating principle," it was, far more than the small disparity in numbers and resources, the main cause of the defeat of the confederate states by the United States (254).

Brownson admits that the written Constitution "is peculiar, and difficult to understand," partly because it is unprecedented (141). One way of expressing its peculiarity is to say, "As there is no union outside of the States, so is there no State outside of the Union; and to be a citizen either of a State or of the United States, it is necessary to be a citizen of a State, and of a State in the Union" (146–47). This peculiarity, Brownson observes, was noticed in an 1830 letter by Madison, where he wrote that the United States is neither a "consolidated" nor a "confederated" government. It is, instead, an unprecedented "mixture of the two" (149). America is a nation, not a confederation, but political authority is not completely centralized or consolidated, because the idea of the nation necessarily includes the political organization of the states. Madison, together with other leading statesmen, speaks only of the written Constitution in understanding that mixture, supposing that it had been "deliberately formed by the people themselves" (148). If that mixture had been deliberately formed, then it could be deliberately undone by sovereign states or sovereign individuals. For Brownson, that mixture is beyond deliberation as part of our organic national solidarity (158). And the American founders, whether they realized it or not, took it as a given when they deliberated about the written Constitution.

However peculiar it may seem, the American nation can be constituted in one peculiar way and in that way only. So "[t]he merit of the statesmen of 1787 is that they did not destroy or deface the work of Providence, but accepted it, and organized the government in harmony with the real order, the real elements given them." By allowing themselves to be governed "by reality, not by theories and speculations," "they proved themselves statesmen." As a result, "their work survives" (173). True statesmen always know, in one way or another, that the providential constitution is real; it cannot be chosen or rejected according to abstract theoretical principles.

The peculiar American division of the powers of government, although not deliberately chosen by the founding statesmen or anyone else, can be understood in terms of its providential purpose. This "American form of government" cannot be comprehended through Aristotelian categories: "It is original, a new contribution to political science." The United States "seeks to attain the end of all wise and just government by means unknown or forbidden to the ancients, and which have been but imperfectly comprehended even by the American political writers themselves" (4). This distinctive and unprecedented form is "an effective safeguard against both feudal disintegration and Roman centralism" (161).

Brownson explains that the American division of power "is not between a *national* government and State governments, but between a *General* government and particular governments" (163). These latter, more philosophical terms highlight his view that our government mirrors the complexity of human nature. The powers of both the general and particular governments are "equally sovereign," and "neither are derived from the other." Neither is subordinate to the other; they are "co-ordinate." They do not check or oppose each other; they work together dialectically to form a whole. The American citizen's loyalty is to the government of the United States, which is the name for American government considered as a whole (164). It is because our loyalty is to that whole that secession is unconstitutional, and all means necessary must be used to resist it.

Brownson holds that the Constitution's division of power between the general government and the particular governments is clear. He even asserts that "the whole controversy on slavery in the territories, which culminated in the civil war, was wholly unnecessary and never could have occurred had the constitution been properly understood and adhered to by both sides." It is clear to him that "the general government never had and has not any power to exclude slavery from the territories, any more to abolish it in the states." So *Dred Scott* was seemingly rightly decided. But Brownson adds that persons migrating to the territories from the states cannot take their slaves with them, because slavery is merely "a local institution, sustained neither by the law of nature nor the law of nations." Slavery is conventional, not natural, and the laws sustaining the enslavement of a particular man are only valid in the states that enact them. Although "Congress could not exclude slavery from the Territory," it is clear to Brownson that "really slavery was virtually excluded" (169). So the pro-slavery argument of Chief Justice Taney in *Dred Scott* is virtually or really wrong.

Brownson's constitutional interpretation was informed by his consistent view "that slavery can exist only under municipal law, can have no existence outside it, for under the law of nature all men are free . . . , as all Christian morality teaches, as was declared by the American Congress of 1776, as is implied by our whole system of jurisprudence, and is assumed as unquestioned by nearly the whole modern world."[84] At the time of Taney's *Dred Scott* opinion, Brownson said he regretted that "the learned judge did not recollect what is taught by his religion, namely, the unity of the human race, that all men by the natural law are equal, and that negroes are men."[85] At the same time, he accepted the Court's decision: "Though we have taken exception to it, and believe it in several respects erroneous . . . we shall not forget our duty as loyal citizens."[86]

Brownson disagreed with the abolitionists mainly over the proper political way to pursue the abolition of slavery in America. They were wrong, he explains, to call for the abolition of slavery "in their sole capacity as men." They forgot that they were also citizens, and that a "purely humanitarian" argument passes a death sentence on "all government and civil society itself." The abolitionists also should not have embraced the "political error" of calling upon the general or national government to abolish slavery, because under the Constitution it "had no jurisdiction in the case." But they could rightly have called upon "the people of the United States" to abolish it through convention or constitutional amendment (206). Had they chosen the correct political means, they would have had Brownson's political support, but as humanitarians the abolitionists were, in his view, incapable of thinking politically.

We can say that Brownson's thoughtful, ingenious, and balanced view of slavery, the Constitution, and citizenship might have fended off war had it been accepted by both sides, but I fear that the alleged compromise would not have impressed the South as a compromise. An institution rooted only in convention and contrary to nature, Brownson says repeatedly, cannot survive. He "never urged emancipation on the ground of the natural equality of all men—never on the ground that slavery is a moral wrong, a crime against society, and a sin against God," but he adds that "we are, and always have been, an anti-slavery man; we do, and always did, regard slavery as a great moral and social wrong, though not the only or the greatest in the country."[87] Brownson believes that antebellum national unity depended on the practical acceptance of slavery in some states through a constitutional interpretation that was in principle anti-slavery and so would virtually prohibit its spread into new territories. On that point, whether he knew it or not, he was in agreement with the leading founders and Lincoln.

Brownson's larger argument is that the whole that is American government mirrors the nature of human beings and protects republican political life from the excesses that threaten it. He provides a philosophical account of the goodness of what came into existence in America historically. Human beings are free as individuals, and that is the partial truth of feudalism. Human individuals are part of and devoted to a whole beyond their making, and that is the partial truth of centralism. Feudalism or freedom as personal assertiveness, embodied to some extent in America in the idea of state sovereignty, is barbaric, selfish, and subpolitical. Centralism, considered as a whole, is universalistic and pantheistic and so radically opposed to the ideas of individual and citizen. The particular human being, for the centralist, is not part of, but rather is totally absorbed into, a whole beyond his making. If the American's loyalty is to be to his nation's republican political life, then it must be to the United States understood as a properly human whole, a whole that does justice to both the individual and the citizen. Brownson the Christian knows, of course, that "[i]n all human governments there will be defects and abuses," but he adds that "the American constitution . . . is the least imperfect that has ever existed" (176).

Brownson's defense of the United States is not just historical, but also philosophical and even theological. It is reminiscent, in fact, of Tocqueville at his most theological. Tocqueville is also critical of both the barbaric injustice of aristocratic particularity and the democratic propensity to prefer generalizations to the complex truth about human liberty. General ideas, he explains, are actually a sign of the weakness of the human mind. God has no need of them. He sees each human being in his likeness with and difference from others. Aristocrats think too particularly, democrats too generally, and so they each see only part of the truth about human beings. The best political order would be based on a divine ability to see what is true about aristocratic particularity and democratic generality. And Tocqueville himself attempts to see with the eyes of God in thinking about aristocracy and democracy. He concludes that the Creator prefers democracy, because in His eyes all human beings are free. But the liberty protected by democracy must be human liberty, and so democracy is good only if it preserves human individuality, if it can manage to avoid its characteristic vices of the tyranny of the majority and evolution toward a soft despotism of "schoolmasters" who control beings so apathetic as to be subhuman. By viewing schoolmaster-despots, or those whom we now call therapeutic experts, as a greater danger than majority tyranny to human liberty in America, Tocqueville corrects the *Federalist*. Madison thought that the main threat to democratic liberty is an aroused majority, but Tocqueville saw that in the long term it is really a general apathy or passivity.[88]

Brownson's defense of the United States is made with this understanding of the strengths and dangers of democracy in mind. Our nation institutionalizes a protection of individuality or particularity against the leveling tendency of the general government, against humanitarianism, Brownson's name for soft despotism. Brownson acknowledges that the constitution he defends seems to leave no protection from a tyrannical majority that might dominate a particular state. He knows that universal suffrage, by itself, is quite ineffective "in securing the freedom and independence of the individual citizen." The truth is that "[t]he ballot of the isolated individual counts for nothing" (174). And the "real practical tendency of universal suffrage is to democratic, instead of an imperial, centralism," with rule by an irresponsible majority party. Experience also shows that "mere paper constitutions" are no "protection against the usurpations of party" (175).

What makes this weakness of the democratic states less "evil" than it seems at first is that in the states themselves power is sometimes once again divided. That is why the best government is found in New England, where each town has control over purely local matters. Brownson predicts, or rather recommends, that with slavery's abolition, "the New England system" will gradually spread throughout the entire nation. Like Tocqueville, Brownson concludes that an indispensable barrier to majority tyranny is as much township localism as is possible without destroying citizens' loyalty to the nation, the United States (175–76).

The fundamental American distinction, for Brownson, is not between the American nation and the several states but between North and South. The two regions are characterized by "opposite" political tendencies (224–25). The North is too democratic, and the South is too aristocratic. The South defended barbaric "personal democracy," and the abolitionists in the North promoted vaguely social and even pantheistic "humanitarian democracy," now the greatest danger to republican government in America. Personal and humanitarian democracy are "each alike hostile to civilization, and tending to destroy the state, and capable of sustaining government only on principles common to all despotisms" (221). "The one loses the race," Brownson explains, "the other the individual" (230). Brownson is, in fact, a severe enough critic of both North and South to have said something, probably many things, to offend the advocates of every form of American partisanship in his time and ours. His standard is the true understanding of our nation as a "territorial democracy," the one that exists between and is equally opposed to both the Southern and Northern extremes.

The South: Personal Democracy and Secession

Brownson, the firmest conceivable opponent of secession, is, strangely enough, not particularly critical of those who favored secession. The argument they used "rests on no assumption of revolutionary principles or abstract rights of man, and on no allegation of real or imaginary wrongs received from the Union" (179). The theory of state sovereignty rested on the prevailing view of the government of the leading framers, and many loyal Americans, as a result, were mistaken concerning the true object of their loyalty. Even Christian antislavery men such as Robert E. Lee wrongly but honestly thought they had a duty as citizens to their state, not their nation. Secession was not, in fact, "the work of a few ambitious and unprincipled leaders." The rebellion was territorial—the overwhelming majority of men in each seceding state favored it on principled, not personal, grounds (188). So the responsibility for the "crime" must be laid not on any particular individuals but on the people of the seceding states as a whole. And their punishment can be no more than their defeat (211). Because they believed themselves "loyal citizens and true patriots" fighting for self-government on constitutional principles, they from one view even deserve the honor always accorded to patriots (178).

Those in rebellion were traitors in "outward act," but they did not have "treasonable intent" (215). The secessionists, because they were merely in error, did not commit "the moral crime of treason." Brownson adds that, in any case, "the civilized world has much relaxed from its former severity toward political offenders." The people of the United States, in their perverse generosity, "have given their moral support to every insurrection in the Old World or New World they discovered." They did so wrongly, and surely they emboldened their own rebels by doing so (211–12).

Brownson concludes that for the people of the North "to treat with severity any portion of the Southern secessionists, who, at the very worst, only acted on the principles the nation had uniformly avowed and pronounced sacred, would be regarded, and justly, by the civilized world, as little less than infamous" (211–12). The cure for the spirit of secession, Brownson holds, is not punishment or revenge but the acceptance by all Americans of the correct view of America's providential constitution. His portrayal of the secessionists as virtuous men who fell prey to an error that was, to some extent, shared by the whole nation is meant to allow them to easily accept, and be accepted by, the American nation.

But Brownson also says that the Civil War was fought by the South as a defense of personal or barbaric democracy (226). The deterioration of territorial democracy into personal democracy was strongest in America in the "slaveholding states," and especially in the "slaveholding class" in those states. That class was "the American imitation of the feudal nobility of medieval Europe" (223). The Southern states have tended "to make all rights and powers personal or individual." So it follows that "as only the white race has been able to assert and maintain its personal freedom, only men of that race are held to have the right to be free" (224). The black has been unable to assert his freedom, and so the Southerner holds he has not the ability to be free: "The tendency of the Southern democrat was to deny the unity of the [whole human] race, as well as all obligations of society to protect the weak and helpless." The Southern democrat has, in other words, denied the doctrine which constitutes the specifically Christian contribution to republican government (225).

The slaveholding men of the South "studied the classics" and "admired Greece and Rome." They imagined they were returning to republican civilization in its pre-Christian purity. But the truth is that Greece and Rome were great *despite* their slavery, and they fell because of "internal weakness caused by the barbarism within." "The infusion of Christian dogma" into "the life, the laws, the jurisprudence of all civilized nations" doomed slavery everywhere. The men of the South did not understand that slavery is "in direct antagonism to American civilization," and that racially based slavery is a particularly monstrous denial of the humanity of a man who might be "literally your brother." Opposed by the "whole force of the national life," the barbarism of slavery was destined for extinction from the nation's beginning (225–27).

Brownson, Christian and civilized defender of the providential constitution, might have been too sanguine about civilization's victory over barbarism. A true statesman might say that Brownson, at times, had too much faith in progress. But that does not mean he thought the victory of the nation on the battlefield was insignificant: "They [the men of the South] and their barbaric democracy have been defeated, and civilization has won its most brilliant victory in all history" (233). Brownson goes even further: "The tendency to individualism has been sufficiently checked by the failure of the rebellion, and no danger from the disintegrating element, either in the particular States or in the United States, is henceforth to be apprehended" (234). Personal assertiveness or the individuality of barbaric freedom is no longer a menace to the American nation. The danger now is to individuality as such.

Southerners, Brownson contends, did not believe they were fighting primarily for the preservation of racially based slavery: "They fought for personal democracy, under the form of state sovereignty, against social democracy; for personal freedom and independence against social or humanitarian despotism." They believed they were fighting for the future of human liberty against the soft despotism Tocqueville had described. The mean between the two extremes of personal democracy and social democracy is, in truth, territorial democracy, and its victory was the beneficent outcome of the war. Patriotism, not socialism, triumphed in America. But there still was something valid about the South's fear concerning humanitarianism's danger to human liberty, and so a certain nobility to their cause that can be appreciated more dispassionately at the war's end. If Southerners could have taken up their cause without assaulting the nation or its providential constitution, Brownson holds, they would have won (228).

Brownson agrees with Tocqueville that the slaveholding Southerners had the virtues and vices common to every aristocracy, and that the political life of territorial democracy depends on the presence of such virtues without the corresponding vices.[89] The South denied liberty to a whole class of human beings purely on the basis of color, but they did cherish and were willing to fight for their own personal liberty or individuality. Brownson acknowledges that the "social" aristocracy had given the South an advantage during the war: "In southern society the people are marshalled under their natural leaders under men who are intrinsically superior to the mass" (242). Southern energy and cohesion came from the fact that those whom Jefferson called the "natural aristocracy" readily rose to the top.[90] That is one reason Brownson opposed the view that the war was between aristocracy and democracy, and that democracy had won. All good government has an aristocratic element; natural leaders ought to lead. But Brownson also observes that the patriotism or political life of a territorial democracy can itself generate aristocratic qualities; thus, "[t]he more aristocratic South proved itself, in both statesmanship and generalship, in no respect superior to the territorial democracy of the North and West" (242). The military spirit, and the honorable profession of the military officer, "supply an element needed in all society, to sustain in it the chivalric and heroic spirit, perpetually endangered by the mercantile and political spirit, which has in it always something low and sordid" (244). Those manly words are surely more aristocratic—and Southern—than Brownson the patriot would want to admit. But as Tocqueville explains, aristocrats or feudal lords are always warriors, and America's Southerners have always been, disproportionately, our nation's hunters and fighters[91]—and, after the question of state sovereignty was settled, our patriots.

In reflecting on our nation's destiny, Brownson asserts that "[t]he United States must henceforth be a great military and naval power, and the old hostility to a standing army and the old attempt to bring the military into disrepute must be abandoned" (246). There must be something noble for natural leaders to do, something to raise the nation above the self-interest that characterizes not only commercial but even ordinary political life. The "depreciation of the military spirit," Brownson contends, comes from the subpolitical, even subhuman sentimentality of humanitarian democracy, is contrary to all republican political life, and is even "[t]he worst tendency in the country" (243).

It should not seem so odd as it undoubtedly does for us to see an orthodox Catholic write so approvingly of heroes and war. It is what comes from the awareness that man is not only a religious or spiritual being, but also a political or national one. Brownson would have appreciated how both world wars and the Cold War energized and disciplined American citizens and statesmen, and he would have appreciated the difficulty Americans have in determining what their nation stands for today. Some military spirit seems to be required for the natural aristocracy to desire and take on positions of political leadership. And the absence of such spirit, experience shows, encourages the evils humanitarians most aim to avoid (243).

The North: Humanitarian Democracy

The tendency in the North, Brownson observes, is to "exaggerate the social element: to overlook the territorial basis of the state and to disregard the rights of individuals." Those among whom this tendency was strongest were called abolitionists. They favor unity over particularity so strongly that they aim to abolish all human distinctions. They see nothing legitimate in territorial democracy, because it divides the world into particular nations, and they also oppose, of course, the division of the United States into particular states. They see the "vague generality" of humanity as superior to particular individuals and particular states, and so they recognize neither individual nor territorial rights. Their despotic opposition to the requirements of active citizenship and personal excellence is rightly called socialism (230–31).

In its denial of individuality and natural rights, abolitionist humanitarianism is as anti-Christian as the individualism or personal democracy of the South (229–30). Despite this moral equivalence, humanitarianism is more dangerous than the egoism of the South, because humanitarians "have the appearance of building on a broader and deeper foundation, of being more Christian, more philosophic and more generous." Their effort is "to persuade the world that humanitarianism is Christianity and so man is God." They are pantheists. All is God, says the pantheist, and so not only are there no particular rights, there is, in truth, no particularity at all. Brownson says that this "philanthropy," the love of humanity in general through the denial of the existence of real men, is the guise Satan takes in our time (229).

Brownson chronicles the extent to which the spirit of humanitarian philanthropy is the spirit of abolition in the service of a pure or consistent equality. The abolition of slavery is to be followed by "negro suffrage, negro equality" and then "female suffrage and the equality of the sexes." (Brownson holds that "God made the man the head of the woman, and the woman for the man, not the man for the woman.") Next comes "equality of property," and because that goal is incompatible with private property, the abolition of property itself. Then natural distinctions concerning beauty and intellect will be attacked. The abolition movement cannot finally end until "all individualities" disappear. Men are to become completely apolitical and indistinguishable members of the species, and the human species will qualitatively be no different from the others (230–31).

Finally, what motivates humanitarianism is the abolition of man; it is based on the mistaken view that "creation itself is a blunder."

Brownson sees that the theory of Rousseau is behind this nihilism, this denial of human reality on behalf of "nullity" (231). It is also "practically a tendency to the savage state, as one may learn even from Jean-Jacques Rousseau."[92] For Brownson, "the essence of social-ism" is in the "assumption that our good lies in the natural order, and is unattainable by individual effort." So the natural good is at odds with individual liberty: "Socialism bids us follow nature, instead of saying with the Gospel, Resist nature."[93] Socialism aims to return human beings to the brutish contentment of Rousseau's natural man.

We might reasonably object to Brownson that the equality of the races is a natural fact, and that suffrage for blacks and women is just, given their natural capabilities. The slippery slope that leads from the abolition of racially based slavery to socialism is for us less than clear; the argument against slave labor is not really particularly compatible with the argument against property. And it is also too simple—unless revelation, contrary to Brownson's view, contradicts reason—to say that God ordained that men should rule over women.[94] We do not have to accept Brownson's view that there is an inevitable movement from the *political* equality of the eighteenth century to the *social* equality of the nineteenth: "Once you concede that even political equality is a good, an object worth seeking, you must concede that social equality is also a good; and social equality is necessarily the annihilation of religion, government, property, and family."[95] Brownson himself seems to have accepted the political equality of the American founding while resolutely opposing those who would abolish all distinctively human institutions. He writes, "We want no political aristocracy. Let all be equal before the law" right before endorsing a "social aristocracy" com-posed of prominent, educated families "to furnish models and leaders for the people."[96] And his opposition to "negro suffrage" was usually prudential and in full confidence that in a civilized, republican, and Christian nation, this opposition would eventually come to an end.

But Tocqueville, while more judiciously affirming the good that is political equality, agrees with Brownson on modern democracy's insatiable desire to abolish human distinctions. The passion, Tocqueville says, that corresponds to the love of equality is really hatred of privilege, or anything that distinguishes one human being from another. When that hatred is turned against all particular beings, all individuals, it is really directed toward the economic, political, and religious life which distinguishes human beings. It is also, of course, directed against human love as it actually exists.[97] That is why Brownson says that modern liberalism "is more disposed to hate than love, and is abler to destroy than to build up."[98] That is also why Brownson fears primarily the humanitarianism of a centralized American government. Socialism, he thinks, will not dominate particular states; "philanthropy, unlike charity, does not begin at home, and is powerless unless it operates at a distance" (236). Charity depends on our real knowledge of particular beings, and that, of course, is strongest at home; philanthropy depends on vision so blurred that we cannot tell one being from another. Brownson's objection to humanitarianism or socialism or pantheism is founded on those ideologies' opposition to truth and virtue. And his defense of the particular states is really a defense of the truth and goodness of human particularity.

Christopher Lasch notices that Brownson's opposition to philanthropy is really opposition to the emptiness of cosmopolitanism. Because Brownson saw so clearly that man is a social being, he favored the fellowship that real men had with each other as friends, fathers and sons, neighbors, and citizens. Although he saw political attachment as primarily to the nation, devotion to a particular territory is, in Brownson's mind, the precondition for the social attachments and ordinary virtues that make life worthwhile. Because human beings have bodies and are inextricably dependent on society, they must approach reality—even what is universally true—through "a particular

set of loyalties." Cosmopolitanism—devotion to a city with no geographical or properly human boundaries—is an oxymoron. Its un-
bridled pursuit leads to lonely solitude, personal impotence, and the
apathy that is the precondition of all despotism. Lasch concludes that
"Man grasps the universal only through the particular: this was the
core of Brownson's Christian radicalism."[99]

Brownson does admit that "[a]ll systems, however erroneous or
false, have an element of truth, because the human intellect, being
created in the image of the divine, and made for the apprehension of
the truth, can never operate with pure falsehood."[100] And so he criticizes Donoso Cortes for his excessive partisanship: Cortes fails to illuminate "the grain of truth" in the socialist "system" he so ably criticizes.[101] The truth of humanitarianism or socialism is that it "faintly
mirrors the Christian doctrine of the unity and solidarity of the race."
It only could have come into being in a Christian nation with some
remnant of the idea of Christian love. Socialism from this view is less
anti-Christian than it is a Christian heresy. "There is," Brownson adds,
"something that will not do to sneer at in that free and noble spirit
that seeks to break down the artificial barriers which separate man
from man and nation from nation, and melt all into one grand brotherhood."[102] He almost acknowledges that there is, finally, something
artificial, if not arbitrary, about the division of the world into political territories or nations. He even goes so far as to say, "Much at least
of what is most living, least groveling, least servile, most manly, and
most elevated, outside the church, is found to-day" in the ranks of the
socialists and the philanthropists.[103]

In his less polemical moments, Brownson acknowledged that the
error of humanitarians is far less moral than it is intellectual and
religious. They believe that the egalitarian, transpolitical principles
that govern human communion with God could supplant the necessities and distinctive goods of our economic and political existence, and

that they could do so, somehow, on a merely natural and social basis, without acknowledging the Creator. The error is in believing that our real spiritual and even rational ends can be achieved through social reform. Although more dangerous, humanitarian liberalism, or socialism, is in some respects more noble and more Christian than Southern feudalism. The Southern defense of liberty understood as assertive individuality is more clearly a cause for real men, but the best humanitarians were and are as manly, free, and noble as the best Southerners. Their fundamental contradiction is in manifesting their individual excellence by struggling to create a world without extraordinary persons such as themselves. The Southerners more consistently, if unjustly, engaged in self-defense.

Brownson's Moral Moderation vs. Middle-Class Incoherence

Brownson sometimes takes the side of both the Southern aristocrats and the Northern humanitarians—not to mention his fellow Catholics—against the restless materialism of American democrats. He does not do so in *The American Republic*, where he tries to ennoble American patriotism. But we cannot appreciate his rhetorical purpose in this volume without attending to what he really believes to be true about American and modern democracy. Brownson's goal is to preserve the distinction between the democratic formula of "equality before the law" and social equality. For he believes that government is best—most republican—when political democracy coexists with social aristocracy as an imperfect but real reflection of the aristocracy rooted in the inequality of natural gifts.

But Brownson is no great friend of the economic inequality not only maintained but also exaggerated by political democracy: American economic liberty "operates practically, almost exclusively, in favor of those who command and employ capital or credit in business, and against the poorer and more numerous classes."[104] Brownson, because he shares the aristocratic and humanitarian dedication to virtue over self-interest, is sometimes, from our view, too hard on men of commerce who act candidly on behalf of their economic good: "The men of wealth, the businessmen, manufacturers and merchants, the bankers and brokers are the men who exert the worst influence in every country, for they always strive to use it as an instrument for advancing their own private interests." Brownson's Christian maxim is, "Let the government take care of the weak, the strong can take care of themselves." And one of his complaints against relying on universal suffrage as an antidote to tyranny is that it "is too weak to prevent private property from having an undue political influence" (242).

Again, Brownson's concern is Tocqueville's: Another danger in democratic societies, besides the tyranny of the majority and soft despotism, is rule by industrialist aristocrats, who generally lack the paternalistic qualities of the older aristocracy.[105] The democratic aristocracy, Brownson writes, "founded on business capacity or capital or credit," is "a thousand times worse and more offensive" than hereditary aristocracy. Consider his most memorable outburst on this matter: "We do not object to a man, or refuse to honor him, because he has risen from the gutter; but we do refuse to honor a man who was born in the gutter and has remained there, but claims respect simply because he has succeeded in gathering a mass of gold around him."[106] Brownson's indignation here is both aristocratic and populist. As Lasch notes, almost everything Brownson wrote is infused with a Christian concern for the souls and moral and intellectual development of ordinary people.[107] It is also worth noting that his argument here was often used by antebellum Southerners to criticize the North: Your aristocracy is more heartless than our aristocracy. And Brownson accepts the Southern view that an aristocracy based simply on money or economic power is not a true aristocracy.

But Brownson, of course, is no socialist; he does not advocate the abolition of property or even its redistribution by the government. He says that all socialism and communism can realistically promise is a dismal equality in poverty, a poverty devoid of moral dignity. Rather, he is concerned about the political and spiritual lives of Americans, which are threatened by the materialistic premises of both capitalism and socialism. His real complaint is that "[b]y excluding the moral element and founding the state on utility, democracy tends to materialize the mind, and to create a passion for sensible goods, or material wealth and well-being."[108] The materialistic passion of Americans is based on the opinion that matter is all there is. The only human distinction or point of honor concerns who has the most stuff.

On the other hand, "it is to the honor of the church that she has always had a special regard and tenderness for the poor; and it is no less to her honor that she has never attempted to remove poverty." Poverty, if anything, "is a blessing." The Bible says the poor "are really the more favored class." Brownson's objection to both capitalism and socialism is that they base the worth or dignity of a man on his wealth;[109] both systems are Hobbesian, not Christian.[110] "One of the great services Christianity has rendered the world," he explains, "has been its consecration of poverty and its elevation of labor to the dignity of a moral duty." But the tendency of modern individualists, North and South, is to "treat poverty as a crime, and hold that honest labor should be endured by none who can escape it."[111] From this perspective, the Southern aristocrats must be lumped with the Hobbesians, and only the Christians are the true democrats.

Brownson sees that "[t]he passion for wealth, so strong in most Americans . . . is at bottom the desire to escape poverty and the disgrace attached to it by democracy." Not material need but the desire not to be pitied or lacking in honor spurs the material restlessness of Americans. They are "discontented," and their poverty is "a real misery" for reasons having little to do with material deprivation. The influence of the Church has always been to see "the honest and virtuous poor . . . respected according to their true worth." And so the influence of the Church in America should be to moderate a restless discontent that ends only in death. The "universal struggle" to escape poverty and gain wealth in America is animated by the attempt to establish *some* form of inequality, to prove one's superiority. Nobody, unfortunately, seems to be content with "moral equality," which exists under God and has nothing to do with wealth.[112]

So important in Brownson's eyes are the moral limitations to the spirit of commerce that he sometimes affirms, with the exception of slavery, the superiority of Southern to Northern society, and he urges the New Englander to imitate the Southerner. The Southerner has the virtues and vices common to every aristocrat, while those of the New Englander are middle-class or bourgeois. "The New Englander has excellent points," Brownson observes, "but is restless in body and mind, always scheming, always in motion, never satisfied with what he has, and always seeking to make all the world like himself, or as uneasy as himself." He is, as Tocqueville says, restless in the midst of prosperity.[113]

The New Englander is "smart, seldom great; educated, but seldom learned; active in mind, but rarely a profound thinker; religious, but thoroughly materialistic." He is clever but not profound because he subordinates the mind to the body; he does not regard the pleasures of the mind or intellectual greatness as good for their own sake.[114] He does what he can to divert himself from deep thought because real, leisurely thought would reveal to him the emptiness of his religious materialism. He is, in fact, miserable in God's absence; he is a member of the "community of the lost rather than that of the blest."[115]

Brownson's general judgment in comparing middle-class democracy with aristocracy also echoes Tocqueville: Democracy at its republican best is more just, but even then it is with a cost in terms of human excellence, especially moral and intellectual excellence.[116] It is true that "education has been more generally diffused than it was in the middle ages, but it is doubtful if the number of thinkers has been increased, or real mental culture extended." Even in the sciences, there are many more known facts, "but little progress has been made in their really scientific classification and explanation." And in an article written at about the same time as *The American Republic,* Brownson contradicts what he says in this book about the unprecedented and progressive character of American territorial democracy. In political science, Aristotle and "the great medieval doctors" have not been surpassed. "He who has read Aristotle's *Politics,*" Brownson observes, "has read the history of American democracy, and the unanswerable refutations of all the democratic theories and tendencies of modern liberals." It is only in our vain modern and democratic chauvinism that we are blind to our general decline.[117] All in all, the world has progressed physically since the fifteenth century, "but progress in the moral and intellectual orders has been in losing rather than in gaining."[118]

Brownson even doubts whether the end of religious persecution and the growth of tolerance are really signs of intellectual or moral progress. We are not more tolerant but "more indifferent than our predecessors, believ[ing] less in mind, and more in matter." We are more indifferent to the truth about the fundamental human questions concerning God and the good.[119] The result has been a certain kind of progress: "Taste has, indeed, been refined, and manners, habits, and sentiments have been softened, and become more humane."[120] But as Rousseau first complained, what we have come to call virtue is really just politeness, or aversion to argument, battle, and candor. Because we are too fearful to fight or even quarrel over the truth, we are short on real men; "characters have been enfeebled and debased, and we find no longer the marked individuality, the personal energy, the manliness, the force, the nobility of thought and purpose, and the high sense of honor, so common in the mediaeval word, and the better periods of antiquity."[121] Brownson's high regard for the noble aristocrats of the South is really for the concern for truth and virtue they shared with the medieval and ancient worlds, the worlds of St. Thomas and Aristotle. Brownson thought of himself, and with good reason, as full of the forceful manliness that comes with nobility of thought and purpose, and he recognized that his best qualities were out of place in his own time.

So one reason Brownson does not want the universal principles of abolitionism or humanitarianism introduced to Southern society is that the South embodies an aristocratic antidote to the democratic excesses engendered by the miserable incoherence of middle-class lives. The Southern aristocracy, recall, is not truly Christian, but it perpetuates a generous love of greatness and a high opinion of the human mind and human destiny that are indispensable for what Brownson predicts will be America's catholic future. The Southerner has an aristocratic preference for the permanent things; he is less in a hurry because he is less obsessed with time, less haunted by his mortality: The New Englander "needs the slower, the more deliberate, and the more patient and enduring man of the South to serve as his counterpoise."[122]

A social order that is both excellent and just—one that both cultivates moral, intellectual, spiritual, and political excellence, and which respects socially and politically the moral equality and dignity of the laboring poor—is partly democratic and partly aristocratic. That mixture—or, in the best case, synthesis—is quite different from the incoherent mixture of freedom and necessity—the free mind working for material satisfaction—that characterizes the mostly Northern American middle class. Brownson, with Tocqueville, is especially impressed with the instability of that incoherence; the democratic antidote to it, they fear, is the soft despotism of pantheism.

America's Political and Religious Destiny

Brownson does not conclude *The American Republic* with Tocquevillian musings about the relationships among democracy, pantheism, and humanitarian despotism. Unlike Tocqueville, he is not tempted by fatalism. He returns instead to his nation's "destiny," or "the special work or mission" it has received from Providence. That mission, as we have seen, is given each nation by its particular historical situation and the limits and possibilities of human nature. Brownson contends that "the special mission of the United States is to continue and complete in the political order the Graeco-Roman civilization" (247). That means, first of all, to continue the Roman work of reconciling law with liberty, or, more precisely, to achieve the Roman idea of the state within the unprecedented political form of the United States. That includes, of course, correcting the Greco-Roman "grand error" of slavery, which is based on the "denial or ignorance of the unity of the human race" (249), without obliterating the territorial distinctions that separate human beings into particular political communities. But the American destiny also includes rivaling or surpassing Greece "in science and philosophy" (3). America has been given the opportunity not only to achieve republican greatness but also to become the highest civilization the world has ever seen.

The United States and the European nations have been given, in principle, the same two goals: to eliminate the residual barbarism of the Roman constitution, and to achieve the "philosophical division of the powers of government." But nowhere in Europe can the second goal now be achieved, and there is "no greater contribution to civilization to be made." It can be done "[n]owhere else than in this New World, and in this New World only in the United States." Brownson goes as far as to say that only in the United States can what "the Greco-Roman republic began be completed" (257).

The United States also has a religious destiny, which corresponds to its political one. In America, church and state are separated, "but the principles in which the state is founded have their origin and ground in the spiritual order—in the principles revealed or affirmed by religion—and are inseparable from them." And just as the United States is sweeping away partial, theoretical accounts of political life with its real political accomplishment, it is replacing religious theories and sectarianism with its movement toward "catholic" or "real religion." It is true that "[a]ll real religion is catholic, and is neither new nor old, but is always and everywhere true" (258–59). Only the United States is in a position to make that truth clear, because only in our nation is government neither hostile to nor one with religion. Only here can religion be seen for what it truly is in relation to the political order (261–63).

Brownson's hopeful observation is that "[i]n the United States, false religions are legally as free as the true religion; but all false religions being one-sided, sophistical, and uncatholic, are opposed by the principles of the state, which tend, by their silent but effective workings, to eliminate them" (262–63). A superficial observer might see in America a mixture of sectarianism and indifferentism. But the American people are "in reality, less uncatholic than the people of any other country," that is, they live intellectually and politically nearer the truth about reality (269).

Brownson goes on to predict that the United States will absorb Canada, Mexico, and the Central American states. That annexation will occur freely, and new states will be the result. All of North and Central America will become one people. Brownson's confidence seems almost unbounded: "[T]he American people need not trouble themselves about their exterior expansion. That will come of itself as fast as desirable." And it will come "without any effort or action on the part of the government" (274–75).

Brownson is no imperialist; republican and catholic example will be sufficient to induce others to accept American expansion. His final mixture of prediction and advice to Americans is, "Let them devote their attention to their internal destiny . . . , and they will gradually see the whole continent coming under their system, forming one grand nation, a really catholic nation, great, glorious and free" (275). Of course, Brownson had earlier produced evidence that this poetic flourish could not be completely true; if it were, America would not need the large standing army he had recommended. But he is clear that a republic's primary task is the cultivation of virtue and devotion to truth, and that all true greatness is dependent on this "internal" accomplishment.

Brownson's prediction regarding America's destiny is not really a prediction at all. It is what America might do if its citizens and statesmen, devoted to truth and virtue, take full advantage of the possibilities given to them by nature and history. Brownson says plenty elsewhere to cause us to doubt whether his nation would actually fulfill its destiny. But the prediction that seems most strange and, in fact, is clearly wrong, is that America was already a catholic nation and destined to become more so. This argument did not move his fellow Americans, and it might be regarded as the greatest impediment to taking his book seriously, both then and now. Indeed, Brownson's catholic prediction had very little influence on Catholic Americans, and just about none at all on non-Catholic Americans. A careful reading of the whole book, together with Brownson's essays, might convince us that much, surprisingly much, of what he has to say is pretty accurate. But his nuanced and philosophical use of the word catholic was doubtless far beyond most of his American readers—even, or especially, Catholics.

Brownson's Influence: Real and Deserved

The American Republic, in truth, attracted little notice on its publication and exerted even less influence. Certainly, a number of Brownson's many essays had been much more influential when they first appeared. Even before the publication of this book, Brownson had come to think of himself, with good reason, as increasingly isolated as a thinker. He knew that he had neither the temperament nor the rhetorical gifts to be a statesman. With characteristic candor he admitted that "[w]e ourselves, we know it well, were never born to lead."[123] He was, he believed, "doomed, Cassandra-like, to utter prophecies which nobody believes" concerning dangers facing the American republic.[124] Near the end of his life, he became increasingly pessimistic about America's future, and he brooded that America and the Catholic Church might not be so compatible after all.[125] He wondered whether his writings would endure.

What Brownson wrote has endured, but there has not been since his death anything like a major Brownson revival. His influence on American political thought has been minimal, much less than he deserves. One reason is that most of his writing is only available in periodicals almost impossible to access today; others of his essays have been reprinted only for very limited audiences. In addition, his defection from Transcendentalism caused its defenders to minimize his influence over that movement and greatly overstate his quirkiness and inconstancy.

As the poet James Russell Lowell wrote of Brownson, "He shifts quite about and then proceeds to expound/ That it's merely the earth, not himself, that turns round."[126] But once Brownson became a Catholic, he did stop shifting. He was a seeker who finally found what he was looking for. Even the rather prosaic and secular Schlesinger "felt the pathos of modernity in this stormy pilgrim, this intellectually displaced person wandering passionately from one system to another until he came to relative rest in the historic certainties of the Catholic Church."[127]

Brownson's Catholicism is probably the most important reason for his neglect. The fact that Brownson believed the teaching of the Catholic Church to be true is bad enough, in many eyes, but his insistence that all Americans should be and even in some sense already are Catholic seemed so strange and illiberal as to cast him to the intellectual margins. Brownson does not fit into the history of progress that is the usual tale of American thought. He was not a progressivist, not an uncritical democrat, not a socialist, not a proponent of laissez-faire—but he was still a defender of the working man and a resolute opponent of slavery. He was neither a progressive nor a reactionary and, in the way the terms are now used, not clearly either a liberal or a conservative. The mature Brownson was associated with no movement, and no movement was associated with him. He did not even fare well with most Catholics of his time, who found him too quarrelsome, too philosophical, too American, too Yankee. He never did find a place of leadership in the largely immigrant Church.

Some American Catholic scholars, especially prior to Vatican II, took Brownson's political thought seriously. They saw its superiority to secular and Protestant liberalism and accordingly made him one of their own. But there have not been many such scholars, and their books and articles are buried in obscure places.[128] None of those scholars had the combination of depth of thought and literary talent required to establish Brownson as a major figure in American political thought. Their main shortcoming, it seems to me, was their inability to locate Brownson in critical relation to the dominant secular, natural-right, humanitarian, and progressivist tendencies in American thought. After Vatican II, Brownson almost, but not quite, disappeared from the work of American Catholic scholars. Only a very few studies since then have taken his claims to tell the truth seriously.[129] Non-Catholic scholars, when they have found something to admire in Brownson, have usually pointed to his passionate devotion to the search for truth and not to what he actually thought.[130] One outstanding exception to this rule was Christopher Lasch. He liked what Brownson had to say about truth being the moral foundation of democracy; he applauded Brownson's refusal to separate completely politics and religion, either in his own thought or that of the American people.

Another remarkable student of Brownson in our time was another Catholic convert, Russell Kirk. Kirk time and again presented Brownson as the model political thinker for Catholic and conservative Americans. He emphasized Brownson's argument that freedom and authority had to be reconciled in justice, and that this could happen only under God. Kirk was also struck by the connection between Brownson's Catholicism and his prescient stands against socialism and other forms of humanitarian despotism, and he called attention to forgotten articles by Brownson critical of the restless anxiety, untutored impulsiveness, and general mediocrity of American life. Kirk saw clearly that what Brownson called humanitarian thought knows no limits, respecting neither territorial limitations nor individual distinctions, and he emphasized Brownson's connection between the disappearance of God and the abolition of man. The "featureless social equality" characteristic of what both Brownson and Tocqueville called democratic despotism requires the absence of both the personal Creator and human individuality.[131] In the same spirit of defense of human particularity against ideological universalism, Kirk favored "territorial democracy"—with its twin limitations of geography and justice—over "plebiscitary democracy."[132] Kirk, also a pioneer in the recovery of Tocqueville's thought for our time, presented a distinctively Tocquevillian view of Brownson.

Kirk's many discussions of Brownson were always suggestive and introductory, written with the intention of leading the reader to

Brownson himself. He, in fact, managed in a very few pages to touch on each of the seven characteristics of Brownson's writing that commend it to us today. First, Brownson is "intellectually one of the most interesting of all Americans." Second, "his examination of order in the United States is an original work." Third, "late in the twentieth century, Americans confront the fundamental problems of personal and social order in which Brownson was passionately interested." Fourth, "he was a considerable political philosopher"—"something rare in the United States." Fifth, "the subtle influence of Brownson's writings . . . has done something to chasten American impulsiveness and materialism." (Kirk, unfortunately, does not trace this influence.) Sixth, he was "one of the shrewder observers of American character and institutions." Finally, "[h]is politics were the politics of a religious man, not of a Benthamite who looks upon the Church as a moral police force."[133] Each of those contributions, I hope, has some place in my commentary on *The American Republic*.

Kirk's promotion of Brownson was unflagging, but it failed to spark a great revival of interest in Brownson, even though Kirk's own thought, of course, has been quite influential. Many Americans who call themselves conservative have come to understand the world in a Kirkian or traditionalist way, and they have become devoted to many of the authors presented in Kirk's *Conservative Mind*, but not very often Brownson. One reason, as Kirk himself admits, is that Brownson's prose is maddeningly redundant and verbose. Brownson, as usual, is honest enough to admit as much. As he says in the preface to *The American Republic*, "My work can lay claim to very little artistic merit." He deliberately filled it with "repetitions," because he has "very little confidence in the memory or industry of readers" (cvi). He clearly had too *much* confidence in the reader's patience.

Kirk sent T. S. Eliot a copy of the anthology of Brownson's political essays he edited. The poet wrote Kirk that he thought it "remarkable that a Yankee a century ago should have held such views as his, and depressing that he has been so ignored and most of us have never heard of him." But Brownson still irritated him: "I am not altogether pleased with Brownson's style, which strikes me as wordy and diffuse."[134] That too is a bit depressing, because perhaps the poet could have learned from Brownson the proper dignity of national or political life in our time.

I might also say that Kirk's own style is too distant from Brownson's really to have been able to convey the most fascinating and controversial elements of Brownson's thought. Often Brownson gets the reader to turn pages not because of how he writes, but because of his bold and brilliant accounts of neglected and fundamental truth. Kirk thought too much of prudence to pronounce that our leading framers were political atheists who were seduced by the anti-Christian doctrines of Hobbes and Locke. He thought it rather un-conservative to take our fathers on directly at all; his critique of the founders can be made out mainly by considering whom he discussed sympathetically and whom he slighted or ignored. Kirk does suggest that the Declaration of Independence, though partly true and Christian, was also partly false and pernicious. But his primary rhetorical task was to show that the Declaration was of no great consequence by reading Jefferson and Locke out of the American tradition rightly understood.

That is not to say that Kirk saw nothing good in the accomplishments of Locke or Jefferson, but he rejected what was distinctive or original about their thought. Kirk approves more of the orthodox theology Congress added to the Declaration (such as the reference to "Divine Providence") than he does of what Jefferson himself wrote.[135] He sees Jefferson's phrase "created equal," for example, as fuzzy, unempirical, and fodder for later demagogues.[136] Kirk argues that Congress did not cross it out only because the phrase was understood sensibly by most of the members in a Christian, not Lockean, context.[137] And so, although Kirk's view of the theory of the founding generation seems at first glance less contentious than Brownson's, it is really not very different.

The goal of Brownson and Kirk is not to do away with Mr. Jefferson's place in American thought. That would be unhistorical and contrary to the facts. Jeffersonianism needs to be in one respect limited and moderated, and in another way completed. Consent or personal sovereignty by itself cannot be the foundation of government, and human liberty needs a better foundation than the abstraction of the Lockean state of nature. Brownson should be viewed as a supplement to Jefferson, and an incomplete one at that. Brownson's thought in some ways is more realistic and political than Jefferson's. But we cannot forget that Jefferson was a formidable statesman, and Brownson never did hold political office, because he was not suited for it. While Brownson rightly criticizes the extremism or political atheism of Jefferson's war against religious tyranny, he also pretty well takes Jefferson's victory in that war for granted in praising the American separation of church and state. Brownson and Jefferson are alike in that both thought and wrote about a wide variety of human issues. Brownson was stronger on theology and metaphysics, but finally we cannot forget the extraordinary political accomplishments of Jefferson and the other leading men of the founding generation. And we cannot forget that Jefferson wrote that the point of democracy is that the natural aristocracy rises to the top.

In his own way Kirk privileged the providential or unwritten constitution over the written one, and he has done more than anyone else in our time to keep Brownson's ideas alive. But he did not quite present Brownson's argument for the American nation in Brownson's own terms. Kirk, for example, changed the meaning of "territorial democracy." For him, such a democracy is simply one "founded upon the local rights of the several states and smaller organs of society."[138] But for Brownson, territorial democracy referred to a nation-state rooted in a particular form of government and not devotion to a particular ruler or ruling group. It was not synonymous with federalism, which is how Kirk tends to use it.

Both Kirk and Brownson agreed that grounding political life in universal principles and not particular territory is destructive of all government, and that the American constitution cannot be understood as a model for all other nations. They also saw that an American nation without vigorous, particularistic states would tend toward despotism. On the one hand, Brownson made more of natural rights and the political relevance of the revealed fact of human equality. And he also made more of both the naturalness and the goodness of the loyalty of citizens to their nation, and therefore more of national greatness and military virtue. On the other hand, Kirk agrees with Brownson that government is not merely repressive, that it achieves justice, secures liberty, and "advance[s] the culture of society."[139] And they also agree "that there was more to America's great expectations than the almighty dollar."[140]

It has been said that "Father John Courtney Murray, S.J., stands with Orestes Brownson as the only two Catholics in American history that one might be prompted to categorize as genuine 'political philosophers.'"[141] Murray, author of *We Hold These Truths*, is recognized by many as the leading and even the authoritative Catholic American teacher on political life in the twentieth century; he, more than anyone else, was responsible for the character of Vatican II's statement on religious liberty (*Dignitatis Humanae*). As far as I know, Murray never acknowledged a debt to Brownson, but the influence has been noticed more than once. The safest thing to say is that the obvious and deep similarities in their thought about the relationship between their Church and their nation shows Brownson's influence on American Catholic thinking and the unity of truth.

Murray, like Brownson, claims that the American founders built better than they knew, for they were providentially more dependent on a tradition of Catholic natural-law thought. What Murray calls "providential" is "the evident coincidence of the principles which inspired the American Republic with the principles which are structural to the Western Christian political tradition."[142] Thus, the founders' written Constitution is admirable, unprecedented, and can be defended with Catholic principles. Catholics, says Murray, can be good Americans with "conscience and conviction."[143] But Murray does not deny that the founders were also heavily influenced by an anti-ecclesiastical Lockeanism, a form of political atheism that culminates in either totalitarian revolution or "impotent nihilism."[144] The founders built better than they knew, but they left their accomplishment more vulnerable than they knew to erosion by theory destructive of all government and, in fact, of human order and human liberty.

The title of Murray's famous book comes, of course, from a particular part of the Declaration of Independence. What makes the American people a whole is our common devotion to the truth. If our republic is really a republic it is because we hold this good in common. But by Murray's time, American intellectuals were no longer convinced that human beings, by nature, could know the truth about the real foundation of political order. Because we are no longer realists, we are no longer really republicans. Murray accepts and if anything radicalizes Brownson's belief that republicans must be realists. Murray, in fact, departs from Brownson by making our civic devotion solely dependent on the truth and not at all dependent on territory.

Murray makes it clear that his model here is Lincoln: "It is classic American doctrine, immortally asserted by Abraham Lincoln, that the new nation which our fathers brought forth on this continent was dedicated to a 'proposition.'"[145] That proposition is found in the Declaration of Independence, and for Murray that inspirational document *must* be used to illuminate the Constitution. But, for Lincoln, that illumination does not necessarily mean being strictly faithful to Jefferson's intentions. One reason that Murray puts more weight on the Declaration than does Brownson is that he is more conscious of a deficiency of our written Constitution: its silence on God. So, he emphasizes that the Declaration, a "landmark of Western political theory," put "this nation under God."[146] Murray agrees with Lincoln that the only way to save the Constitution from the moral superficiality or excessive selfishness of secularism is to constitutionalize the Declaration. Brownson might object, of course, that the Declaration, being so theoretical and Lockean, is actually more dangerously atheistic than the Constitution's pedestrian and political "We, the people of the United States." And so the written Constitution's sacred foundation is better located in the providential constitution alone. But Murray might respond that, since Lincoln at least, referring to our unwritten constitution rather than the Declaration to buttress a correct understanding of the American order has become all but impossible.

Today, Murray contends, the most imperiled part of the American proposition is the belief that the principles we hold in common are true, that is, that they actually correspond to the created nature of human beings. If this faith in a "realist epistemology is denied," then "the American proposition is eviscerated . . . in one stroke."[147] Murray's realism teaches that human beings are oriented by nature toward the discovery of truth. That view now seems to be denied everywhere, and one main reason is that we can see so clearly that the contract theory of Locke was based on realism's denial. Social and political reality, Locke and his successors argue, is created out of nothing by sovereign beings. In order to defend our principles, Murray recommends that we abandon Locke in favor of the realist St. Thomas. Fortunately, writes Murray, echoing Brownson, our fathers' belief in Locke's teaching concerning the state of nature is no longer credible anywhere. Their "serene, and often naïve, certainties of the eighteenth century" are our nonsense. The deconstruction of Lockeanism points the way to a realism that would truly make sense of the American proposition.[148]

More even than Brownson, Murray contends that Americans now need to employ reason to become conscious of their purpose. With the waning of Lockeanism, our ability to appeal to our political "fathers" for guidance is now quite limited. The problem of human freedom "stands revealed to us" in a way it was not to our fathers, because we, not they, are in a position to see the "naked essence," the nihilistic individualism, at the core of the modern experiment to which they contributed.[149] We have no choice but to confront what they did not have to confront.

As Brownson also believed, Murray contends that the modern idea of freedom has been primarily destructive. It has left human beings dissatisfied with all traditional or natural or "given" answers to the question, "What is man?" We no longer know why being human is good at all. Human beings have deconstructed themselves as purposeful and rational beings in theory, and they have worked, in our time, in various ways to do so in practice.[150] Brownson's fears about the Rousseauistic theory and practice that informs abolitionist humanitarianism are confirmed by the experience on which Murray reflects. Communism, Murray says, was "political modernity carried to its logical conclusion," by which he means "all that is implicit or unintentional in modernity" became "explicit or deliberate in the Communist system."[151]

Well before the revolution of 1989, Murray knew that communism was the end of modern history, but not the end of history itself. Hope for history's end has always been a misanthropic "mirage." Now, at the end of the destructive modern era, human beings feel a "spiritual vacuum . . . at the heart of human existence." Murray observes that "postmodern" man cannot help but engage in "anxious reflection" about how our "hollow emptiness [should] be filled." We have no choice but to confront "the nature and structure of reality itself," and by so doing make "a metaphysical decision about the nature of man."[152] In one sense, we are better situated in Murray's time than in Brownson's: We now know that we cannot do without metaphysical and theological reflection, because the modern era did not succeed in destroying the thoughtful and anxious human individual. The good news, in a way, is that Brownson's Tocquevillian observations about the restless mediocrity of Americans are more true than ever.

The decision that will free us from impotent nihilism is for "a metaphysics of right," a standard that is not "subjective" or based merely on human decision. In other words, we must turn to the idea of natural law. For Murray, natural law doctrine is without "presuppositions." It is completely verifiable empirically. Nature is a "teleological concept" that can guide human beings as rational, moral, and spiritual beings.[153] To "choose" the natural law is to choose to recognize the truth about being and human being, and to reject ideological lies and Lockean abstractions.

Murray seems at times to differ from Brownson by affirming the rational self-sufficiency of natural law. But actually he, like Brownson, seems to direct us to philosophic inquiry in the confidence that reason, properly employed, will find its own limits. He agrees with Brownson that a true understanding of human liberty depends upon revelation or belief in a Creator, and that this belief can be affirmed by reason as the best of the plausible alternative explanations of a mystery that eludes rational comprehension. Revelation leads human beings beyond what they would know by nature alone, teaching "the equality of all men, and the unity of the human race."[154] It is only through revelation, however, that we can know the truth that we are more than political and rational animals, that we are creatures with a duty to the Creator. It is only through revelation, as Brownson says, that we know that natural law is law.

By centering his concern on the truth and the being who can know it by nature, and, finally, on the dependence of reason on revelation, Murray, whether he knows it or not, follows in Brownson's footsteps. With Brownson and Murray, we can say that there is an American tradition of Thomistic realism, which opposes itself in theory to the dominant tradition of contractualism and pragmatism while resolutely affirming the achievement of American constitutionalism. We might add to the American Thomist tradition the great literary artists Walker Percy and Flannery O'Connor, who like Brownson affirmed the truth of man against the excesses of both the American North and the American South. Both Percy and O'Connor recognize the truth of the aristocratic criticism of democracy while still agreeing with the Christian affirmation of democracy, despite all its mediocrity and derangement. We also find in Percy, not only a novelist but also a philosopher, a realistic affirmation of the truth and goodness of science balanced with a rejection of any scientific claims that do not acknowledge the reality of the distinctive excellences and destiny of human beings.

Brownson certainly differs from Lincoln and even from Murray in his consistent subordination of equality to truth. We can fault Brownson for not caring enough about slavery's extinction—although he criticized Lincoln for not declaring emancipation immediately after war broke out. But Brownson wrote mainly in terms of the danger Americans would face after the war. And he viewed humanitarian sentimentalism and pantheism as greater dangers to the truth than the pagan aristocracy of the South. The century just ended confirms Brownson's view, and it does so without engaging in any obfuscation of the evil that permeated the antebellum South. The truth is that Southern barbarism paled in comparison to the barbaric assaults against truth

and human dignity mounted by totalitarianism in the twentieth century.

In thinking about Brownson's privileging of the truth, we should
remember that the great anticommunist dissidents Aleksandr
Solzhenitsyn and Václav Havel said that the revolution of 1989 was
against the lie of ideology and on behalf of the truth, by which they
meant on behalf of the being who can know and live in light of the
truth. We must also remember that the leading American professor of
philosophy, Richard Rorty, says we ought to prefer comfort to truth,
and the best way to do that is to label anything that makes us com-
fortable as true. Rorty quite rightly traces this preference to Jefferson,
as indicated in his preference for Unitarianism over Calvinism and
Catholicism. We could also say something about the growth of pantheism in our time, about the view that human beings are qualitatively no different from the other animals. We have every reason to
fear that the deepest goal of the emerging biotechnological revolution
will be to make that otherwise incredible view true. Because pantheism is the most radical form of egalitarianism imaginable, it is easy
for us to say that we must to some extent do battle against egalitarianism on behalf of the truth. But in doing so we must follow Brownson
in not opposing the truth of revelation to scientific truth. When the
Declaration says all men are created equal, it preserves as true the
natural distinctions that separate man from both the other animals
and God. And the Declaration, as a political assertion of a particular
people and not an invitation for revolution everywhere, also preserves
the distinction between political particularity and spiritual universality.

Brownson and Murray agree that human liberty must be understood as freedom for the person to discover the truth embodied in the
Church. As Murray explains, the pre-Christian West was marked by
a "monism" that had no place for the church and so no place for the

transpolitical individual. And the post-Christian West attempts in incipiently totalitarian fashion to restore that unity at the expense of individuality or particularity. The Church teaches that God has given men freedom so that they can pursue the truth about God, and so that the Church can perform its mission of evangelization, thus aiding man in that pursuit. Truth, by its nature, is catholic. Understanding truth in subjective or sentimental terms, in Protestant or Transcendentalist fashion, does not give it the dignity required to defend itself against despotic politicization. The truths we Americans hold in common must really be true if our liberty is to be really defensible.

Brownson is more emphatic than Murray about the political dimension of the human being and the virtue of loyalty. But Murray's criticism of the principles of our fathers is more cautious and indirect than Brownson's. Our founding liberals, whatever their faults, are superior to contemporary liberals. The natural-law tradition in decline in their time has completely lost its hold on American liberals in our time. The way back to Thomistic realism, the path Murray devoted himself to tracing, must be through a critical appreciation of our fathers. Perhaps Brownson could be bolder in opposing Lockeanism because he was more confident that through his writing it could be replaced by something better. Murray knew that too aggressive an attack on Lockean individualism would give too much aid and comfort to socialists, relativists, and nihilists, because American Lockeanism is embedded in the American form of constitutionalism, which is, in fact, more than Locke. On the latter point, of course, Brownson agrees. But there is nothing Brownson says against Lockeanism and its theoretical and American implications with which Murray does not agree.

Brownson's defense of the nation or territorial democracy was, in its way, offered in opposition to the universalism of the French Revolution; thus does Brownson's nationalism remind us of Tocqueville's and even de Gaulle's French nationalism. The most able defender of the nation today is the French Catholic Tocquevillian Pierre Manent. Manent observes that France came into its own in the nineteenth century in opposition to universalistic political efforts. In this respect Brownson was a characteristic nineteenth-century thinker. Manent also sees that the nation has in large measure been discredited by the world wars and totalitarianism. The result: "Today universal humanity tends to overwhelm difference so much that it sometimes seems that between the individual and the world ('we are the world') nothing intrudes except maybe a void where various ethnic, religious, and sexual 'identities' float, each demanding respect."[155]

The political or republican dimension of human life, genuine concern with the common good, has almost disappeared. Manent sees that the "popular term *identity* is a terribly impoverished substitute for the older term *community*." And the decline in community has been caused by the decline in what "was traditionally considered to be the community par excellence, the 'supreme' community, as Aristotle famously noted," the political community.[156] The truth is, Manent agrees with Brownson, that "[m]an as a free and rational being cannot fulfill himself outside a political community, with all the consequences (not all of them pleasant) that this entails. It is in the political body, and only in the political body, that we seriously put things in common." The city or *polis*, where deliberation over justice occurs, is qualitatively different from the family, and it, more than the family, is the model for distinctively human community.[157]

Manent notices that, despite its desire for self-sufficiency, even modern democracy needs a "body" to actually exist. It needs limits, a "territorial framework" that may seem arbitrary but is indispensable for the existence of political life. The modern European, Manent explains, wanted the principle of consent to govern everything, for everything to be the product of his will, for nothing to be given or providential. The result is a paradox: "The European wanted only what he himself willed; he rejected as arbitrary and outdated the nation, the political instrument that allowed him, by giving him limits, to exercise his sovereignty or will." The willful escape from limits paradoxically made the exercise of political will much less possible: "The European as a citizen finds himself able to accomplish less and less."[158]

Republican government must be territorial; the nation may well be the indispensable modern form of the state or *polis*, loyalty more than consent must be the foundation of good government and political life, and the withering away of the state will be at the expense of all that human beings rightly regard as good. The truth, as Manent says, is that people cannot "live long within civilization alone without some sense of political belonging (which is necessarily exclusive), and thus without some definition of what we hold in common."[159] And what we hold in common, given what we have inherited from the Greeks, Romans, and Christians, must be partly particular, or exclusive to us as citizens, and partly universal, or an expression of the solidarity of all human beings. The modern nation, with its mixture of the exclusivity of citizenship and openness to universal truth embodied in religion and transnational civilization and culture, mirror, if only very imperfectly, the complexity which is human nature. In this respect, Brownson's political analysis, in its insistence on respect for particularity, has held up well.

What Manent views as the proper role of political philosophy today is nothing more than what Brownson saw in his time. The political thinker, in Manent's words, "legitimates the city before the church"; he "affirms the human virtues" and "maintains the legitimacy of human affirmation." He affirms the naturalness of political life and the reality of the particular human individual against empty and impotent cosmopolitanism, and human liberty against the lies of socialism and pantheism. But that affirmation must be under God. So the political thinker must also affirm "the universality of the church

against the particularity of the city" and display "a skepticism toward every human self-assertion that remains particular."[160] He defends the republic, civilization, and the church against barbarism, and
he defends the truth—and thus the freedom of thought, the individual,
and the church—against the despotism that all nations tend toward
when uninfluenced by the truth of revelation.

Notes

1. This biographical sketch is indebted, most of all, to Thomas R. Ryan,
   Orestes A. Brownson: A Definitive Biography (Huntington, Ind.: Our Sunday
   Visitor, 1976). This massive book is very thorough and sympathetic, and is
   informed throughout by the author's considerable learning. I have also
   benefited from Patrick Allitt, *Catholic Converts* (Ithaca, N.Y.: Cornell
   University Press, 1997) and R. A. Herrera, *Orestes Brownson: Signs of
   Contradiction* (Wilmington, Del.: ISI Books, 1999).

2. Gregory S. Butler, *In Search of the American Spirit: The Political Thought of
   Orestes Brownson* (Carbondale, Ill.: Southern Illinois Press, 1992) is particularly good in chronicling Brownson's gnostic humanitarianism and his
   rejection of it in favor of Catholic theology. Butler illuminates Brownson
   with Voegelin.

3. Ibid., 79.

4. Arthur M. Schlesinger Jr., *A Life in the Twentieth Century* (New York:
   Houghton Mifflin, 2000), 177.

5. Butler, *In Search of the American Spirit*, 75–76. The last quote is from
   Brownson, *The Convert*, as quoted by Butler, 76.

6. Brownson, *The Convert*, as quoted by Allitt, 66.

7. Butler, *In Search of the American Spirit*, 83.

8. Schlesinger, *A Life in the Twentieth Century*, 177.

9. Alvan S. Ryan, "Orestes A. Brownson, 1803-76: The Critique of Transcendentalism," *American Classics Reconsidered*, ed. Harold S. Gardiner (New
   York: Scribner's, 1958), 115.

10. Russell Kirk, "Introduction," *Orestes Brownson: Selected Political Essays*, ed.
    Russell Kirk (New Brunswick, N.J.: Transaction, 1990; originally pub-
    lished, 1955), 3.

11. Schlesinger, *A Life in the Twentieth Century*, 177. Schlesinger's first book
    was a revision of his senior thesis at Harvard on Brownson (*Orestes A.
    Brownson: A Pilgrim's Progress* [Boston: Little Brown, 1939]).

12. Quoted in Ryan, *Orestes A. Brownson*, 728.

13. Ryan, *Orestes A. Brownson*, 626.

14. Brownson, as quoted by Ryan, *Orestes A. Brownson*, 646.

15. Page references in the text are to this edition of *The American Republic.*

16. Isaac T. Hecker, "Dr. Brownson and Catholicity," *Catholic World* 46 (1887): 222–35.

17. See my "The Dissident Criticism of America," *The American Experiment: Essays on the Theory and Practice of Liberty* (Lanham, Md.: Rowman and Littlefield, 1994).

18. Orestes Brownson, "Catholic Schools," *The Brownson Reader*, ed. A. Ryan (New York: P.J. Kennedy and Sons, 1955), 138.

19. Orestes Brownson, "Rationalism and Traditionalism" (1860), *The Works of Orestes Brownson* (Detroit: Thorndike Nourse, 1882-87), vol. 1, 491. Armand Mauer's "Orestes Brownson's Christian Philosophy," *Monist* (July 1992), 341–54 called this passage and several others to my attention. Mauer's article is easily the best account of Brownson's view of the relationship between reason and revelation.

20. Brownson, "Rationalism and Traditionalism," 490.

21. Ibid., 500.

22. Ibid., 501–02 with the context set throughout Mauer's article.

23. Brownson, "Science and the Sciences," *The Brownson Reader*, 245. Emphasis added.

24. Brownson, "An Old Quarrel" (1867), *Works*, vol. 2, 303.

25. Brownson, "Refutation of Atheism" (1873–74), *Works*, vol. 2, 100.

26. Brownson, "Schools of Philosophy" (1854), *Works*, vol. 1, 302–03.

27. Brownson, "Our Lady of Lourdes" (1875), *Orestes A. Brownson: Selected Writings*, ed. Patrick W. Carey (New York: Paulist Press, 1991), 272.

28. Brownson, "Rationalism and Traditionalism," 519.

29. Orestes Brownson, "Liberalism and Progress," *Selected Political Essays*, 172.

30. Brownson, "Nature and Grace" (1868), *Selected Writings*, 286.

31. Brownson, "Our Lady of Lourdes," 272.

32. Brownson, "Catholic Polemics" (1861), *The Brownson Reader*, 334.

33. Ibid., 335.

34. Christopher Lasch, *The True and Only Heaven: Progress and Its Critics* (New York: W.W. Norton, 1991), 184–97.

35. Alexis de Tocqueville, *Democracy in America*, vol. 2, pt. 1, ch. 16.

36. Lasch, *The True and Only Heaven*, 186–89.

37. Thomas Jefferson, *Notes on the State of Virginia*, Query XVII.

38. After a fair and judicious consideration of Jefferson's writings on religious liberty, John G. West, Jr. remarks that "[o]ne might conclude from all this that the real reason Jefferson supported religious liberty was that he thought it would bring about the triumph of his demythologized Unitarianism. This undercurrent is plainly present in Jefferson and much more so

than many realize" (*The Politics of Reason and Revelation: Religion and Civic Life in the New Nation* [Lawrence, Kans.: University Press of Kansas, 1996], 64).

39. Brownson, "Catholic Schools" (1862), *The Brownson Reader*, 139.

40. Tocqueville, *Democracy*, vol. 2, pt. 1, ch. 6 and 7.

41. Brownson, "Liberalism and Socialism," *Selected Political Essays*, 126.

42. Tocqueville, *Democracy*, vol. 2, pt. 1, ch. 7.

43. Brownson, "Nature and Grace," 302.

44. Ibid., 286.

45. Orestes Brownson, *Essays and Reviews Chiefly on Theology, Politics, and Religion* (New York: D. and J. Sadlier, 1852), 367.

46. Brownson, *The Convert*, as excerpted in *The Brownson Reader*, 298–99.

47. Alexis de Tocqueville, *The Old Regime and the Revolution*.

48. Tocqueville, *Democracy*, vol. 1, pt. 2, ch. 9 with vol. 2, pt. 1, ch. 6.

49. Brownson, "Liberalism and Socialism," 144.

50. On Madison's atheism, as well as on his noble attempt to reconcile the Lockeanism of the founders with Christian premises, see Thomas Lindsay, "Religion and the Founders' Intentions," *The American Experiment*, 119–34. For a longer and more technical version, Lindsay, "James Madison on Religion and Politics: Rhetoric and Reality," *American Political Science Review* 85 (1991): 1321–37. For a more elegant version, Gary Rosen, *American Compact: James Madison and the Problem of Founding* (Lawrence, Kans.: University Press of Kansas, 1999), 18–26. Rosen notes, in effect, that Madison's teaching on conscience or religion was proto-Transcendentalist: "Religious truth becomes a particular sort of experience rather than a doctrine" (23). It is personal, even idiosyncratic, rather than shared.

51. Aristotle, *Nicomachean Ethics*, book 1, section 2.

52. Tocqueville, *Democracy*, vol. 2, pt. 1, ch. 3.

53. Brownson, letter to George Bancroft (22 October 1866), quoted in Robert E. Moffit, "Constitutional Politics: The Political Theory of Orestes Brownson," *The Political Science Reviewer* 8 (1978), 146, note 23.

54. Brownson, "Are the United States a Nation?" (1864), *Works*, vol. 17, 560.

55. Brownson, "Public and Parochial Schools" (1859), *The Brownson Reader*, 131–32.

56. Brownson, "Liberalism and Socialism," 128.

57. Brownson is clearly wrong on the connection between *polis* and polished, as Paul Seaton demands, quite rightly, that I observe.

58. Brownson, *Essays and Reviews*, 307.

59. Brownson, "Luther and Reformation," *Works*, vol. 10, 471. I am indebted to Patrick Allitt for calling this quote and the next to my attention. See *Catholic Converts*, 82.

60. Brownson, "Luther and Reformation," 475.

61. Brownson, *Essays and Reviews*, 306–07.

62. Thomas Jefferson, *Notes on the State of Virginia*, Query XVIII.

63. Brownson, *Essays and Reviews*, 310.

64. Brownson, "Liberalism and Socialism," 128–29.

65. Brownson, "The Democratic Principle," *Selected Political Essays*, 200–02.

66. Ibid., 204.

67. Ibid., 195.

68. Brownson, "Are the United States a Nation?" 562–63.

69. Ibid., 561.

70. Ibid., 562.

71. Brownson, "Liberalism and Progress," 174.

72. Brownson, *Essays and Reviews*, 305.

73. Ibid., 312.

74. Tocqueville, *Democracy*, "Introduction."

75. Brownson, "The Democratic Principle," 199–200.

76. Ibid., 197.

77. Ibid., 197.

78. Ibid., 218.

79. Brownson, "Liberalism and Socialism," 157.

80. This paragraph is a Brownsonian reflection on the criticism of Maistre found in Harry V. Jaffa, *A New Birth of Freedom: Abraham Lincoln and the Coming of the Civil War* (Lanham, Md.: Rowman and Littlefield, 2000).

81. Brownson, "The Federal Constitution," 498–99.

82. Brownson, "Are the United States a Nation?" 564–65.

83. Ibid., 566.

84. Ryan, *Orestes A. Brownson*, 614.

85. Brownson, "The Slavery Question Once More," *Works*, vol. 17 (1857), 92.

86. Ibid., 92.

87. Brownson, "Are the United States a Nation?" 581.

88. Tocqueville, *Democracy in America*, vol. 2, pt. 1, ch. 3, vol. 2, pt. 4, ch. 6–8.

89. On the Southerners, see Tocqueville, *Democracy*, vol. 1, pt. 2, ch. 10. On the need for aristocratic qualities to fend off illiberal democratic extremism, see, for example, vol. 2, pt. 1, ch. 15 and 20; vol. 2, pt. 2, ch. 4 and 15.

90. Brownson, "Liberalism and Progress," *Selected Political Essays*, 166.

91. Tocqueville, *Democracy*, vol. 1, pt. 2, ch. 10, especially concerning the implicit comparison between the Southern masters and the Native Americans as aristocratic hunters and fighters.

92. Brownson, "Liberalism and Progress," 186.

93. Brownson, "Socialism and the Church," *Selected Political Essays*, 98.

94. But it makes no sense to say that the man who once cavorted with Fanny Wright could be filled with patriarchal prejudices. As Herrera says, "At first sympathetic to feminism, Brownson later opposed it," thinking, not without

reason, that it would "ineluctably move on to victimize the very structure of the family" (191).

95. Brownson, "Socialism and the Church," 81. I have corrected two obvious typos in this version of Brownson's essay.

96. Brownson, "Liberalism and Progress," 186.

97. See my "Tocqueville on the Doctrine of Interest," *Government and Opposition* 30 (Spring 1995).

98. Brownson, "Liberalism and Progress," 173.

99. Lasch, *The True and Only Heaven*, 189–94.

100. Brownson, "Liberalism and Socialism," 132.

101. Ibid., 126.

102. Ibid., 141.

103. Ibid., 135.

104. Brownson, "The Democratic Principle," 207.

105. Tocqueville, *Democracy*, vol. 2, pt. 2, ch. 20.

106. Brownson, "The Democratic Principle," 208–09.

107. Lasch, *The True and Only Heaven*, 185–86.

108. Brownson, "The Democratic Principle," 208.

109. Ibid., 210–12.

110. Ibid., 210–11.

111. Brownson, "Liberalism and Progress," 176.

112. Brownson, "The Democratic Principle," 211–12.

113. Tocqueville, *Democracy*, vol. 2, pt. 2, ch. 13.

114. Tocqueville, *Democracy*, vol. 2, pt. 1, ch. 10.

115. Brownson, "Liberalism and Progress," 166–67.

116. Tocqueville, *Democracy*, vol. 1, pt. 1, ch. 3 with vol. 2, pt. 1 generally.

117. Brownson, "Liberalism and Progress," 176–78.

118. Ibid., 175.

119. Ibid., 179.

120. Ibid., 175.

121. Ibid., 177.

122. Ibid., 167.

123. Ibid., 187.

124. Ibid., 188.

125. Ibid., 198.

126. Quoted by Schlesinger, *A Life in the Twentieth Century*, 178.

127. Schlesinger, *A Life in the Twentieth Century*, 178.

128. For most of these articles, consult the bibliography at the end of Butler's book. Particularly informative are Thomas I. Cook and Arnaud B. Leavelle, "Orestes Brownson's *The American Republic*," *Review of Politics* 4

(1942): 77–90, 173–93; Francis E. McMahon, "Orestes Brownson on Church and State," *Theological Studies* 15 (1954): 175–228; and Stanley J. Parry, "The Premises of Brownson's Political Theory," *Review of Politics* 16 (1954): 194–211.

129. Here I would place the work by Gregory Butler and Armand A. Mauer already cited. In addition, see Mauer, "Orestes Brownson: Philosopher of Freedom," *No Divided Allegiance*, 84–99 for the ways in which Brownson was not a Thomist. Brownson was in fact a Thomist only in the relatively loose sense of affirming the harmony of reason and revelation and the natural goodness of political life. In other words, Brownson was, roughly, a Thomist in the sense Walker Percy was. See my *Postmodernism Rightly Understood: The Return to Realism in American Thought* (Lanham, Md.: Rowman and Littlefield, 1999), chapter 3. A subtle treatment of a side of Brownson's thought that I all but ignore is Patrick W. Carey, "Introduction: Orestes A. Brownson's Spirituality," *Orestes A. Brownson: Selected Writings*, 7–58. Carey agrees with Mauer that, most deeply, Brownson may be more Augustinian than Thomistic. But for Brownson what unites these two Catholic thinkers is more important than what separates them. Soon after finishing *The American Republic*, Brownson wrote to his son Henry: "I am about to commence another work, *The Problem of the Age*, designed to show the principle in which [the following] meet and are reconciled: Faith & Reason, Revelation & Science, Theology & Philosophy. I wish to do some thing for my age similar to what St. Augustine did in his *de Civitate Dei* for his age, & St. Thomas in his *Contra Gentiles* did for his age. You see my ambition is great, greater than my ability, but I will do the best I can" (quoted in Ryan, *Orestes A. Brownson*, 841, note 35). Walker Percy was working on a very similar book for his age at the time of his death, tentatively titled *Contra Gentiles*.

130. The best of these studies, I think, is Schlesinger's first book. Again, consult Butler's bibliography. Also particularly well regarded is Theodore Maynard, *Orestes Brownson: Yankee, Radical, Catholic* (New York: Macmillan, 1943).

131. Russell Kirk, *Redeeming the Time* (Wilmington, Del.: ISI Books, 1996), 171–72.

132. Ibid., 217.

133. Kirk, *The Roots of American Order* (Washington, D.C.: Regnery, 1991), 460.

134. This letter is quoted in Russell Kirk, "Orestes Brownson and T.S. Eliot," *No Divided Allegiance*, 164–65.

135. Kirk, *The Roots of American Order*, 404.

136. Ibid., 406–07.

137. Ibid., 408–09.

138. Kirk, "Preface," 8.

139. Kirk, *The Roots of American Order*, 465.

140. Ibid., 468.

141. "Preface," *We Hold These Truths and More: Further Catholic Reflections on the*

American Proposition, ed. Donald J. D'Elia and Stephen M. Krason (Steubenville, Ohio: Franciscan University Press, 1993), vii.

142. John Courtney Murray, *We Hold These Truths: Catholic Reflections on the American Proposition* (New York: Sheed and Ward, 1960), 30, 43.

143. Ibid., 43.

144. Ibid., 12, 310–16.

145. Ibid., viii.

146. Ibid., 28–30.

147. Ibid., viii-ix.

148. Ibid., viii, 310–16.

149. Ibid., 321, 308.

150. Ibid., 126–28, 200.

151. Ibid., 211.

152. Ibid., 215–16, 319.

153. Ibid., 327, 109.

154. Ibid., 131.

155. Pierre Manent, *Modern Liberty and Its Discontents*, ed. D. Mahoney and P. Seaton (Lanham, Md.: Rowman and Littlefield, 1998), 186.

156. Ibid., 190.

157. Ibid., 190–91.

158. Ibid., 193.

159. Ibid., 156.

160. Ibid., 214.

Preface

*I*n the volume which, with much diffidence, is here offered to the public, I have given, as far as I have considered it worth giving, my whole thought in a connected form on the nature, necessity, extent, authority, origin, ground, and constitution of government, and the unity, nationality, constitution, tendencies, and destiny of the American Republic. Many of the points treated have been from time to time discussed or touched upon, and many of the views have been presented, in my previous writings; but this work is newly and independently written from beginning to end, and is as complete on the topics treated as I have been able to make it.

I have taken nothing bodily from my previous essays, but I have used their thoughts as far as I have judged them sound and they came within the scope of my present work. I have not felt myself bound to adhere to my own past thoughts or expressions any farther than they coincide with my present convictions, and I have written as freely and as independently as if I had never written or published any thing before. I have never been the slave of my own past, and truth has always been dearer to me than my own opinions. This work is not only my latest, but will be my last on politics or government, and must be taken as the authentic, and the only authentic statement of my political views and convictions, and whatever in any of my previous writings conflicts with the principles defended in its pages, must be regarded as retracted, and rejected.

The work now produced is based on scientific principles; but it is an essay rather than a scientific treatise, and even good-natured critics will, no doubt, pronounce it an article or a series of articles designed for a review, rather than a book. It is hard to overcome the habits of a lifetime. I have taken some pains to exchange the reviewer for the author, but am fully conscious that I have not succeeded. My work can lay claim to very little artistic merit. It is full of repetitions; the same thought is frequently recurring,—the result, to some extent, no doubt, of carelessness and the want of artistic skill; but to a greater extent, I fear, of "malice aforethought." In composing my work I have followed, rather than directed, the course of my thought, and, having very little confidence in the memory or industry of readers, I have preferred, when the completeness of the argument required it, to repeat myself to encumbering my pages with perpetual references to what has gone before.

That I attach some value to this work is evident from my consenting to its publication; but how much or how little of it is really mine, I am quite unable to say. I have, from my youth up, been reading, observing, thinking, reflecting, talking, I had almost said writing, at least by fits and starts, on political subjects, especially in their connection with philosophy, theology, history, and social progress, and have assimilated to my own mind what it would assimilate, without keeping any notes of the sources whence the materials assimilated were derived. I have written freely from my own mind as I find it now formed; but how it has been so formed, or whence I have borrowed, my readers know as well as I. All that is valuable in the thoughts set forth, it is safe to assume has been appropriated from others. Where I have been distinctly conscious of borrowing what has not become common property, I have given credit, or, at least, mentioned the author's name, with three important exceptions which I wish to note more formally.

I am principally indebted for the view of American nationality and the Federal Constitution I present, to hints and suggestions furnished by the remarkable work of John C. Hurd, Esq., on *The Law of Freedom and Bondage in the United States*, a work of rare learning and profound philosophic views. I could not have written my work without the aid derived from its suggestions, any more than I could without Plato, Aristotle, St. Augustine, St. Thomas, Suarez, Pierre Leroux, and the Abbate Gioberti. To these two last-named authors, one a humanitarian sophist, the other a Catholic priest, and certainly one of the profoundest philosophical writers of this century, I am much indebted, though I have followed the political system of neither. I have taken from Leroux the germs of the doctrine I set forth on the solidarity of the race, and from Gioberti the doctrine I defend in relation to the creative act, which is, after all, simply that of the *Credo* and the first verse of *Genesis*.

In treating the several questions which the preparation of this volume has brought up, in their connection, and in the light of first principles, I have changed or modified, on more than one important point, the views I had expressed in my previous writings, especially on the distinction between civilized and barbaric nations, the real basis of civilization itself, and the value to the world of the Græco-Roman civilization. I have ranked feudalism under the head of barbarism, rejected every species of political aristocracy, and represented the English constitution as essentially antagonistic to the American, not as its type. I have accepted universal suffrage in principle, and defended American democracy, which I define to be territorial democracy, and carefully distinguish from pure individualism on the one hand, and from pure socialism or humanitarianism on the other.

I reject the doctrine of State sovereignty, which I held and defended from 1828 to 1861, but still maintain that the sovereignty of the American Republic vests in the States, though in the States collectively, or united, not severally, and thus escape alike consolidation and disintegration. I find, with Mr. Madison, our most philosophic statesman, the originality of the American system in the division of powers between a General government having sole charge of the foreign and general, and particular or State governments having, within their respective territories, sole charge of the particular relations and interests of the American people; but I do not accept his concession that this division is of conventional origin, and maintain that it enters into the original Providential constitution of the American state, as I have done in my Review for October, 1863, and January and October, 1864.

I maintain, after Mr. Senator Sumner, one of the most philosophic and accomplished living American statesmen, that "State secession is State suicide," but modify the opinion I too hastily expressed that the political death of a State dissolves civil society within its territory and abrogates all rights held under it, and accept the doctrine that the laws in force at the time of secession remain in force till superseded or abrogated by competent authority, and also that, till the State is revived and restored as a State in the Union, the only authority, under the American system, competent to supersede or abrogate them is the United States, not Congress, far less the Executive. The error of the Government is not in recognizing the territorial laws as surviving secession, but in counting a State that has seceded as still a State in the Union, with the right to be counted as one of the United States in amending the Constitution. Such State goes *out* of the Union, but comes *under* it.

I have endeavored throughout to refer my particular political views to their general principles and to show that the general principles asserted have their origin and ground in the great, universal, and unchanging principles of the universe itself. Hence, I have labored to show the scientific relations of political to theological principles, the real principles of all science, as of all reality. An atheist, I have said, may be a politician; but if there were no God, there could be no politics. This may offend the sciolists of the age, but I must follow science where it leads, and cannot be arrested by those who mistake their darkness for light.

I write throughout as a Christian, because I am a Christian; as a Catholic, because all Christian principles, nay, all real principles are catholic, and there is nothing sectarian either in nature or revelation. I am a Catholic by God's grace and great goodness, and must write as I am. I could not write otherwise if I would, and would not if I could. I have not obtruded my religion, and have referred to it only where my argument demanded it; but I have had neither the weakness nor the bad taste to seek to conceal or disguise it. I could never have written my book without the knowledge I have, as a Catholic, of Catholic theology, and my acquaintance, slight as it is, with the great fathers and doctors of the church, the great masters of all that is solid or permanent in modern thought, either with Catholics or non-Catholics.

Moreover, though I write for all Americans, without distinction of sect or party, I have had more especially in view the people of my own religious communion. It is no discredit to a man in the United States at the present day to be a firm, sincere, and devout Catholic. The old sectarian prejudice may remain with a few, "whose eyes," as Emerson says, "are in their hind-head, not in their fore-head;" but the American people are not at heart sectarian, and the nothingarianism so prevalent among them only marks their state of transition from sectarian opinions to positive Catholic faith. At any rate, it can no longer be denied that Catholics are an integral, living, and growing element in the American population, quite too numerous, too wealthy, and too influential to be ignored. They have played too conspicuous a part in the late troubles of the country, and poured out too freely and too much of their richest and noblest blood in defence of the unity of the nation and the integrity of its domain, for that. Catholics henceforth must be treated as standing, in all respects, on a footing of equality with any other class of American citizens, and their views of political science, or of any other science, be counted of equal importance, and listened to with equal attention.

I have no fears that my book will be neglected because avowedly by a Catholic author, and from a Catholic publishing house. They who are not Catholics will read it, and it will enter into the current of American literature, if it is one they must read in order to be up with the living and growing thought of the age. If it is not a book of that sort, it is not worth reading by any one.

Furthermore, I am ambitious, even in my old age, and I wish to exert an influence on the future of my country, for which I have made, or, rather, my family have made, some sacrifices, and which I tenderly love. Now, I believe that he who can exert the most influence on our Catholic population, especially in giving tone and direction to our Catholic youth, will exert the most influence in forming the character and shaping the future destiny of the American Republic. Ambition and patriotism alike, as well as my own Catholic faith and sympathies, induce me to address myself primarily to Catholics. I quarrel with none of the sects; I honor virtue wherever I see it, and accept truth wherever I find it; but, in my belief, no sect is destined to a long life, or a permanent possession. I engage in no controversy with any one not of my religion, for, if the positive, affirmative truth is brought out and placed in a clear light before the public, whatever is sectarian in any of the sects will disappear as the morning mists before the rising sun.

I expect the most intelligent and satisfactory appreciation of my book from the thinking and educated classes among Catholics; but I speak to my countrymen at large. I could not personally serve my country in the field: my habits as well as my infirmities prevented, to say nothing of my age; but I have endeavored in this humble work to add my contribution, small though it may be, to political science, and to discharge, as far as I am able, my debt of loyalty and patriotism. I would the book were more of a book, more worthy of my countrymen, and a more weighty proof of the love I bear them, and with which I have written it. All I can say is, that it is an honest book, a sincere book, and contains my best thoughts on the subjects treated. If well received, I shall be grateful; if neglected, I shall endeavor to practise resignation, as I have so often done.

— *O. A. Brownson*
Elizabeth, N. J.
September 16, 1865

I

Introduction

$\mathcal{T}$he ancients summed up the whole of human wisdom in the maxim, Know Thyself, and certainly there is for an individual no more important as there is no more difficult knowledge, than knowledge of himself, whence he comes, whither he goes, what he is, what he is for, what he can do, what he ought to do, and what are his means of doing it.

Nations are only individuals on a larger scale. They have a life, an individuality, a reason, a conscience, and instincts of their own, and have the same general laws of development and growth, and, perhaps, of decay, as the individual man. Equally important, and no less difficult than for the individual, is it for a nation to know itself, understand its own existence, its own powers and faculties, rights and duties, constitution, instincts, tendencies, and destiny. A nation has a spiritual as well as a material, a moral as well as a physical existence, and is subjected to internal as well as external conditions of health and virtue, greatness and grandeur, which it must in some measure understand and observe, or become weak and infirm, stunted in its growth, and end in premature decay and death.

Among nations, no one has more need of full knowledge of itself than the United States, and no one has hitherto had less. It has hardly had a distinct consciousness of its own national existence, and has lived the irreflective life of the child, with no severe trial, till the recent rebellion, to throw it back on itself and compel it to reflect on its own constitution, its own separate existence, individuality, tendencies, and end. The defection of the slaveholding States, and the fearful struggle that has followed for national unity and integrity, have brought it at once to a distinct recognition of itself, and forced it to pass from thoughtless, careless, heedless, reckless adolescence to grave and reflecting manhood. The nation has been suddenly compelled to study itself, and henceforth must act from reflection, understanding, science, statesmanship, not from instinct, impulse, passion, or caprice, knowing well what it does, and wherefore it does it. The change which four years of civil war have wrought in the nation is great, and is sure to give it the seriousness, the gravity, the dignity, the manliness it has heretofore lacked.

Though the nation has been brought to a consciousness of its own existence, it has not, even yet, attained to a full and clear understanding of its own national constitution. Its vision is still obscured by the floating mists of its earlier morning, and its judgment rendered indistinct and indecisive by the wild theories and fancies of its childhood. The national mind has been quickened, the national heart has been opened, the national disposition prepared, but there remains the important work of dissipating the mists that still linger, of brushing away these wild theories and fancies, and of enabling it to form a clear and intelligent judgment of itself, and a true and just appreciation of its own constitution, tendencies, and destiny; or, in other words, of enabling the nation to understand its own idea, and the means of its actualization in space and time.

Every living nation has an idea given it by Providence to realize, and whose realization is its special work, mission, or destiny. Every nation is, in some sense, a chosen people of God. The Jews were the chosen people of God, through whom the primitive traditions were to be preserved in their purity and integrity, and the Messiah was to come. The Greeks were the chosen people of God, for the development and realization of the beautiful or the divine splendor in art, and of the true in science and philosophy; and the Romans, for the development of the state, law, and jurisprudence. The great despotic nations of Asia were never properly nations; or if they were nations with a mission, they proved false to it, and count for nothing in the progressive development of the human race. History has not recorded their mission, and as far as they are known they have contributed only to the abnormal development or corruption of religion and civilization. Despotism is barbaric and abnormal.

The United States, or the American Republic, has a mission, and is chosen of God for the realization of a great idea. It has been chosen not only to continue the work assigned to Greece and Rome, but to accomplish a greater work than was assigned to either. In art, it will prove false to its mission if it does not rival Greece; and in science and philosophy, if it does not surpass it. In the state, in law, in jurisprudence, it must continue and surpass Rome. Its idea is liberty, indeed, but liberty with law, and law with liberty. Yet its mission is not so much the realization of liberty as the realization of the true idea of the state, which secures at once the authority of the public and the freedom of the individual—the sovereignty of the people without social despotism, and individual freedom without anarchy. In other words, its mission is to bring out in its life the dialectic union of authority and liberty, of the natural rights of man and those of society. The Greek and Roman republics asserted the state to the detriment of individual freedom; modern republics either do the same, or assert individual freedom to the detriment of the state. The American republic has been instituted by Providence to realize the freedom of each with advantage to the other.

The real mission of the United States is to introduce and establish a political constitution, which, while it retains all the advantages of the constitutions of states thus far known, is unlike any of them, and secures advantages which none of them did or could possess. The American constitution has no prototype in any prior constitution. The American form of government can be classed throughout with none of the forms of government described by Aristotle, or even by later authorities. Aristotle knew only four forms of government: Monarchy, Aristocracy, Democracy, and Mixed Governments. The American form is none of these, nor any combination of them. It is original, a new contribution to political science, and seeks to attain the end of all wise and just government by means unknown or forbidden to the ancients, and which have been but imperfectly comprehended even by American political writers themselves. The originality of the American constitution has been overlooked by the great majority even of our own statesmen, who seek to explain it by analogies borrowed from the constitutions of other states rather than by a profound study of its own principles. They have taken too low a view of it, and have rarely, if ever, appreciated its distinctive and peculiar merits.

As the United States have vindicated their national unity and integrity, and are preparing to take a new start in history, nothing is more important than that they should take that new start with a clear and definite view of their national constitution, and with a distinct understanding of their political mission in the future of the world. The citizen who can help his countrymen to do this will render them an important service and deserve well of his country, though he may have been unable to serve in her armies and defend her on the battlefield. The work now to be done by American statesmen is even more difficult and more delicate than that which has been accomplished by our brave armies. As yet the people are hardly better prepared for the political work to be done than they were at the outbreak of the civil war for the military work they have so nobly achieved. But, with time, patience, and good-will, the difficulties may be overcome, the errors of the past corrected, and the Government placed on the right track for the future.

It will hardly be questioned that either the constitution of the United States is very defective or it has been very grossly misinterpreted by all parties. If the slave States had not held that the States are severally sovereign, and the Constitution of the United States a simple agreement or compact, they would never have seceded; and if the Free States had not confounded the Union with the General government, and shown a tendency to make it the entire national government, no occasion or pretext for secession would have been given. The great problem of our statesmen has been from the first, How to assert union without consolidation, and State rights without disintegration? Have they, as yet, solved that problem? The war has silenced the State sovereignty doctrine, indeed, but has it done so without lesion to State rights? Has it done it without asserting the General government as the supreme, central, or national government? Has it done it without striking a dangerous blow at the federal element of the constitution? In suppressing by armed force the doctrine that the States are severally sovereign, what barrier is left against consolidation? Has not one danger been removed only to give place to another?

But perhaps the constitution itself, if rightly understood, solves the problem; and perhaps the problem itself is raised precisely through misunderstanding of the constitution. Our statesmen have recognized no constitution of the American people themselves; they have confined their views to the written constitution, as if that constituted the American people a state or nation, instead of being, as it is, only a law ordained by the nation already existing and constituted. Perhaps, if they had recognized and studied the constitution which preceded that drawn up by the Convention of 1787, and which is intrinsic, inherent in the republic itself, they would have seen that it solves the problem, and asserts national unity without consolidation, and the rights of the several States without danger of disintegration. The whole controversy, possibly, has originated in a misunderstanding of the real constitution of the United States, and that misunderstanding itself in the misunderstanding of the origin and constitution of government in general. The constitution, as will appear in the course of this essay, is not defective; and all that is necessary to guard against either danger is to discard all our theories of the constitution, and return and adhere to the constitution itself, as it really is and always has been.

There is no doubt that the question of Slavery had much to do with the rebellion, but it was not its sole cause. The real cause must be sought in the progress that had been made, especially in the States themselves, in forming and administering their respective governments, as well as the General government, in accordance with political theories borrowed from European speculators on government, the so-called Liberals and Revolutionists, which have and can have no legitimate application in the United States. The tendency of American politics, for the last thirty or forty years, has been, within the several States themselves, in the direction of centralized democracy, as if the American people had for their mission only the reproduction of ancient Athens. The American system is not that of any of the simple forms of government, nor any combination of them. The attempt to bring it under any of the simple or mixed forms of government recognized by political writers, is an attempt to clothe the future in the cast-off garments of the past. The American system, wherever practicable, is better than monarchy, better than aristocracy, better than simple democracy, better than any possible combination of these several forms, because it accords more nearly with the principles of things, the real order of the universe.

But American statesmen have studied the constitutions of other states more than that of their own, and have succeeded in obscuring the American system in the minds of the people, and giving them in its place pure and simple democracy, which is its false development or corruption. Under the influence of this false development, the people were fast losing sight of the political truth that, though the people are sovereign, it is the organic, not the inorganic people, the territorial people, not the people as simple population, and were beginning to assert the absolute God-given right of the majority to govern. All the changes made in the bosom of the States themselves have consisted in removing all obstacles to the irresponsible will of the majority, leaving minorities and individuals at their mercy. This tendency to a centralized democracy had more to do with provoking secession and rebellion than the anti-slavery sentiments of the Northern, Central, and Western States.

The failure of secession and the triumph of the National cause, in spite of the short-sightedness and blundering of the Administration, have proved the vitality and strength of the national constitution, and the greatness of the American people. They say nothing for or against the democratic theory of our demagogues, but every thing in favor of the American system or constitution of government, which has found a firmer support in American instincts than in American statesmanship. In spite of all that had been done by theorists, radicals, and revolutionists, no-government men, non-resistants, humanitarians, and sickly sentimentalists to corrupt the American people in mind, heart, and body, the native vigor of their national constitution has enabled them to come forth triumphant from the trial. Every American patriot has reason to be proud of his country men, and every American lover of freedom to be satisfied with the institutions of his country. But there is danger that the politicians and demagogues will ascribe the merit, not to the real and living national constitution, but to their miserable theories of that constitution, and labor to aggravate the several evils and corrupt tendencies which caused the rebellion it has cost so much to suppress.

What is now wanted is, that the people, whose instincts are right, should understand the American constitution as it is, and so understand it as to render it impossible for political theorists, no matter of what school or party, to deceive them again as to its real import, or induce them to depart from it in their political action.

A work written with temper, without passion or sectional prejudice, in a philosophical spirit, explaining to the American people their own national constitution, and the mutual relations of the General government and the State governments, cannot, at this important crisis in our affairs, be inopportune, and, if properly executed, can hardly fail to be of real service. Such a work is now attempted—would it were by another and abler hand—which, imperfect as it is, may at least offer some useful suggestions, give a right direction to political thought, although it should fail to satisfy the mind of the reader.

This much the author may say in favor of his own work, that it sets forth no theory of government in general, or of the United States in particular. The author is not a monarchist, an aristocrat, a democrat, a feudalist, nor an advocate of what are called mixed governments like the English, at least for his own country; but is simply an American, devoted to the real, living, and energizing constitution of the American republic as it is, not as some may fancy it might be, or are striving to make it. It is, in his judgment, what it ought to be, and he has no other ambition than to present it as it is to the understanding and love of his countrymen.

Perhaps simple artistic unity and propriety would require the author to commence his essay directly with the United States; but while the constitution of the United States is original and peculiar, the government of the United States has necessarily something in common with all legitimate governments, and he has thought it best to precede his discussion of the American republic, its constitution, tendencies, and destiny, by some considerations on government in general. He does this because he believes, whether rightly or not, that while the American people have received from Providence a most truly profound and admirable system of government, they are more or less infected with the false theories of government which have been broached during the last two centuries. In attempting to realize these theories, they have already provoked or rendered practicable a rebellion which has seriously threatened the national existence, and come very near putting an end to the American order of civilization itself. These theories have received already a shock in the minds of all serious and thinking men; but the men who think are in every nation a small minority, and it is necessary to give these theories a public refutation, and bring back those who do not think, as well as those who do, from the world of dreams to the world of reality. It is hoped, therefore, that any apparent want of artistic unity or symmetry in the essay will be pardoned for the sake of the end the author has had in view.

II

Government

*M*an is a dependent being, and neither does nor can suffice for himself. He lives not in himself, but lives and moves and has his being in God. He exists, develops, and fulfils his existence only by communion with God, through which he participates of the divine being and life. He communes with God through the divine creative act and the Incarnation of the Word, through his kind, and through the material world. Communion with God through Creation and Incarnation is religion, distinctively taken, which binds man to God as his first cause, and carries him onward to God as his final cause; communion through the material world is expressed by the word property; and communion with God through humanity is society. Religion, society, property, are the three terms that embrace the whole of man's life, and express the essential means and conditions of his existence, his development, and his perfection, or the fulfilment of his existence, the attainment of the end for which he is created.

Though society, or the communion of man with his Maker through his kind, is not all that man needs in order to live, to grow, to actualize the possibilities of his nature, and to attain to his beatitude, since humanity is neither God nor the material universe, it is yet a necessary and essential condition of his life, his progress, and the completion of his existence. He is born and lives in society, and can be born and live nowhere else. It is one of the necessities of his nature. "God saw that it was not good for man to be alone." Hence, wherever man is found he is found in society, living in more or less strict intercourse with his kind.

But society never does and never can exist without government of some sort. As society is a necessity of man's nature, so is government a necessity of society. The simplest form of society is the family—Adam and Eve. But though Adam and Eve are in many respects equal, and have equally important though different parts assigned them, one or the other must be head and governor, or they cannot form the society called family. They would be simply two individuals of different sexes, and the family would fail for the want of unity. Children cannot be reared, trained, or educated without some degree of family government, of some authority to direct, control, restrain, or prescribe. Hence the authority of the husband and father is recognized by the common consent of mankind. Still more apparent is the necessity of government the moment the family develops and grows into the tribe, and the tribe into the nation. Hence no nation exists without government; and we never find a savage tribe, however low or degraded, that does not assert somewhere, in the father, in the elders, or in the tribe itself, the rude outlines or the faint reminiscences of some sort of government, with authority to demand obedience and to punish the refractory. Hence, as man is nowhere found out of society, so nowhere is society found without government.

Government is necessary: but let it be remarked by the way, that its necessity does not grow exclusively or chiefly out of the fact that the human race by sin has fallen from its primitive integrity, or original righteousness. The fall asserted by Christian theology, though often misinterpreted, and its effects underrated or exaggerated, is a fact too sadly confirmed by individual experience and universal history; but it is not the cause why government is necessary, though it may be an additional reason for demanding it. Government would have been necessary if man had not sinned, and it is needed for the good as well as for the bad. The law was promulgated in the Garden, while man retained his innocence and remained in the integrity of his nature. It exists in heaven as well as on earth, and in heaven in its perfection. Its office is not purely repressive, to restrain violence, to redress wrongs, and to punish the transgressor. It has something more to do than to restrict our natural liberty, curb our passions, and maintain justice between man and man. Its office is positive as well as negative. It is needed to render effective the solidarity of the individuals of a nation, and to render the nation an organism, not a mere organization—to combine men in one living body, and to strengthen all with the strength of each, and each with the strength of all—to develop, strengthen, and sustain individual liberty, and to utilize and direct it to the promotion of the common weal—to be a social providence, imitating in its order and degree the action of the divine providence itself, and, while it provides for the common good of all, to protect each, the lowest and meanest, with the whole force and majesty of society. It is the minister of wrath to wrong-doers, indeed, but its nature is beneficent, and its action defines and protects the right of property, creates and maintains a medium in which religion can exert her supernatural energy, promotes learning, fosters science and art, advances civilization, and contributes as a powerful means to the fulfilment by man of the Divine purpose in his existence. Next after religion, it is man's greatest good; and even religion without it can do only a small portion of her work. They wrong it who call it a necessary evil; it is a great good, and, instead of being distrusted, hated, or resisted, except in its abuses, it should be loved, respected, obeyed, and, if need be, defended at the cost of all earthly goods, and even of life itself.

The nature or essence of government is to govern. A government that does not govern, is simply no government at all. If it has not the ability to govern and governs not, it may be an agency, an instrument in the hands of individuals for advancing their private interests, but it is not government. To be government, it must govern both individuals and the community. If it is a mere machine for making prevail the will of one man, of a certain number of men, or even of the community, it may be very effective sometimes for good, sometimes for evil, oftenest for evil, but government in the proper sense of the word it is not. To govern is to direct, control, restrain, as the pilot controls and directs his ship. It necessarily implies two terms, governor and governed, and a real distinction between them. The denial of all real distinction between governor and governed is an error in politics analogous to that in philosophy or theology of denying all real distinction between creator and creature, God and the universe, which all the world knows is either pantheism or pure atheism—the supreme sophism. If we make governor and governed one and the same, we efface both terms; for there is no governor nor governed, if the will that governs is identically the will that is governed. To make the controller and the controlled the same, is precisely to deny all control. There must, then, if there is government at all, be a power, force, or will that governs, distinct from that which is governed. In those governments in which it is held that the people govern, the people governing do and must act in a diverse relation from the people governed, or there is no real government.

Government is not only that which governs, but that which has the right or authority to govern. Power without right is not government. Governments have the right to use force at need, but might does not make right, and not every power wielding the physical force of a nation is to be regarded as its rightful government. Whatever resort to physical force it may be obliged to make, either in defence of its authority or of the rights of the nation, the government itself lies in the moral order, and politics is simply a branch of ethics—that branch which treats of the rights and duties of men in their public relations, as distinguished from their rights and duties in their private relations.

Government being not only that which governs, but that which has the right to govern, obedience to it becomes a moral duty, not a mere physical necessity. The right to govern and the duty to obey are correlatives, and the one cannot exist or be conceived without the other. Hence loyalty is not simply an amiable sentiment, but a duty, a moral virtue. Treason is not merely a difference in political opinion with the governing authority, but a crime against the sovereign, and a moral wrong, therefore a sin against God, the Founder of the Moral Law. Treason, if committed in other countries, unhappily, has been more frequently termed by our countrymen patriotism and loaded with honor than branded as a crime, the greatest of crimes, as it is, that human governments have authority to punish. The American people have been chary of the word loyalty, perhaps because they regard it as the correlative of royalty; but loyalty is rather the correlative of law, and is, in its essence, love and devotion to the sovereign authority, however constituted or wherever lodged. It is as necessary, as much a duty, as much a virtue in republics as in monarchies; and nobler examples of the most devoted loyalty are not found in the world's history than were exhibited in the ancient Greek and Roman republics, or than have been exhibited by both men and women in the young republic of the United States. Loyalty is the highest, noblest, and most generous of human virtues, and is the human element of that sublime love or charity which the inspired Apostle tells us is the fulfilment of the law. It has in it the principle of devotion, of self-sacrifice, and is, of all human virtues, that which renders man the most Godlike. There is nothing great, generous, good, or heroic of which a truly loyal people are not capable, and nothing mean, base, cruel, brutal, criminal, detestable, not to be expected of a really disloyal people. Such a people no generous sentiment can move, no love can bind. It mocks at duty, scorns virtue, tramples on all rights, and holds no person, no thing, human or divine, sacred or inviolable.

The assertion of government as lying in the moral order, defines civil liberty, and reconciles it with authority. Civil liberty is freedom to do whatever one pleases that authority permits or does not forbid. Freedom to follow in all things one's own will or inclination, without any civil restraint, is license, not liberty. There is no lesion to liberty in repressing license, nor in requiring obedience to the commands of the authority that has the right to command. Tyranny or oppression is not in being subjected to authority, but in being subjected to usurped authority—to a power that has no right to command, or that commands what exceeds its right or its authority. To say that it is contrary to liberty to be forced to forego our own will or inclination in any case whatever, is simply denying the right of all government, and falling into no-governmentism. Liberty is violated only when we are required to forego our own will or inclination by a power that has no right to make the requisition; for we are bound to obedience as far as authority has right to govern, and we can never have the right to disobey a rightful command. The requisition, if made by rightful authority, then, violates no right that we have or can have, and where there is no violation of our rights there is no violation of our liberty. The moral right of authority, which involves the moral duty of obedience, presents, then, the ground on which liberty and authority may meet in peace and operate to the same end.

This has no resemblance to the slavish doctrine of passive obedience, and that the resistance to power can never be lawful. The tyrant may be lawfully resisted, for the tyrant, by force of the word itself, is a usurper, and without authority. Abuses of power may be resisted even by force when they become too great to be endured, when there is no legal or regular way of redressing them, and when there is a reasonable prospect that resistance will prove effectual and substitute something better in their place. But it is never lawful to resist the rightful sovereign, for it can never be right to resist right, and the rightful sovereign in the constitutional exercise of his power can never be said to abuse it. Abuse is the unconstitutional or wrongful exercise of a power rightfully held, and when it is not so exercised there is no abuse or abuses to redress. All turns, then, on the right of power, or its legitimacy. Whence does government derive its right to govern? What is the origin and ground of sovereignty? This question is fundamental, and without a true answer to it politics cannot be a science, and there can be no scientific statesmanship. Whence, then, comes the sovereign right to govern?

III

Origin of Government

Government is both a fact and a right. Its origin as a fact, is simply a question of history; its origin as a right or authority to govern, is a question of ethics. Whether a certain territory and its population are a sovereign state or nation, or not—whether the actual ruler of a country is its rightful ruler, or not—is to be determined by the historical facts in the case; but whence the government derives its right to govern, is a question that can be solved only by philosophy, or, philosophy failing, only by revelation.

Political writers, not carefully distinguishing between the fact and the right, have invented various theories as to the origin of government, among which may be named—

I. Government originates in the right of the father to govern his child.

II. It originates in convention, and is a social compact.

III. It originates in the people, who, collectively taken, are sovereign.

IV. Government springs from the spontaneous development of nature.

V. It derives its right from the immediate and express appointment of God;—

VI. From God through the Pope, or visible head of the spiritual society;—

VII. From God through the people;—

VIII. From God through the natural law.

I. The first theory is sound, if the question is confined to the origin of government as a fact. The patriarchal system is the earliest known system of government, and unmistakable traces of it are found in nearly all known governments—in the *tribes* of Arabia and Northern Africa, the Irish *septs* and the Scottish *clans*, the Tartar *hordes*, the Roman *gentes*, and the Russian and Hindoo *villages*. The right of the father was held to be his right to govern his family or household, which, with his children, included his wife and servants. From the family to the tribe the transition is natural and easy, as also from the tribe to the nation. The father is chief of the family; the chief of the eldest family is chief of the tribe; the chief of the eldest tribe becomes chief of the nation, and, as such, king or monarch. The heads of families collected in a senate form an aristocracy, and the families themselves, represented by their delegates, or publicly assembling for public affairs, constitute a democracy. These three forms, with their several combinations, to wit, monarchy, aristocracy, democracy, and mixed governments, are all the forms known to Aristotle, and have generally been held to be all that are possible.

Historically, all governments have, in some sense, been developed from the patriarchal, as all society has been developed from the family. Even those governments, like the ancient Roman and the modern feudal, which seem to be founded on landed property, may be traced back to a patriarchal origin. The patriarch is sole proprietor, and the possessions of the family are vested in him, and he governs as proprietor as well as father. In the tribe, the chief is the proprietor, and in the nation, the king is the landlord, and holds the domain. Hence, the feudal baron is invested with his fief by the suzerain, holds it from him, and to him it escheats when forfeited or vacant. All the great Asiatic kings of ancient or modern times hold the domain and govern as proprietors; they have the authority of the father and the owner; and their subjects, though theoretically their children, are really their slaves.

In Rome, however, the proprietary right undergoes an important transformation. The father retains all the power of the patriarch within his family, the patrician in his *gens* or house, but, outside of it, is met and controlled by the city or state. The heads of houses are united in the senate, and collectively constitute and govern the state. Yet, not all the heads of houses have seats in the senate, but only the tenants of the sacred territory of the city, which has been surveyed and marked by the god Terminus. Hence the great plebeian houses, often richer and nobler than the patrician, were excluded from all share in the government and the honors of the state, because they were not tenants of any portion of the sacred territory. There is here the introduction of an element which is not patriarchal, and which transforms the patriarch or chief of a tribe into the city or state, and founds the civil order, or what is now called civilization. The city or state takes the place of the private proprietor, and territorial rights take the place of purely personal rights.

In the theory of the Roman law, the land owns the man, not the man the land. When land was transferred to a new tenant, the practice in early times was to bury him in it, in order to indicate that it took possession of him, received, accepted, or adopted him; and it was only such persons as were taken possession of, accepted or adopted by the sacred territory or domain that, though denizens of Rome, were citizens with full political rights. This, in modern language, means that the state is territorial, not personal, and that the citizen appertains to the state, not the state to the citizen. Under the patriarchal, the tribal, and the Asiatic monarchical systems, there is, properly speaking, no state, no citizens, and the organization is economical rather than political. Authority—even the nation itself—is personal, not territorial. The patriarch, the chief of the tribe, or the king, is the only proprietor. Under the Græco-Roman system all this is transformed. The nation is territorial as well as personal, and the real proprietor is the city or state. Under the Empire, no doubt, what lawyers call the eminent domain was vested in the emperor, but only as the representative and trustee of the city or state.

When or by what combination of events this transformation was effected, history does not inform us. The first-born of Adam, we are told, built a city, and called it after his son Enoch; but there is no evidence that it was constituted a municipality. The earliest traces of the *civil* order proper are found in the Greek and Italian republics, and its fullest and grandest developments are found in Rome, imperial as well as republican. It was no doubt preceded by the patriarchal system, and was historically developed from it, but by way of accretion, rather than by simple explication. It has in it an element that, if it exists in the patriarchal constitution, exists there only in a different form, and the transformation marks the passage from the economical order to the political, from the barbaric to the civil constitution of society, or from barbarism to civilization.

The word civilization stands opposed to barbarism, and is derived from *civitas*—city or state. The Greeks and Romans call all tribes and nations in which authority is vested in the chief, as distinguished from the state, barbarians. The origin of the word *barbarian, barbarus,* or *barbaroz,* is unknown, and its primary sense can be only conjectured. Webster regards its primary sense as foreign, wild, fierce; but this could not have been its original sense; for the Greeks and Romans never termed all foreigners barbarians, and they applied the term to nations that had no inconsiderable culture and refinement of manners, and that had made respectable progress in art and science—as the Indians, Persians, Medians, Chaldeans, and Assyrians. They applied the term evidently in a political, not an ethical or an æsthetical sense, and as it would seem to designate a social order in which the state was not developed, and in which the nation was personal, not territorial, and authority was held as a private right, not as a public trust, or in which the domain vests in the chief or tribe, and not in the state; for they never term any others barbarians.

Republic is opposed not to monarchy, in the modern European sense, but to monarchy in the ancient or absolute sense. Lacedæmon had kings; yet it was no less republican than Athens; and Rome was called and was a republic under the emperors no less than under the consuls. Republic, *respublica*, by the very force of the term, means the public wealth, or, in good English, the commonwealth; that is, government founded not on personal or private wealth, but on the public wealth, public territory, or domain, or a government that vests authority in the nation, and attaches the nation to a certain definite territory. France, Spain, Italy, Holland, Belgium, Denmark, even Great Britain in substance though not in form, are all, in the strictest sense of the word, republican states; for the king or emperor does not govern in his own private right, but solely as representative of the power and majesty of the state. The distinctive mark of republicanism is the substitution of the state for the personal chief, and public authority for personal or private right. Republicanism is really civilization as opposed to barbarism, and all civility, in the old sense of the word, or *civiltà* in Italian, is republican, and is applied in modern times to breeding, or refinement of manners, simply because these are characteristics of a republican, or polished [from *poliz*, city] people. Every people that has a real civil order, or a fully developed state or polity, is a republican people; and hence the church and her great doctors, when they speak of the state as distinguished from the church, call it the *republic*, as may be seen by consulting even a late Encyclical of Pius IX., which some have interpreted wrongly in an anti-republican sense.

All tribes and nations in which the patriarchal system remains, or is developed without transformation, are barbaric, and really so regarded by all Christendom. In civilized nations the patriarchal authority is transformed into that of the city or state, that is, of the republic; but in all barbarous nations it retains its private and personal character. The nation is only the family or tribe, and is called by the name of its ancestor, founder, or chief, not by a geographical denomination. Race has not been supplanted by country; they are a people, not a state. They are not fixed to the soil, and though we may find in them ardent love of family, the tribe, or the chief, we never find among them that pure love of country or patriotism which so distinguished the Greeks and Romans, and is no less marked among modern Christian nations. They have a family, a race, a chief or king, but no *patria*, or country. The barbarians who overthrew the Roman Empire, whether of the West or the East, were nations, or confederacies of nations, but not states. The nation with them was personal, not territorial. Their country was wherever they fed their flocks and herds, pitched their tents, and encamped for the night. There were Germans, but no German state, and even to-day the German finds his "father-land" wherever the German speech is spoken. The Polish, Sclavonian, Hungarian, Illyrian, Italian, and other provinces held by German states, in which the German language is not the mother-tongue, are excluded from the Germanic Confederation. The Turks, or Osmanlis, are a race, not a state, and are encamped, not settled, on the site of the Eastern Roman or Greek Empire.

Even when the barbaric nations have ceased to be nomadic, pastoral, or predatory nations, as the ancient Assyrians and Persians or modern Chinese, and have their geographical boundaries, they have still no state, no country. The nation defines the boundaries, not the boundaries the nation. The nation does not belong to the territory, but the territory to the nation or its chief. The Irish and Anglo-Saxons, in former times, held the land in gavelkind, and the territory belonged to the tribe or sept; but if the tribe held it as indivisible, they still held it as private property. The shah of Persia holds the whole Persian territory as private property, and the landholders among his subjects are held to be his tenants. They hold it from him, not from the Persian state. The public domain of the Greek empire is in theory the private domain of the Ottoman emperor or Turkish sultan. There is in barbaric states no republic, no commonwealth; authority is parental, without being tempered by parental affection. The chief is a despot, and rules with the unlimited authority of the father and the harshness of the proprietor. He owns the land and his subjects.

Feudalism, established in Western Europe after the downfall of the Roman Empire, however modified by the Church and by reminiscences of Græco-Roman civilization retained by the conquered, was a barbaric constitution. The feudal monarch, as far as he governed at all, governed as proprietor or landholder, not as the representative of the commonwealth. Under feudalism there are estates, but no state. The king governs as an estate, the nobles hold their power as an estate, and the commons are represented as an estate. The whole theory of power is, that it is an estate; a private right, not a public trust. It is not without reason, then, that the common sense of civilized nations terms the ages when it prevailed in Western Europe barbarous ages.

It may seem a paradox to class democracy with the barbaric constitutions, and yet as it is defended by many stanch democrats, especially European democrats and revolutionists, and by French and Germans settled in our own country, it is essentially barbaric and anti-republican. The characteristic principle of barbarism is, that power is a private or personal right, and when democrats assert that the elective franchise is a natural right of man, or that it is held by virtue of the fact that the elector is a man, they assert the fundamental principle of barbarism and despotism. This says nothing in favor of restricted suffrage, or against what is called universal suffrage. To restrict suffrage to property-holders helps nothing, theoretically or practically. Property has of itself advantages enough, without clothing its holders with exclusive political rights and privileges, and the laboring classes any day are as trustworthy as the business classes. The wise statesman will never restrict suffrage, or exclude the poorer and more numerous classes from all voice in the government of their country. General suffrage is wise, and if Louis Philippe had had the sense to adopt it, and thus rally the whole nation to the support of his government, he would never have had to encounter the revolution of 1848. The barbarism, the despotism, is not in universal suffrage, but in defending the elective franchise as a private or personal right. It is not a private, but a political right, and, like all political rights, a public trust. Extremes meet, and thus it is that men who imagine that they march at the head of the human race and lead the civilization of the age, are really in principle retrograding to the barbarism of the past, or taking their place with nations on whom the light of civilization has never yet dawned. All is not gold that glisters.

The characteristic of barbarism is, that it makes all authority a private or personal right; and the characteristic of civilization is, that it makes it a public trust. Barbarism knows only persons; civilization asserts and maintains the state. With barbarians the authority of the patriarch is developed simply by way of explication; in civilized states it is developed by way of transformation. Keeping in mind this distinction, it may be maintained that all systems of government, as a simple historical fact, have been developed from the patriarchal. The patriarchal has preceded them all, and it is with the patriarchal that the human race has begun its career. The family or household is not a state, a civil polity, but it is a government, and, historically considered, is the initial or inchoate state as well as the initial or inchoate nation. But its simple direct development gives us barbarism, or what is called Oriental despotism, and which nowhere exists, or can exist, in Christendom. It is found only in pagan and Mohammedan nations; Christianity in the secular order is republican, and continues and completes the work of Greece and Rome. It meets with little permanent success in any patriarchal or despotic nation, and must either find or create civilization, which has been developed from the patriarchal system by way of transformation.

But, though the patriarchal system is the earliest form of government, and all governments have been developed or modified from it, the right of government to govern cannot be deduced from the right of the father to govern his children, for the parental right itself is not ultimate or complete. All governments that assume it to be so, and rest on it as the foundation of their authority, are barbaric or despotic, and, therefore, without any legitimate authority. The right to govern rests on ownership or dominion. Where there is no proprietorship, there is no dominion; and where there is no dominion, there is no right to govern. Only he who is sovereign proprietor is sovereign lord.

Property, ownership, dominion rests on creation. The maker has the right to the thing made. He, so far as he is sole creator, is sole proprietor, and may do what he will with it. God is sovereign lord and proprietor of the universe, because He is its sole creator. He hath the absolute dominion, because He is absolute maker. He has made it, He owns it; and one may do what he will with his own. His dominion is absolute, because He is absolute creator, and He rightly governs as absolute and universal lord; yet is like no despot, because He exercises only His sovereign right, and His own essential wisdom, goodness, justness, rectitude, and immutability, are the highest of all conceivable guaranties that His exercise of His power will always be right, wise, just, and good. The despot is a man attempting to be God upon earth, and to exercise a usurped power. Despotism is based on the parental right, and the parental right is assumed to be absolute. Hence, your despotic rulers claim to reign, and to be loved and worshipped as gods. Even the Roman emperors, in the fourth and fifth centuries, were addressed as divinities; and Theodosius the Great, a Christian, was addressed as "Your Eternity," *Eternitas vestras*—so far did barbarism encroach on civilization, even under Christian emperors.

The right of the father over his child is an imperfect right, for he is the generator, not the creator of his child. Generation is in the order of second causes, and is simply the development or explication of the race. The early Roman law, founded on the confusion of generation with creation, gave the father absolute authority over the child—the right of life and death, as over his servants or slaves; but this was restricted under the Empire, and in all Christian nations the authority of the father is treated, like all power, as a trust. The child, like the father himself, belongs to the state, and to the state the father is answerable for the use he makes of his authority. The law fixes the age of majority, when the child is completely emancipated; and even during his nonage, takes him from the father and places him under guardians, in case the father is incompetent to fulfil or grossly abuses his trust. This is proper, because society contributes to the life of the child, and has a right as well as an interest in him. Society, again, must suffer if the child is allowed to grow up a worthless vagabond or a criminal; and has a right to intervene, both in behalf of itself and of the child, in case his parents neglect to train him up in the nurture and admonition of the Lord, or are training him up to be a liar, a thief, a drunkard, a murderer, a pest to the community. How, then, base the right of society on the right of the father, since, in point of fact, the right of society is paramount to the right of the parent?

But even waiving this, and granting what is not the fact, that the authority of the father is absolute, unlimited, it cannot be the ground of the right of society to govern. Assume the parental right to be perfect and inseparable from the parental relation, it is no right to govern where no such relation exists. Nothing true, real, solid in government can be founded on what Carlyle calls a "sham." The statesman, if worthy of the name, ascertains and conforms to the realities, the verities of things; and all jurisprudence that accepts legal fictions is imperfect, and even censurable. The presumptions or assumptions of law or politics must have a real and solid basis, or they are inadmissible. How, from the right of the father to govern his own child, born from his loins, conclude his right to govern one not his child? Or how, from my right to govern my child, conclude the right of society to found the state, institute government, and exercise political authority over its members?

IV

Origin of Government
(continued)

II. Rejecting the patriarchal theory as untenable, and shrinking from asserting the divine origin of government, lest they should favor theocracy, and place secular society under the control of the clergy, and thus disfranchise the laity, modern political writers have sought to render government purely human, and maintain that its origin is conventional, and that it is founded in compact or agreement. Their theory originated in the seventeenth century, and was predominant in the last century and the first third of the present. It has been, and perhaps is yet, generally accepted by American politicians and statesmen, at least so far as they ever trouble their heads with the question at all, which it must be confessed is not far.

The moral theologians of the Church have generally spoken of government as a social pact or compact, and explained the reciprocal rights and obligations of subjects and rulers by the general law of contracts; but they have never held that government originates in a voluntary agreement between the people and their rulers, or between the several individuals composing the community. They have never held that government has only a conventional origin or authority. They have simply meant, by the social compact, the mutual relations and reciprocal rights and duties of princes and their subjects, as implied in the very existence and nature of civil society. Where there are rights and duties on each side, they treat the fact, not as an agreement voluntarily entered into, and which creates them, but as a compact which binds alike sovereign and subject; and in determining whether either side has sinned or not, they inquire whether either has broken the terms of the social compact. They were engaged, not with the question whence does government derive its authority, but with its nature, and the reciprocal rights and duties of governors and the governed. The compact itself they held was not voluntarily formed by the people themselves, either individually or collectively, but was imposed by God, either immediately, or mediately, through the law of nature. "Every man," says Cicero, "is born in society, and remains there." They held the same, and maintained that every one born into society contracts by that fact certain obligations to society, and society certain obligations to him; for under the natural law, every one has certain rights, as life, liberty, and the pursuit of happiness, and owes certain duties to society for the protection and assistance it affords him.

But modern political theorists have abused the phrase borrowed from the theologians, and made it cover a political doctrine which they would have been the last to accept. These theorists or political speculators have imagined a state of nature antecedently to civil society, in which men lived without government, law, or manners, out of which they finally came by entering into a voluntary agreement with some one of their number to be king and to govern them, or with one another to submit to the rule of the majority. Hobbes, the English materialist, is among the earliest and most distinguished of the advocates of this theory. He held that men lived, prior to the creation of civil society, in a state of nature, in which all were equal, and every one had an equal right to every thing, and to take any thing on which he could lay his hands and was strong enough to hold. There was no law but the will of the strongest. Hence, the state of nature was a state of continual war. At length, wearied and disgusted, men sighed for peace, and, with one accord, said to the tallest, bravest, or ablest among them: Come, be our king, our master, our sovereign lord, and govern us; we surrender our natural rights and our natural independence to you, with no other reserve or condition than that you maintain peace among us, keep us from robbing and plundering one another or cutting each other's throats.

Locke followed Hobbes, and asserted virtually the same theory, but asserted it in the interests of liberty, as Hobbes had asserted it in the interests of power. Rousseau, a citizen of Geneva, followed in the next century with his *Contrat Social*, the text-book of the French revolutionists—almost their Bible—and put the finishing stroke to the theory. Hitherto the compact or agreement had been assumed to be between the governor and the governed; Rousseau supposes it to be between the people themselves, or a compact to which the people are the only parties. He adopts the theory of a state of nature in which men lived, antecedently to their forming themselves into civil society, without government or law. All men in that state were equal, and each was independent and sovereign proprietor of himself. These equal, independent, sovereign individuals met, or are held to have met, in convention, and entered into a compact with themselves, each with all, and all with each, that they would constitute government, and would each submit to the determination and authority of the whole, practically of the fluctuating and irresponsible majority. Civil society, the state, the government, originates in this compact, and the government, as Mr. Jefferson asserts in the Declaration of American Independence, "derives its just powers from the consent of the governed."

This theory, as so set forth, or as modified by asserting that the individual delegates instead of surrendering his rights to civil society, was generally adopted by the American people in the last century, and is still the more prevalent theory with those among them who happen to have any theory or opinion on the subject. It is the political tradition of the country. The state, as defined by the elder Adams, is held to be a voluntary association of individuals. Individuals create civil society, and may uncreate it whenever they judge it advisable. Prior to the Southern Rebellion, nearly every American asserted with Lafayette, "the sacred right of insurrection" or revolution, and sympathized with insurrectionists, rebels, and revolutionists, wherever they made their appearance. Loyalty was held to be the correlative of royalty, treason was regarded as a virtue, and traitors were honored, feasted, and eulogized as patriots, ardent lovers of liberty, and champions of the people. The fearful struggle of the nation against a rebellion which threatened its very existence may have changed this.

That there is, or ever was, a state of nature such as the theory assumes, may be questioned. Certainly nothing proves that it is, or ever was, a real state. That there is a law of nature is undeniable. All authorities in philosophy, morals, politics, and jurisprudence assert it; the state assumes it as its own immediate basis, and the codes of all nations are founded on it; universal jurisprudence, the *jus gentium* of the Romans, embodies it, and the courts recognize and administer it. It is the reason and conscience of civil society, and every state acknowledges its authority. But the law of nature is as much in force in civil society as out of it. Civil law does not abrogate or supersede natural law, but presupposes it, and supports itself on it as its own ground and reason. As the natural law, which is only natural justice and equity dictated by the reason common to all men, persists in the civil law, municipal or international, as its informing soul, so does the state of nature persist in the civil state, natural society in civil society, which simply develops, applies, and protects it. Man in civil society is not out of nature, but is in it—is in his most natural state; for society is natural to him, and government is natural to society, and in some form inseparable from it. The state of nature under the natural law is not, as a separate state, an actual state, and never was; but an abstraction, in which is considered, apart from the concrete existence called society, what is derived immediately from the natural law. But as abstractions have no existence out of the mind that forms them, the state of nature has no actual existence in the world of reality as a separate state.

But suppose with the theory the state of nature to have been a real and separate state, in which men at first lived, there is great difficulty in understanding how they ever got out of it. Can a man divest himself of his nature, or lift himself above it? Man is in his nature, and inseparable from it. If his primitive state was his natural state, and if the political state is supernatural, preternatural, or subnatural, how passed he alone, by his own unaided powers, from the former to the latter? The ancients, who had lost the primitive tradition of creation, asserted, indeed, the primitive man as springing from the earth, and leading a mere animal life, living in caves or hollow trees, and feeding on roots and nuts, without speech, without science, art, law, or sense of right and wrong; but prior to the prevalence of the Epicurean philosophy, they never pretended that man could come out of that state alone by his own unaided efforts. They ascribed the invention of language, art, and science, the institution of civil society, government, and laws, to the intervention of the gods. It remained for the Epicureans—who, though unable, like their modern successors, the Positivists or Developmentists, to believe in a first cause, believed in effects without causes, or that things make or take care of themselves—to assert that men could, by their own unassisted efforts, or by the simple exercise of reason, come out of the primitive state, and institute what in modern times is called *civiltà*, civility, or civilization.

The partisans of this theory of the state of nature from which men have emerged by the voluntary and deliberate formation of civil society, forget that if government is not the sole condition, it is one of the essential conditions of progress. The only progressive nations are civilized or republican nations. Savage and barbarous tribes are unprogressive. Ages on ages roll over them without changing any thing in their state; and Niebuhr has well remarked with others, that history records no instance of a savage tribe or people having become civilized by its own spontaneous or indigenous efforts. If savage tribes have ever become civilized, it has been by influences from abroad, by the aid of men already civilized, through conquest, colonies, or missionaries; never by their own indigenous efforts, nor even by commerce, as is so confidently asserted in this mercantile age. Nothing in all history indicates the ability of a savage people to pass of itself from the savage state to the civilized. But the primitive man, as described by Horace in his *Satires*, and asserted by Hobbes, Locke, Rousseau, and others, is far below the savage. The lowest, most degraded, and most debased savage tribe that has yet been discovered has at least some rude outlines or feeble reminiscences of a social state, of government, morals, law, and religion, for even in superstition the most gross there is a reminiscence of true religion; but the people in the alleged state of nature have none.

The advocates of the theory deceive themselves by transporting into their imaginary state of nature the views, habits, and capacities of the civilized man. It is, perhaps, not difficult for men who have been civilized, who have the intelligence, the arts, the affections, and the habits of civilization, if deprived by some great social convulsion of society, and thrown back on the so-called state of nature, or cast away on some uninhabited island in the ocean, and cut off from all intercourse with the rest of mankind, to reconstruct civil society, and re-establish and maintain civil government. They are civilized men, and bear civil society in their own life. But these are no representatives of the primitive man in the alleged state of nature. These primitive men have no experience, no knowledge, no conception even of civilized life, or of any state superior to that in which they have thus far lived. How then can they, since, on the theory, civil society has no root in nature, but is a purely artificial creation, even conceive of civilization, much less realize it?

These theorists, as theorists always do, fail to make a complete abstraction of the civilized state, and conclude from what they feel they could do in case civil society were broken up, what men may do and have done in a state of nature. Men cannot divest themselves of themselves, and, whatever their efforts to do it, they think, reason, and act as they are. Every writer, whatever else he writes, writes himself. The advocates of the theory, to have made their abstraction complete, should have presented their primitive man as below the lowest known savage, unprogressive, and in himself incapable of developing any progressive energy. Unprogressive, and, without foreign assistance, incapable of progress, how is it possible for your primitive man to pass, by his own unassisted efforts, from the alleged state of nature to that of civilization, of which he has no conception, and towards which no innate desire, no instinct, no divine inspiration pushes him?

But even if, by some happy inspiration, hardly supposable without supernatural intervention repudiated by the theory—if by some happy inspiration, a rare individual should so far rise above the state of nature as to conceive of civil society and of civil government, how could he carry his conception into execution? Conception is always easier than its realization, and between the design and its execution there is always a weary distance. The poetry of all nations is a wail over unrealized ideals. It is little that even the wisest and most potent statesman can realize of what he conceives to be necessary for the state: political, legislative, or judicial reforms, even when loudly demanded, and favored by authority, are hard to be effected, and not seldom generations come and go without effecting them. The republics of Plato, Sir Thomas More, Campanella, Harrington, as the communities of Robert Owen and M. Cabet, remain Utopias, not solely because intrinsically absurd, though so in fact, but chiefly because they are innovations, have no support in experience, and require for their realization the modes of thought, habits, manners, character, life, which only their introduction and realization can supply. So to be able to execute the design of passing from the supposed state of nature to civilization, the reformer would need the intelligence, the habits, and characters in the public which are not possible without civilization itself. Some philosophers suppose men have invented language, forgetting that it requires language to give the ability to invent language.

Men are little moved by mere reasoning, however clear and convincing it may be. They are moved by their affections, passions, instincts, and habits. Routine is more powerful with them than logic. A few are greedy of novelties, and are always for trying experiments; but the great body of the people of all nations have an invincible repugnance to abandon what they know for what they know not. They are, to a great extent, the slaves of their own vis inertiæ, and will not make the necessary exertion to change their existing mode of life, even for a better. Interest itself is powerless before their indolence, prejudice, habits, and usages. Never were philosophers more ignorant of human nature than they, so numerous in the last century, who imagined that men can be always moved by a sense of interest, and that enlightened self-interest, *···intérêt bien entendu*, suffices to found and sustain the state. No reform, no change in the constitution of government or of society, whatever the advantages it may promise, can be successful, if introduced, unless it has its root or germ in the past. Man is never a creator; he can only develop and continue, because he is himself a creature, and only a second cause. The children of Israel, when they encountered the privations of the wilderness that lay between them and the promised land flowing with milk and honey, fainted in spirit, and begged Moses to lead them back to Egypt, and permit them to return to slavery.

In the alleged state of nature, at the philosophers describe it, there is no germ of civilization, and the transition to civil society would not be a development, but a complete rupture with the past, and an entire new creation. When it is with the greatest difficulty that necessary reforms are introduced in old and highly civilized nations, and when it can seldom be done at all without terrible political and social convulsions, how can we suppose men without society, and knowing nothing of it, can deliberately, and, as it were, with "malice aforethought," found society? Without government, and destitute alike of habits of obedience and habits of command, how can they initiate, establish, and sustain government? To suppose it, would be to suppose that men in a state of nature, without culture, without science, without any of the arts, even the most simple and necessary, are infinitely superior to the men formed under the most advanced civilization. Was Rousseau right in asserting civilization as a fall, as a deterioration of the race?

But suppose the state of nature, even suppose that men, by some miracle or other, can get out of it and found civil society, the origin of government as authority in compact is not yet established. According to the theory, the rights of civil society are derived from the rights of the individuals who form or enter into the compact. But individuals cannot give what they have not, and no individual has in himself the right to govern another. By the law of nature all men have equal rights, are equals, and equals have no authority one over another. Nor has an individual the sovereign right even to himself, or the right to dispose of himself as he pleases. Man is not God, independent, self-existing, and self-sufficing. He is dependent, and dependent not only on his Maker, but on his fellow-men, on society, and even on nature, or the material world. That on which he depends, in the measure in which he depends on it, contributes to his existence, to his life, and to his well-being, and has, by virtue of its contribution, a right in him and to him; and hence it is that nothing is more painful to the proud spirit than to receive a favor that lays him under an obligation to another. The right of that on which man depends, and by communion with which he lives, limits his own right over himself.

Man does not depend exclusively on society, for it is not his only medium of communion with God, and therefore its right to him is neither absolute nor unlimited; but still he depends on it, lives in it, and cannot live without it. It has, then, certain rights over him, and he cannot enter into any compact, league, or alliance that society does not authorize, or at least permit. These rights of society override his rights to himself, and he can neither surrender them nor delegate them. Other rights, as the rights of religion and property, which are held directly from God and nature, and which are independent of society, are included in what are called the natural rights of man; and these rights cannot be surrendered in forming civil society, for they are rights of man only before civil society, and therefore not his to cede, and because they are precisely the rights that government is bound to respect and protect. The compact, then, cannot be formed as pretended, for the only rights individuals could delegate or surrender to society to constitute the sum of the rights of government are hers already, and those which are not hers are those which cannot be delegated or surrendered, and in the free and full enjoyment of which, it is the duty, the chief end of government to protect each and every individual.

The convention not only is not a fact, but individuals have no authority without society, to meet in convention, and enter into the alleged compact, because they are not independent, sovereign individuals. But pass over this: suppose the convention, suppose the compact, it must still be conceded that it binds and can bind only those who voluntarily and deliberately enter into it. This is conceded by Mr. Jefferson and the American Congress of 1776, in the assertion that government derives its "just powers from the consent of the governed." This consent, as the matter is one of life and death, must be free, deliberate, formal, explicit, not simply an assumed, implied, or constructive consent. It must be given personally, and not by one for another without his express authority.

It is usual to infer the consent or the acceptance of the terms of the compact from the silence of the individual, and also from his continued residence in the country and submission to its government. But residence is no evidence of consent, because it may be a matter of necessity. The individual may be unable to emigrate, if he would; and by what right can individuals form an agreement to which I must consent or else migrate to some strange land? Can my consent, under such circumstances, even if given, be any thing but a forced consent, a consent given under duress, and therefore invalid? Nothing can be inferred from one's silence, for he may have many reasons for being silent besides approval of the government. He may be silent because speech would avail nothing; because to protest might be dangerous— cost him his liberty, if not his life; because he sees and knows nothing better, and is ignorant that he has any choice in the case; or because, as very likely is the fact with the majority, he has never for a moment thought of the matter, or ever had his attention called to it, and has no mind on the subject.

But however this may be, there certainly must be excluded from the compact or obligation to obey the government created by it all the women of a nation, all the children too young to be capable of giving their consent, and all who are too ignorant, too weak of mind to be able to understand the terms of the contract. These several classes cannot be less than three-fourths of the population of any country. What is to be done with them? Leave them without government? Extend the power of the government over them? By what right? Government derives its just powers from the consent of the governed, and that consent they have not given. Whence does one-fourth of the population get its right to govern the other three-fourths?

But what is to be done with the rights of minorities? Is the rule of unanimity to be insisted on in the convention, and in the government, when it goes into operation? Unanimity is impracticable, for where there

are many men there will be differences of opinion. The rule of unanimity gives to each individual a veto on the whole proceeding, which
was the grand defect of the Polish constitution. Each member of the
Polish Diet, which included the whole body of the nobility, had an
absolute veto, and could, alone, arrest the whole action of the government. Will you substitute the rule of the majority, and say the majority must govern? By what right? It is agreed to in the convention.
Unanimously, or only by a majority? The right of the majority to
have their will is, on the social compact theory, a conventional right,
and therefore cannot come into play before the convention is completed, or the social compact is framed and accepted. How, in settling
the terms of the compact, will you proceed? By majorities? But suppose a minority objects, and demands two-thirds, three-fourths, or
four-fifths, and votes against the majority rule, which is carried only
by a simple plurality of votes, will the proceedings of the convention
bind the dissenting minority? What gives to the majority the right to
govern the minority who dissent from its action?

On the supposition that society has rights not derived from individuals, and which are intrusted to the government, there is a good
reason why the majority should prevail within the legitimate sphere of
government, because the majority is the best representative practicable
of society itself; and if the constitution secures to minorities and dissenting individuals their natural rights and their equal rights as citizens, they have no just cause of complaint, for the majority in such case
has no power to tyrannize over them or to oppress them. But the theory
under examination denies that society has any rights except such as it
derives from individuals who all have equal rights. According to it, society is itself conventional, and created by free, independent, equal, sovereign individuals. Society is a congress of sovereigns, in which no one
has authority over another, and no one can be rightfully forced to submit to any decree against his will. In such a congress the rule of the

majority is manifestly improper, illegitimate, and invalid, unless adopted by unanimous consent.

But this is not all. The individual is always the equal of himself, and if the government derives its powers from the consent of the governed, he governs in the government, and parts with none of his original sovereignty. The government is not his master, but his agent, as the principal only delegates, not surrenders, his rights and powers to the agent. He is free at any time he pleases to recall the powers he has delegated, to give new instructions, or to dismiss him. The sovereignty of the individual survives the compact, and persists through all the acts of his agent, the government. He must, then, be free to withdraw from the compact whenever he judges it advisable. Secession is perfectly legitimate if government is simply a contract between equals. The disaffected, the criminal, the thief the government would send to prison, or the murderer it would hang, would be very likely to revoke his consent, and to secede from the state. Any number of individuals large enough to count a majority among themselves, indisposed to pay the government taxes, or to perform the military service exacted, might hold a convention, adopt a secession ordinance, and declare themselves a free, independent, sovereign state, and bid defiance to the tax-collector and the provost-marshal, and that, too, without forfeiting their estates or changing their domicile. Would the government employ military force to coerce them back to their allegiance? By what right? Government is their agent, their creature, and no man owes allegiance to his own agent, or creature.

The compact could bind only temporarily, and could at any moment be dissolved. Mr. Jefferson saw this, and very consistently maintained that one generation has no power to bind another; and, as if this was not enough, he asserted the right of revolution, and gave it as his opinion that in every nation a revolution once in every generation is desirable, that is, according to his reckoning, once every nineteen years. The doctrine that one generation has no power to bind its successor is not only a logical conclusion from the theory that governments derive their just powers from the consent of the governed, since a generation cannot give its consent before it is born, but is very convenient for a nation that has contracted a large national debt; yet, perhaps, not so convenient to the public creditor, since the new generation may take it into its head not to assume or discharge the obligations of its predecessor, but to repudiate them. No man, certainly, can contract for any one but himself; and how then can the son be bound, without his own personal or individual consent, freely given, by the obligations entered into by his father?

The social compact is necessarily limited to the individuals who form it, and as necessarily, unless renewed, expires with them. It thus creates no state, no political corporation, which survives in all its rights and powers, though individuals die. The state is on this theory a voluntary association, and in principle, except that it is not a secret society, in no respect differs from the Carbonari, or the Knights of the Golden Circle. When Orsini attempted to execute the sentence of death on the Emperor of the French, in obedience to the order of the Carbonari, of which the Emperor was a member, he was, if the theory of the origin of government in compact be true, no more an assassin than was the officer who executed on the gallows the rebel spies and incendiaries Beal and Kennedy.

Certain it is that the alleged social compact has in it no social or civil element. It does not and cannot create society. It can give only an aggregation of individuals, and society is not an aggregation nor even an organization of individuals. It is an organism, and individuals live in its life as well as it in theirs. There is a real living solidarity, which makes individuals members of the social body, and members one of another. There is no society without individuals, and there are no individuals without society; but in society there is that which is not individual, and is more than all individuals. The social compact is an attempt to substitute for this real living solidarity, which gives to society at once unity of life and diversity of members, an artificial solidarity, a fictitious unity for a real unity, and membership by contract for real living membership, a cork leg for that which nature herself gives. Real government has its ground in this real living solidarity, and represents the social element, which is not individual, but above all individuals, as man is above men. But the theory substitutes a simple agency for government, and makes each individual its principal. It is an abuse of language to call this agency a government. It has no one feature or element of government. It has only an artificial unity, based on diversity; its authority is only personal, individual, and in no sense a public authority, representing a public will, a public right, or a public interest. In no country could government be adopted and sustained if men were left to the wisdom or justness of their theories, or in the general affairs of life acted on them. Society, and government as representing society, has a real existence, life, faculties, and organs of its own, not derived or derivable from individuals. As well might it be maintained that the human body consists in and derives all its life from the particles of matter it assimilates from its food, and which are constantly escaping, as to maintain that society derives its life, or government its powers, from individuals. No mechanical aggregation of brute matter can make a living body, if there is no living and assimilating principle within; and no aggregation of individuals, however closely bound together by pacts or oaths, can make society where there is no informing social principle that aggregates and assimilates them to a living body, or produce that mystic existence called a state or commonwealth.

The origin of government in the *Contrat Social* supposes the nation to be a purely personal affair. It gives the government no territorial status, and clothes it with no territorial rights or jurisdiction. The government that could so originate would be, if any thing, a barbaric, not a republican government. It has only the rights conferred on it, surrendered or delegated to it by individuals, and therefore, at best, only individual rights. Individuals can confer only such rights as they have in the supposed state of nature. In that state there is neither private nor public domain. The earth in that state is not property, and is open to the first occupant, and the occupant can lay no claim to any more than he actually occupies. Whence, then, does government derive its territorial jurisdiction, and its right of eminent domain claimed by all national governments? Whence its title to vacant or unoccupied lands? How does any particular government fix its territorial boundaries, and obtain the right to prescribe who may occupy, and on what conditions, the vacant lands within those boundaries? Whence does it get its jurisdiction of navigable rivers, lakes, bays, and the seaboard within its territorial limits, as appertaining to its domain? Here are rights that it could not have derived from individuals, for individuals never possessed them in the so-called state of nature. The concocters of the theory evidently overlooked these rights, or considered them of no importance. They seem never to have contemplated the existence of territorial states, or the division of mankind into nations fixed to the soil. They seem not to have supposed the earth could be appropriated; and, indeed, many of their followers pretend that it cannot be, and that the public lands of a nation are open lands, and whoso chooses may occupy them, without leave asked of the national authority or granted. The American people retain more than one reminiscence of the nomadic and predatory habits of their Teutonic or Scythian ancestors before they settled on the banks of the Don or the Danube, on the Northern Ocean, in Scania, or came in contact with the Græco-Roman civilization.

Yet mankind are divided into nations, and all civilized nations are fixed to the soil. The territory is defined, and is the domain of the state, from which all private proprietors hold their title-deeds. Individual proprietors hold under the state, and often hold more than they occupy; but it retains in all private estates the eminent domain, and prohibits the alienation of land to one who is not a citizen. It defends its domain, its public unoccupied lands, and the lands owned by private individuals, against all foreign powers. Now whence, if government has only the rights ceded it by individuals, does it get this domain, and hold the right to treat settlers on even its unoccupied lands as trespassers? In the state of nature the territorial rights of individuals, if any they have, are restricted to the portion of land they occupy with their rude culture, and with their flocks and herds, and in civilized nations to what they hold from the state, and, therefore, the right as held and defended by all nations, and without which the nation has no status, no fixed dwelling, and is and can be no state, could never have been derived from individuals. The earliest notices of Rome show the city in possession of the sacred territory, to which the state and all political power are attached. Whence did Rome become a landholder, and the governing people a territorial people? Whence does any nation become a territorial nation and lord of the domain? Certainly never by the cession of individuals, and hence no civilized government ever did or could originate in the so-called social compact.

V

Origin of Government
(continued)

III. The tendency of the last century was to individualism; that of the present is to socialism. The theory of Hobbes, Locke, Rousseau, and Jefferson, though not formally abandoned, and still held by many, has latterly been much modified, if not wholly transformed. Sovereignty, it is now maintained, is inherent in the people; not individually, indeed, but collectively, or the people as society. The constitution is held not to be simply a compact or agreement entered into by the people as individuals creating civil society and government, but a law ordained by the sovereign people, prescribing the constitution of the state and defining its rights and powers.

This transformation, which is rather going on than completed, is, under one aspect at least, a progress, or rather a return to the sounder principles of antiquity. Under it government ceases to be a mere agency, which must obtain the assassin's consent to be hung before it can rightfully hang him, and becomes authority, which is one and imperative. The people taken collectively are society, and society is a living organism, not a mere aggregation of individuals. It does not, of course, exist without individuals, but it is something more than individuals, and has rights not derived from them, and which are paramount to theirs. There is more truth, and truth of a higher order, in this than in the theory of the social compact. Individuals, to a certain extent, derive their life from God through society, and so far they depend on her, and they are hers; she owns them, and has the right to do as she will with them. On this theory the state emanates from society, and is supreme. It coincides with the ancient Greek and Roman theory, as expressed by Cicero, already cited. Man is born in society and remains there, and it may be regarded as the source of ancient Greek and Roman patriotism, which still commands the admiration of the civilized world. The state with Greece and Rome was a living reality, and loyalty a religion. The Romans held Rome to be a divinity, gave her statues and altars, and offered her divine worship. This was superstition, no doubt, but it had in it an element of truth. To every true philosopher there is something divine in the state, and truth in all theories. Society stands nearer to God, and participates more immediately of the Divine essence, and the state is a more lively image of God than the individual. It was man, the generic and reproductive man, not the isolated individual, that was created in the image and likeness of his Maker. "And God created man in his own image; in the image of God created he him; male and female created he them." This theory is usually called the democratic theory, and it enlists in its support the instincts, the intelligence, the living forces, and active tendencies of the age. Kings, kaisers, and hierarchies are powerless before it, and war against it in vain. The most they can do is to restrain its excesses, or to guard against its abuses. Its advocates, in returning to it, sometimes revive in its name the old pagan superstition. Not a few of the European democrats recognize in the earth, in heaven, or in hell, no power superior to the people, and say not only people-king, but people-God. They say absolutely, without any qualification, the voice of the people is the voice of God, and make their will the supreme law, not only in politics, but in religion, philosophy, morals, science, and the arts. The people not only found the state, but also the church. They inspire or reveal the truth, ordain or prohibit worships, judge of doctrines, and decide cases of conscience. Mazzini said, when at the head of the Roman Republic in 1848, the question of religion must be remitted to the judgment of the people. Yet this theory is the dominant theory of the age, and is in all civilized nations advancing with apparently irresistible force.

But this theory has its difficulties. Who are the collective people that have the rights of society, or, who are the sovereign people? The word *people* is vague, and in itself determines nothing. It may include a larger or a smaller number; it may mean the political people, or it may mean simply population; it may mean peasants, artisans, shopkeepers, traders, merchants, as distinguished from the nobility; hired laborers or workmen as distinguished from their employer, or slaves as distinguished from their master or owner. In which of these senses is the word to be taken when it is said, "The people are sovereign?" The people are the population or inhabitants of one and the same country. That is something. But who or what determines the country? Is the country the whole territory of the globe? That will not be said, especially since the dispersion of mankind and their division into separate nations. Is the territory indefinite or undefined? Then indefinite or undefined are its inhabitants, or the people invested with the rights of society. Is it defined and its boundaries fixed? Who has done it? The people. But who are the people? We are as wise as we were at starting. The logicians say that the definition of *idem* per *idem*, or the same by the same, is simply no definition at all.

The people are the nation, undoubtedly, if you mean by the people the sovereign people. But who are the people constituting the nation? The sovereign people? This is only to revolve in a vicious circle. The nation is the tribe or the people living under the same regimen, and born of the same ancestor, or sprung from the same ancestor or progenitor. But where find a nation in this the primitive sense of the word?

Migration, conquest, and intermarriage, have so broken up and inter-mingled the primitive races, that it is more than doubtful if a single nation, tribe, or family of unmixed blood now exists on the face of the earth. A Frenchman, Italian, Spaniard, German, or Englishman, may have the blood of a hundred different races coursing in his veins. The nation is the people inhabiting the same country, and united under one and the same government, it is further answered. The nation, then, is not purely personal, but also territorial. Then, again, the question comes up, who or what determines the territory? The government? But not before it is constituted, and it cannot be constituted till its territorial limits are determined. The tribe doubtless occupies territory, but is not fixed to it, and derives no jurisdiction from it, and therefore is not terri-torial. But a nation, in the modern or civilized sense, is fixed to the territory, and derives from it its jurisdiction, or sovereignty; and, there-fore, till the territory is determined, the nation is not and cannot be determined.

The question is not an idle question. It is one of great practical importance; for, till it is settled, we can neither determine who are the sovereign people, nor who are united under one and the same govern-ment. Laws have no extra-territorial force, and the officer who should attempt to enforce the national laws beyond the national territory would be a trespasser. If the limits are undetermined, the government is not territorial, and can claim as within its jurisdiction only those who choose to acknowledge its authority. The importance of the question has been recently brought home to the American people by the secession of eleven or more States from the Union. Were these States a part of the Ameri-can nation, or were they not? Was the war which followed secession, and which cost so many lives and so much treasure, a civil war or a foreign war? Were the secessionists traitors and rebels to their sover-eign, or were they patriots fighting for the liberty and independence of their country and the right of self-government? All on both sides agreed that the nation is sovereign; the dispute was as to the existence of the nation itself, and the extent of its jurisdiction. Doubtless, when a nation has a generally recognized existence as an historical fact, most of the difficulties in determining who are the sovereign people can be got over; but the question here concerns the institution of government, and determining who constitute society and have the right to meet in person, or by their delegates in convention, to institute it. This question, so important, and at times so difficult, the theory of the origin of government in the people collectively, or the nation, does not solve, or furnish any means of solving.

But suppose this difficulty surmounted, there is still another, and a very grave one, to overcome. The theory assumes that the people collectively, "in their own native right and might," are sovereign. According to it the people are ultimate, and free to do whatever they please. This sacrifices individual freedom. The origin of government in a compact entered into by individuals, each with all and all with each, sacrificed the rights of society, and assumed each individual to be in himself an independent sovereignty. If logically carried out, there could be no such crime as treason, there could be no state, and no public authority. This new theory transfers to society the sovereignty which that asserted for the individual, and asserts social despotism, or the absolutism of the state. It asserts with sufficient energy public authority, or the right of the people to govern; but it leaves no space for individual rights, which society must recognize, respect, and protect. This was the grand defect of the ancient Græco-Roman civilization. The historian explores in vain the records of the old Greek and Roman republics for any recognition of the rights of individuals not held as privileges or concessions from the state. Society recognized no limit to her authority, and the state claimed over individuals all the authority of the patriarch over his household, the chief over his tribe, or the absolute monarch over his subjects. The direct and indirect influence of the body of freemen admitted to a voice in public affairs, in determining the resolutions and action of the state, no doubt tempered in practice to some extent the authority of the state, and prevented acts of gross oppression; but in theory the state was absolute, and the people individually were placed at the mercy of the people collectively, or, rather, the majority of the collective people.

Under ancient republicanism, there were rights of the state and rights of the citizen, but no rights of man, held independently of society, and not derived from God through the state. The recognition of these rights by modern society is due to Christianity: some say to the barbarians, who overthrew the Roman empire; but this last opinion is not well founded. The barbarian chiefs and nobles had no doubt a lively sense of personal freedom and independence, but for themselves only. They had no conception of personal freedom as a general or universal right, and men never obtain universal principles by generalizing particulars. They may give a general truth a particular application, but not a particular truth—understood to be a particular truth—a general or universal application. They are too good logicians for that. The barbarian individual freedom and personal independence was never generalized into the doctrine of the rights of man, any more than the freedom of the master has been generalized into the right of his slaves to be free. The doctrine of individual freedom before the state is due to the Christian religion, which asserts the dignity and worth of every human soul, the accountability to God of each man for himself, and lays it down as law for every one that God is to be obeyed rather than men. The church practically denied the absolutism of the state, and asserted for every man rights not held from the state, in converting the empire to Christianity, in defiance of the state authority, and the imperial edicts punishing with death the profession of the Christian faith. In this she practically, as well as theoretically, overthrew state absolutism, and infused into modern

society the doctrine that every individual, even the lowest and meanest, has rights which the state neither confers nor can abrogate; and it
will only be by extinguishing in modern society the Christian faith,
and obliterating all traces of Christian civilization, that state absolutism can be revived with more than a partial and temporary success.

The doctrine of individual liberty may be abused, and so explained
as to deny the rights of society, and to become pure individualism; but
no political system that runs to the opposite extreme, and absorbs the
individual in the state, stands the least chance of any general or permanent success till Christianity is extinguished. Yet the assertion of principles which logically imply state absolutism is not entirely harmless,
even in Christian countries. Error is never harmless, and only truth can
give a solid foundation on which to build. Individualism and socialism
are each opposed to the other, and each has only a partial truth. The
state founded on either cannot stand, and society will only alternate
between the two extremes. To-day it is torn by a revolution in favor of
socialism; to-morrow it will be torn by another in favor of individualism, and without effecting any real progress by either revolution. Real
progress can be secured only by recognizing and building on the truth,
not as it exists in our opinions or in our theories, but as it exists in the
world of reality, and independent of our opinions.

Now, social despotism or state absolutism is not based on truth or
reality. Society has certain rights over individuals, for she is a medium
of their communion with God, or through which they derive life from
God, the primal source of all life; but she is not the only medium of
man's life. Man, as was said in the beginning, lives by communion with
God, and he communes with God in the creative act and the Incarnation, through his kind, and through nature. This threefold communion
gives rise to three institutions—religion or the church, society or the
state, and property. The life that man derives from God through religion and property, is not derived from him through society, and conse-

quently so much of his life he holds independently of society; and this constitutes his rights as a man as distinguished from his rights as a citizen. In relation to society, as not held from God through her, these are termed his natural rights, which she must hold inviolable, and government protect for every one, whatever his complexion or his social position. These rights—the rights of conscience and the rights of property, with all their necessary implications—are limitations of the rights of society, and the individual has the right to plead them against the state. Society does not confer them, and it cannot take them away, for they are at least as sacred and as fundamental as her own.

But even this limitation of popular sovereignty is not all. The people can be sovereign only in the sense in which they exist and act. The people are not God, whatever some theorists may pretend—are not independent, self-existent, and self-sufficing. They are as dependent collectively as individually, and therefore can exist and act only as second cause, never as first cause. They can, then, even in the limited sphere of their sovereignty, be sovereign only in a secondary sense, never absolute sovereign in their own independent right. They are sovereign only to the extent to which they impart life to the individual members of society, and only in the sense in which she imparts it, or is its cause. She is not its first cause or creator, and is the medial cause or medium through which they derive it from God, not its efficient cause or primary source. Society derives her own life from God, and exists and acts only as dependent on him. Then she is sovereign over individuals only as dependent on God. Her dominion is then not original and absolute, but secondary and derivative.

This third theory does not err in assuming that the people collectively are more than the people individually, or in denying society to be a mere aggregation of individuals with no life, and no rights but what it derives from them; nor even in asserting that the people in the sense of society are sovereign, but in asserting that they are sovereign in their own native or underived right and might. Society has not in herself the absolute right to govern, because she has not the absolute dominion either of herself or her members. God gave to man dominion over the irrational creation, for he made irrational creatures for man; but he never gave him either individually or collectively the dominion over the rational creation. The theory that the people are absolutely sovereign in their own independent right and might, as some zealous democrats explain it, asserts the fundamental principle of despotism, and all despotism is false, for it identifies the creature with the Creator. No creature is creator, or has the rights of creator, and consequently no one in his own right is or can be sovereign. This third theory, therefore, is untenable.

IV. A still more recent class of philosophers, if philosophers they may be called, reject the origin of government in the people individually or collectively. Satisfied that it has never been instituted by a voluntary and deliberate act of the people, and confounding government as a fact with government as authority, maintain that government is a spontaneous development of nature. Nature develops it as the liver secretes bile, as the bee constructs her cell, or the beaver builds his dam. Nature, working by her own laws and inherent energy, develops society, and society develops government. That is all the secret. Questions as to the origin of government or its rights, beyond the simple positive fact, belong to the theological or metaphysical stage of the development of nature, but are left behind when the race has passed beyond that stage, and has reached the epoch of positive science, in which all, except the positive fact, is held to be unreal and non-existent. Government, like every thing else in the universe, is simply a positive development of nature. Science explains the laws and conditions of the development, but disdains to ask for its origin or ground in any order that transcends the changes of the world of space and time.

These philosophers profess to eschew all theory, and yet they only oppose theory to theory. The assertion that reality for the human mind is restricted to the positive facts of the sensible order, is purely theoretic, and is any thing but a positive fact. Principles are as really objects of science as facts, and it is only in the light of principles that facts themselves are intelligible. If the human mind had no science of reality that transcends the sensible order, or the positive fact, it could have no science at all. As things exist only in their principles or causes, so can they be known only in their principles and causes; for things can be known only as they are, or as they really exist. The science that pretends to deduce principles from particular facts, or to rise from the fact by way of reasoning to an order that transcends facts, and in which facts have their origin, is undoubtedly chimerical, and as against that the positivists are unquestionably right. But to maintain that man has no intelligence of any thing beyond the fact, no intuition or intellectual apprehension of its principle or cause, is equally chimerical. The human mind cannot have all science, but it has real science as far as it goes, and real science is the knowledge of things as they are, not as they are not. Sensible facts are not intelligible by themselves, because they do not exist by themselves; and if the human mind could not penetrate beyond the individual fact, beyond the mimetic to the methexic, or transcendental principle, copied or imitated by the individual fact, it could never know the fact itself. The error of modern philosophers, or philosopherlings, is in supposing the principle is deduced or inferred from the fact, and in denying that the human mind has direct and immediate intuition of it.

Something that transcends the sensible order there must be, or there could be no development; and if we had no science of it, we could never assert that development is development, or scientifically explain the laws and conditions of development. Development is explication, and supposes a germ which precedes it, and is not itself a development; and development, however far it may be carried, can never do more than realize the possibilities of the germ. Development is not creation, and cannot supply its own germ. That at least must be given by the Creator, for from nothing nothing can be developed. If authority has not its germ in nature, it cannot be developed from nature spontaneously or otherwise. All government has a governing will; and without a will that commands, there is no government; and nature has in her spontaneous developments no will, for she has no personality. Reason itself, as distinguished from will, only presents the end and the means, but does not govern; it prescribes a rule, but cannot ordain a law. An imperative will, the will of a superior who has the right to command what reason dictates or approves, is essential to government; and that will is not developed from nature, because it has no germ in nature. So something above and beyond nature must be asserted, or government itself cannot be asserted, even as a development. Nature is no more self-sufficing than are the people, or than is the individual man.

No doubt there is a natural law, which is law in the proper sense of the word law; but this is a positive law under which nature is placed by a sovereign above herself, and is never to be confounded with those laws of nature so-called, according to which she is productive as second cause, or produces her effects, which are not properly laws at all. Fire burns, water flows, rain falls, birds fly, fishes swim, food nourishes, poisons kill, one substance has a chemical affinity for another, the needle points to the pole, by a natural law, it is said; that is, the effects are produced by an inherent and uniform natural force. Laws in this sense are simply physical forces, and are nature herself. The natural law, in an ethical sense, is not a physical law, is not a natural force, but a law imposed by the Creator on all moral creatures, that is, all creatures endowed with reason and free-will, and is called *natural* because promulgated in natural reason, or the reason common and essential to all moral creatures. This is the moral law. It is what the French call *le droit naturel*, natural right, and, as the theologians teach us, is the transcript of the eternal law, the eternal will or reason of God. It is the foundation of all law, and all acts of a state that contravene it are, as St. Augustine maintains, violences rather than laws. The moral law is no development of nature, for it is above nature, and is imposed on nature. The only development there is about it is in our understanding of it.

There is, of course, development in nature, for nature considered as creation has been created in germ, and is completed only in successive developments. Hence the origin of space and time. There would have been no space if there had been no external creation, and no time if the creation had been completed externally at once, as it was in relation to the Creator. Ideal space is simply the ability of God to externize his creative act, and actual space is the relation of coexistence in the things created; ideal time is the ability of God to create existences with the capacity of being completed by successive developments, and actual time is the relation of these in the order of succession, and when the existence is completed or consummated development ceases, and time is no more. In relation to himself the Creator's works are complete from the first, and hence with him there is no time, for there is no succession. But in relation to itself creation is incomplete, and there is room for development, which may be continued till the whole possibility of creation is actualized. Here is the foundation of what is true in the modern doctrine of progress. Man is progressive, because the possibilities of his nature are successively unfolded and actualized.

Development is a fact, and its laws and conditions may be scientifically ascertained and defined. All generation is development, as is all growth, physical, moral, or intellectual. But every thing is developed in its own order, and after its kind. The Darwinian theory of the development of species is not sustained by science. The development starts from the germ, and in the germ is given the law or principle of the development. From the acorn is developed the oak, never the pine or the linden. Every kind generates its kind, never another. But no development is, strictly speaking, spontaneous, or the result alone of the inherent energy or force of the germ developed. There is not only a solidarity of race, but in some sense of all races, or species; all created things are bound to their Creator, and to one another. One and the same law or principle of life pervades all creation, binding the universe together in a unity that copies or imitates the unity of the Creator. No creature is isolated from the rest, or absolutely independent of others. All are parts of one stupendous whole, and each depends on the whole, and the whole on each, and each on each. All creatures are members of one body, and members one of another. The germ of the oak is in the acorn, but the acorn left to itself alone can never grow into the oak, any more than a body at rest can place itself in motion. Lay the acorn away in your closet, where it is absolutely deprived of air, heat, and moisture, and in vain will you watch for its germination. Germinate it cannot without some external influence, or communion, so to speak, with the elements from which it derives its sustenance and support.

There can be no absolutely spontaneous development. All things are doubtless active, for nothing exists except in so far as it is an active force of some sort; but only God himself alone suffices for his own activity. All created things are dependent, have not their being in themselves, and are real only as they participate, through the creative act, of the Divine being. The germ can no more be developed than it could exist without God, and no more develop itself than it could create itself. What is called the law of development is in the germ; but that law or force can operate only in conjunction with another force or other forces. All development, as all growth, is by accretion or assimilation. The assimilating force is, if you will, in the germ, but the matter assimilated comes and must come from abroad. Every herdsman knows it, and knows that to rear his stock he must supply them with appropriate food;

every husbandman knows it, and knows that to raise a crop of corn, he must plant the seed in a soil duly prepared, and which will supply the gases needed for its germination, growth, flowering, bolling, and ripening. In all created things, in all things not complete in themselves, in all save God, in whom there is no development possible, for He is, as say the schoolmen, most pure act, in whom there is no unactualized possibility, the same law holds good. Development is always the resultant of two factors, the one the thing itself, the other some external force co-operating with it, exciting it, and aiding it to act. Hence the *præmotio physica* of the Thomists, and the *prævenient* and *adjuvant* grace of the theologians, without which no one can begin the Christian life, and which must needs be supernatural when the end is supernatural. The principle of life in all orders is the same, and human activity no more suffices for itself in one order than in another.

Here is the reason why the savage tribe never rises to a civilized state without communion in some form with a people already civilized, and why there is no moral or intellectual development and progress without education and instruction, consequently without instructors and educators. Hence the value of tradition; and hence, as the first man could not instruct himself, Christian theologians, with a deeper philosophy than is dreamed of by the sciolists of the age, maintain that God himself was man's first teacher, or that he created Adam a full-grown man, with all his faculties developed, complete, and in full activity. Hence, too, the heathen mythologies, which always contain some elements of truth, however they may distort, mutilate, or travesty them, make the gods the first teachers of the human race, and ascribe to their instruction even the most simple and ordinary arts of every-day life. The gods teach men to plough, to plant, to reap, to work in iron, to erect a shelter from the storm, and to build a fire to warm them and to cook their food. The common sense, as well as the common traditions of mankind, refuses to accept the doctrine that men are developed without foreign aid, or progressive without divine assistance. Nature of herself can no more develop government than it can language. There can be no language without society, and no society without language. There can be no government without society, and no society without government of some sort.

But even if nature could spontaneously develop herself, she could never develop an institution that has the right to govern, for she has not herself that right. Nature is not God, has not created us, therefore has not the right of property in us. She is not and cannot be our sovereign. We belong not to her, nor does she belong to herself, for she is herself creature, and belongs to her Creator. Not being in herself sovereign, she cannot develop the right to govern, nor can she develop government as a fact, to say nothing of its right, for government, whether we speak of it as fact or as authority, is distinct from that which is governed; but natural developments are nature, and indistinguishable from her. The governor and the governed, the restrainer and the restrained, can never as such be identical. Self-government, taken strictly, is a contradiction in terms. When an individual is said to govern himself, he is never understood to govern himself in the sense in which he is governed. He by his reason and will governs or restrains his appetites and passions. It is man as spirit governing man as flesh, the spiritual mind governing the carnal mind.

Natural developments cannot in all cases be even allowed to take their own course without injury to nature herself. "Follow nature" is an unsafe maxim, if it means, leave nature to develop herself as she will, and follow thy natural inclinations. Nature is good, but inclinations are frequently bad. All our appetites and passions are given us for good, for a purpose useful and necessary to individual and social life, but they become morbid and injurious if indulged without restraint. Each has its special object, and naturally seeks it exclusively, and thus generates discord and war in the individual, which immediately find expression in society, and also in the state, if the state be a simple natural development. The Christian maxim, Deny thyself, is far better than the Epicurean maxim, Enjoy thyself, for there is no real enjoyment without self-denial. There is deep philosophy in Christian asceticism, as the Positivists themselves are aware, and even insist. But Christian asceticism aims not to destroy nature, as voluptuaries pretend, but to regulate, direct, and restrain its abnormal developments for its own good. It forces nature in her developments to submit to a law which is not in her, but above her. The Positivists pretend that this asceticism is itself a natural development, but that cannot be a natural development which directs, controls, and restrains natural development.

The Positivists confound nature at one time with the law of nature, and at another the law of nature with nature herself, and take what is called the natural law to be a natural development. Here is their mistake, as it is the mistake of all who accept naturalistic theories. Society, no doubt, is authorized by the law of nature to institute and maintain government. But the law of nature is not a natural development, nor is it in nature, or any part of nature. It is not a natural force which operates in nature, and which is the developing principle of nature. Do they say reason is natural, and the law of nature is only reason? This is not precisely the fact. The natural law is law proper, and is reason only in the sense that reason includes both intellect and will, and nobody can pretend that nature in her spontaneous developments acts from intelligence and volition. Reason, as the faculty of knowing, is subjective and natural; but in the sense in which it is coincident with the natural law, it is neither subjective nor natural, but objective and divine, and is God affirming himself and promulgating his law to his creature, man. It is, at least, an immediate participation of the divine light, by which He reveals himself and His will to the human understanding, and is not natural, but supernatural, in the sense that God himself is supernatural. This is wherefore reason is law, and every man is bound to submit or conform to reason.

That legitimate governments are instituted under the natural law is frankly conceded, but this is by no means the concession of government as a natural development. The reason and will of which the natural law is the expression are the reason and will of God. The natural law is the divine law as much as the revealed law itself, and equally obligatory. It is not a natural force developing itself in nature, like the law of generation, for instance, and therefore proceeding from God as first cause, but it proceeds from God as final cause, and is, therefore, theological, and strictly a moral law, founding moral rights and duties. Of course, all morality and all legitimate government rest on this law, or, if you will, originate in it. But not therefore in nature, but in the Author of nature. The authority is not the authority of nature, but of Him who holds nature in the hollow of His hand.

V. In the seventeenth century a class of political writers who very well understood that no creature, no man, no number of men, not even nature herself, can be inherently sovereign, defended the opinion that governments are founded, constituted, and clothed with their authority by the direct and express appointment of God himself. They denied that rulers hold their power from the nation; that, however oppressive may be their rule, that they are justiciable by any human tribunal, or that power, except by the direct judgment of God, is amissible. Their doctrine is known in history as the doctrine of "the divine right of kings, and passive obedience." All power, says St. Paul, is from God, and the powers that be are ordained of God, and to resist them is to resist the ordination of God. They must be obeyed for conscience' sake.

It would, perhaps, be rash to say that this doctrine had never been broached before the seventeenth century, but it received in that century, and chiefly in England, its fullest and most systematic developments. It was patronized by the Anglican divines, asserted by James I. of England, and lost the Stuarts the crown of three kingdoms. It crossed the Channel, into France, where it found a few hesitating and stammering defenders among Catholics, under Louis XIV., but it has never been very generally held, though it has had able and zealous supporters. In England it was opposed by all the Presbyterians, Puritans, Independents, and Republicans, and was forgotten or abandoned by the Anglican divines themselves in the Revolution of 1688, that expelled James II. and crowned William and Mary. It was ably refuted by the Jesuit Suarez in his reply to a *Remonstrance for the Divine Right of Kings* by the James I.; and a Spanish monk who had asserted it in Madrid, under Philip II., was compelled by the Inquisition to retract it publicly in the place where he had asserted it. All republicans reject it, and the Church has never sanctioned it. The Sovereign Pontiffs have claimed and exercised the right to deprive princes of their principality, and to absolve their subjects from the oath of fidelity. Whether the Popes rightly claimed and exercised that power is not now the question; but their having claimed and exercised it proves that the Church does not admit the inamissibility of power and passive obedience; for the action of the Pope was judicial, not legislative. The Pope has never claimed the right to depose a prince till by his own act he has, under the moral law or the constitution of his state, forfeited his power, nor to absolve subjects from their allegiance till their oath, according to its true intent and meaning, has ceased to bind. If the Church has always asserted with the Apostle there is no power but from God—*non est potestas nisi a Deo*—she has always through her doctors maintained that it is a trust to be exercised for the public good, and is forfeited when persistently exercised in a contrary sense. St. Augustine, St. Thomas, and Suarez all maintain that unjust laws are violences rather than laws, and do not oblige, except in charity or prudence, and that the republic may change its magistrates, and even its constitution, if it sees proper to do so.

That God, as universal Creator, is Sovereign Lord and proprietor of all created things or existences, visible or invisible, is certain; for the maker has the absolute right to the thing made; it is his, and he may do with it as he will. As he is sole creator, he alone hath dominion; and as he is absolute creator, he has absolute dominion over all the things which he has made. The guaranty against oppression is his own essential nature, is in the plenitude of his own being, which is the plenitude of wisdom and goodness. He cannot contradict himself, be other than he is, or act otherwise than according to his own essential nature. As he is, in his own eternal and immutable essence, supreme reason and supreme good, his dominion must always in its exercise be supremely good and supremely reasonable, therefore supremely just and equitable. From him certainly is all power; he is unquestionably King of kings, and Lord of lords. By him kings reign and magistrates decree just things. He may, at his will, set up or pull down kings, rear or overwhelm empires, foster the infant colony, and make desolate the populous city. All this is unquestionably true, and a simple dictate of reason common to all men. But in what sense is it true? Is it true in a supernatural sense? Or is it true only in the sense that it is true that by him we breathe, perform any or all of our natural functions, and in him live, and move, and have our being?

Viewed in their first cause, all things are the immediate creation of God, and are supernatural, and from the point of view of the first cause the Scriptures usually speak, for the great purpose and paramount object of the sacred writers, as of religion itself, is to make prominent the fact that God is universal creator, and supreme governor, and therefore the first and final cause of all things. But God creates second causes, or substantial existences, capable themselves of acting and producing effects in a secondary sense, and hence he is said to be *causa causarum*, cause of causes. What is done by these second causes or creatures is done eminently by him, for they exist only by his creative act, and produce only by virtue of his active presence, or effective concurrence. What he does through them or through their agency is done by him, not immediately, but mediately, and is said to be done naturally, as what he does immediately is said to be done supernaturally. Natural is what God does through second causes, which he creates; supernatural is that which he does by himself alone, without their intervention or agency. Sovereignty, or the right to govern, is in him, and he may at his will delegate it to men either mediately or immediately, by a direct and express appointment, or mediately through nature. In the absence of all facts proving its delegation direct and express, it must be assumed to be mediate, through second causes. The natural is always to be presumed, and the supernatural is to be admitted only on conclusive proof.

The people of Israel had a supernatural vocation, and they received their law, embracing their religious and civil constitution and their ritual directly from God at the hand of Moses, and various individuals from time to time appear to have been specially called to be their judges, rulers, or kings. Saul was so called, and so was David. David and his line appear, also, to have been called not only to supplant Saul and his line, but to have been supernaturally invested with the kingdom forever; but it does not appear that the royal power with which David and his line were invested was inamissible. They lost it in the Babylonish captivity, and never afterwards recovered it. The Asmonean princes were of another line, and when our Lord came the sceptre was in the hands of Herod, an Idumean or Edomite. The promise made to David and his house is generally held by Christian commentators to have received its fulfilment in the everlasting spiritual royalty of the Messiah, sprung through Mary from David's line.

The Christian Church is supernaturally constituted and supernaturally governed, but the persons selected to exercise powers supernaturally defined, from the Sovereign Pontiff down to the humblest parish priest are selected and inducted into office through human agency. The Gentiles very generally claimed to have received their laws from the gods, but it does not appear, save in exceptional cases, that they claimed that their princes were designated and held their powers by the direct and express appointment of the god. Save in the case of the Jews, and that of the Church, there is no evidence that any particular government exists or ever has existed by direct or express appointment, or otherwise than by the action of the Creator through second causes, or what is called his ordinary providence. Except David and his line, there is no evidence of the express grant by the Divine Sovereign to any individual or family, class or caste of the government of any nation or country. Even those Christian princes who professed to reign "by the grace of God," never claimed that they received their principalities from God otherwise than through his ordinary providence, and meant by it little more than an acknowledgment of their dependence on him, their obligation to use their power according to his law, and their accountability to him for the use they make of it.

The doctrine is not favorable to human liberty, for it recognizes no rights of man in face of civil society. It consecrates tyranny, and makes God the accomplice of the tyrant, if we suppose all governments have actually existed by his express appointment. It puts the king in the place of God, and requires us to worship in him the immediate representative of the Divine Being. Power is irresponsible and inamissible, and however it may be abused, or however corrupt and oppressive may be its exercise, there is no human redress. Resistance to power is resistance to God. There is nothing for the people but passive obedience and unreserved submission. The doctrine, in fact, denies all *human* government, and allows the people no voice in the management of their own affairs, and gives no place for human activity. It stands opposed to all republicanism, and makes power an hereditary and indefeasible right, not a trust which he who holds it may forfeit, and of which he may be deprived if he abuses it.

VI

Origin of Government
(concluded)

VI. The theory which derives the right of government from the direct and express appointment of God is sometimes modified so as to mean that civil authority is derived from God through the spiritual authority. The patriarch combined in his person both authorities, and was in his own household both priest and king, and so originally was in his own tribe the chief, and in his kingdom the king. When the two offices became separated is not known. In the time of Abraham they were still united. Melchisedech, king of Salem, was both priest and king, and the earliest historical records of kings present them as offering sacrifices. Even the Roman emperor was Pontifex Maximus as well as Imperator, but that was so not because the two offices were held to be inseparable, but because they were both conferred on the same person by the republic. In Egypt, in the time of Moses, the royal authority and the priestly were separated, and held by different persons. Moses, in his legislation for his nation, separated them, and instituted a sacerdotal order or caste. The heads of tribes and the heads of families are, under his law, princes, but not priests, and the priesthood is conferred on and restricted to his own tribe of Levi, and more especially the family of his own brother Aaron.

The priestly office by its own nature is superior to the kingly, and in all primitive nations with a separate organized priesthood, whether a true priesthood or a corrupt, the priest is held to be above the king, elects or establishes the law by which is selected the temporal chief, and inducts him into his office, as if he received his authority from God through the priesthood. The Christian priesthood is not a caste, and is transmitted by the election of grace, not as with the Israelites and all sacerdotal nations, by natural generation. Like Him whose priests they are, Christian priests are priests after the order of Melchisedech, who was without priestly descent, without father or mother of the priestly line. But in being priests after the order of Melchisedech, they are both priests and kings, as Melchisedech was, and as was our Lord himself, to whom was given by his Father all power in heaven and in earth. The Pope, or Supreme Pontiff, is the vicar of our Lord on earth, his representative—the representative not only of him who is our invisible High-Priest, but of him who is King of kings and Lord of lords, therefore of both the priestly and the kingly power. Consequently, no one can have any mission to govern in the state any more than in the church, unless derived from God directly or indirectly through the Pope or Supreme Pontiff. Many theologians and canonists in the Middle Ages so held, and a few perhaps hold so still. The bulls and briefs of several Popes, as Gregory VII., Innocent III., Gregory IX., Innocent IV., and Boniface VIII., have the appearance of favoring it.

At one period the greater part of the mediæval kingdoms and principalities were fiefs of the Holy See, and recognized the Holy Father as their suzerain. The Pope revived the imperial dignity in the person of Charlemagne, and none could claim that dignity in the Western world unless elected and crowned by him, that is, unless elected directly by the Pope or by electors designated by him, and acting under his authority. There can be no question that the spiritual is superior to the temporal, and that the temporal is bound in the very nature of things to conform to the spiritual, and any law enacted by the civil power in contravention of the law of God is null and void from the beginning. This is what Mr. Seward meant by the higher law, a law higher even than the Constitution of the United States. Supposing this higher law, and supposing that kings and princes hold from God through the spiritual society, it is very evident that the chief of that society would have the right to deprive them, and to absolve their subjects, as on several occasions he actually has done.

But this theory has never been a dogma of the Church, nor, to any great extent, except for a brief period, maintained by theologians or canonists. The Pope conferred the imperial dignity on Charlemagne and his successors, but not the civil power, at least out of the Pope's own temporal dominions. The emperor of Germany was at first elected by the Pope, and afterwards by hereditary electors designated or accepted by him, but the king of the Germans with the full royal authority could be elected and enthroned without the papal intervention or permission. The suzerainty of the Holy See over Italy, Naples, Aragon, Muscovy, England, and other European states, was by virtue of feudal relations, not by virtue of the spiritual authority of the Holy See or the vicarship of the Holy Father. The right to govern under feudalism was simply an estate, or property; and as the church could acquire and hold property, nothing prevented her holding fiefs, or her chief from being suzerain. The expressions in the papal briefs and bulls, taken in connection with the special relations existing between the Pope and emperor in the Middle Ages, and his relations with other states as their feudal sovereign, explained by the controversies concerning rights growing out of these relations, will be found to give no countenance to the theory in question.

These relations really existed, and they gave the Pope certain temporal rights in certain states, even the temporal supremacy, as he has still in what is left him of the States of the Church; but they were ex-

ceptional or accidental relations, not the universal and essential relations between the church and the state. The rights that grew out of
these relations were real rights, sacred and inviolable, but only where
and while the relations subsisted. They, for the most part, grew out of
the feudal system introduced into the Roman empire by its barbarian
conquerors, and necessarily ceased with the political order in which they
originated. Undoubtedly the church consecrated civil rulers, but this
did not imply that they received their power or right to govern from
God through her; but implied that their persons were sacred, and that
violence to them would be sacrilege; that they held the Christian faith,
and acknowledged themselves bound to protect it, and to govern their
subjects justly, according to the law of God.

The church, moreover, has always recognized the distinction of the
two powers, and although the Pope owes to the fact that he is chief of
the spiritual society, his temporal principality, no theologian or canonist
of the slightest respectability would argue that he derives his rights as
temporal sovereign from his rights as pontiff. His rights as pontiff depend on the express appointment of God; his rights as temporal prince
are derived from the same source from which other princes derive their
rights, and are held by the same tenure. Hence canonists have maintained that the subjects of other states may even engage in war with the
Pope as prince, without breach of their fidelity to him as pontiff or
supreme visible head of the church.

The church not only distinguishes between the two powers, but
recognizes as legitimate, governments that manifestly do not derive from
God through her. St. Paul enjoins obedience to the Roman emperors for
conscience' sake, and the church teaches that infidels and heretics may
have legitimate government; and if she has ever denied the right of any
infidel or heretical prince, it has been on the ground that the constitution and laws of his principality require him to profess and protect the
Catholic faith. She tolerates resistance in a non-Catholic state no more

than in a Catholic state to the prince; and if she has not condemned and cut off from her communion the Catholics who in our struggle have joined the Secessionists and fought in their ranks against the United States, it is because the prevalence of the doctrine of State sovereignty has seemed to leave a reasonable doubt whether they were really rebels fighting against their legitimate sovereign or not.

No doubt, as the authority of the church is derived immediately from God in a supernatural manner, and as she holds that the state derives its authority only mediately from him, in a natural mode, she asserts the superiority of her authority, and that, in case of conflict between the two powers, the civil must yield. But this is only saying that supernatural is above natural. But—and this is the important point—she does not teach, nor permit the faithful to hold, that the supernatural abrogates the natural, or in any way supersedes it. Grace, say the theologians, supposes nature, *gratia supponit naturam.* The church in the matter of government accepts the natural, aids it, elevates it, and is its firmest support.

VII. St. Augustine, St. Gregory Magnus, St. Thomas, Bellarmine, Suarez, and the theologians generally, hold that princes derive their power from God through the people, or that the people, though not the source, are the medium of all political authority, and therefore rulers are accountable for the use they make of their power to both God and the people.

This doctrine agrees with the democratic theory in vesting sovereignty in the people, instead of the king or the nobility, a particular individual, family, class, or caste; and differs from it, as democracy is commonly explained, in understanding by the people, the people collectively, not individually—the organic people, or people fixed to a given territory, not the people as a mere population—the people in the republican sense of the word nation, not in the barbaric or despotic sense;

and in deriving the sovereignty from God, from whom is all power, and except from whom there is and can be no power, instead of asserting it as the underived and indefeasible right of the people in their "own native right and might." The people not being God, and being only what philosophers call a second cause, they are and can be sovereign only in a secondary and relative sense. It asserts the divine origin of power, while democracy asserts its human origin. But as, under the law of nature, all men are equal, or have equal rights as men, one man has and can have in himself no right to govern another; and as man is never absolutely his own, but always and everywhere belongs to his Creator, it is clear that no government originating in humanity alone can be a legitimate government. Every such government is founded on the assumption that man is God, which is a great mistake—is, in fact, the fundamental sophism which underlies every error and every sin.

The divine origin of government, in the sense asserted by Christian theologians, is never found distinctly set forth in the political writings of the ancient Greek and Roman writers. Gentile philosophy had lost the tradition of creation, as some modern philosophers, in so-called Christian nations, are fast losing it, and were as unable to explain the origin of government as they were the origin of man himself. Even Plato, the profoundest of all ancient philosophers, and the most faithful to the traditionary wisdom of the race, lacks the conception of creation, and never gets above that of generation and formation. Things are produced by the Divine Being impressing his own ideas, eternal in his own mind, on a pre-existing matter, as a seal on wax. Aristotle teaches substantially the same doctrine. Things eternally exist as matter and form, and all the Divine Intelligence does, is to unite the form to the matter, and change it, as the schoolmen say, from *materia informis* to *materia formata*. Even the Christian Platonists and Peripatetics never as philosophers assert creation; they assert it, indeed, but as theologians, as a fact of revelation, not as a fact of science; and hence it is that their theology and their philosophy never thoroughly harmonize, or at least are not shown to harmonize throughout.

Speaking generally, the ancient Gentile philosophers were pantheists, and represented the universe either as God or as an emanation from God. They had no proper conception of Providence, or the action of God in nature through natural agencies, or as modern physicists say, natural laws. If they recognized the action of divinity at all, it was a supernatural or miraculous intervention of some god. They saw no divine intervention in any thing naturally explicable, or explicable by natural laws. Having no conception of the creative act, they could have none of its immanence, or the active and efficacious presence of the Creator in all his works, even in the action of second causes themselves. Hence they could not assert the divine origin of government, or civil authority, without supposing it supernaturally founded, and excluding all human and natural agencies from its institution. Their writings may be studied with advantage on the constitution of the state, on the practical workings of different forms of government, as well as on the practical administration of affairs, but never on the origin of the state, and the real ground of its authority.

The doctrine is derived from Christian theology, which teaches that there is no power except from God, and enjoins civil obedience as a religious duty. Conscience is accountable to God alone, and civil government, if it had only a natural or human origin, could not bind it. Yet Christianity makes the civil law, within its legitimate sphere, as obligatory on conscience as the divine law itself, and no man is blameless before God who is not blameless before the state. No man performs faithfully his religious duties who neglects his civil duties, and hence the law of the church allows no one to retire from the world and enter a religious order, who has duties that bind him or her to the family or the state; though it is possible that the law is not always strictly observed, and that individuals sometimes enter a convent for the sake of getting rid of those duties, or the equally important duty of taking care of themselves. But by asserting the divine origin of government, Christianity consecrates civil authority, clothes it with a religious character, and makes civil disobedience, sedition, insurrection, rebellion, revolution, civil turbulence of any sort or degree, sins against God as well as crimes against the state. For the same reason she makes usurpation, tyranny, oppression of the people by civil rulers, offences against God as well as against society, and cognizable by the spiritual authority.

After the establishment of the Christian church, after its public recognition, and when conflicting claims arose between the two powers—the civil and the ecclesiastical—this doctrine of the divine origin of civil government was abused, and turned against the church with most disastrous consequences. While the Roman Empire of the West subsisted, and even after its fall, so long as the emperor of the East asserted and practically maintained his authority in the Exarchate of Ravenna and the Duchy of Rome, the Popes comported themselves, in civil matters, as subjects of the Roman emperor, and set forth no claim to temporal independence. But when the emperor had lost Rome, and all his possessions in Italy, had abandoned them, or been deprived of them by the barbarians, and ceased to make any efforts to recover them, the Pope was no longer a subject, even in civil matters, of the emperor, and owed him no civil allegiance. He became civilly independent of the Roman Empire, and had only spiritual relations with it. To the new powers that sprang up in Europe he appears never to have acknowledged any civil subjection, and uniformly asserted, in face of them, his civil as well as spiritual independence.

This civil independence the successors of Charlemagne, who pretended to be the successors of the Roman Emperors of the West, and called their empire the Holy Roman Empire, denied, and maintained that the Pope owed them civil allegiance, or that, in temporals, the emperor was the Pope's superior. If, said the emperor, or his lawyers for him, the civil power is from God, as it must be, since *non est potestas nisi a Deo*, the state stands on the same footing with the church, and the imperial power emanates from as high a source as the pontifical. The emperor is then as supreme in temporals as the Pope in spirituals; and as the emperor is subject to the Pope in spirituals, so must the Pope be subject to the emperor in temporals. As, at the time when the dispute arose, the temporal interests of churchmen were so interwoven with their spiritual rights, the pretensions of the emperor amounted practically to the subjection in spirituals as well as temporals of the ecclesiastical authority to the civil, and absorbed the church in the state, the reasoning was denied, and churchmen replied: The Pope represents the spiritual order, which is always and everywhere supreme over the temporal, since the spiritual order is the divine sovereignty itself. Always and everywhere, then, is the Pope independent of the emperor, his superior, and to subject him in any thing to the emperor would be as repugnant to reason as to subject the soul to the body, the spirit to the flesh, heaven to earth, or God to man.

If the universal supremacy claimed for the Pope, rejoined the imperialists, be conceded, the state would be absorbed in the church, the autonomy of civil society would be destroyed, and civil rulers would have no functions but to do the bidding of the clergy. It would establish a complete theocracy, or, rather, clerocracy, of all possible governments the government the most odious to mankind, and the most hostile to social progress. Even the Jews could not, or would not, endure it, and prayed God to give them a king, that they might be like other nations.

In the heat of the controversy neither party clearly and distinctly perceived the true state of the question, and each was partly right and partly wrong. The imperialists wanted room for the free activity of civil society, the church wanted to establish in that society the supremacy of the moral order, or the law of God, without which governments can have no stability, and society no real well-being. The real solution of the difficulty was always to be found in the doctrine of the church herself, and had been given time and again by her most approved theologians. The Pope, as the visible head of the spiritual society, is, no doubt, superior to the emperor, not precisely because he represents a superior order, but because the church, of which he is the visible chief, is a supernatural institution, and holds immediately from God; whereas civil society, represented by the emperor, holds from God only mediately, through second causes, or the people. Yet, though derived from God only through the people, civil authority still holds from God, and derives its right from Him through another channel than the church or spiritual society, and, therefore, has a right, a sacredness, which the church herself gives not, and must recognize and respect. This she herself teaches in teaching that even infidels, as we have seen, may have legitimate government, and since, though she interprets and applies the law of God, both natural and revealed, she makes neither.

Nevertheless, the imperialists or the statists insisted on their false charge against the Pope, that he labored to found a purely theocratic or clerocratic government, and finding themselves unable to place the representative of the civil society on the same level with the representative of the spiritual, or to emancipate the state from the law of God while they conceded the divine origin or right of government, they sought to effect its independence by asserting for it only a natural or purely human origin. For nearly two centuries the most popular and influential writers on government have rejected the divine origin and ground of civil authority, and excluded God from the state. They have refused to look beyond second causes, and have labored to derive authority from man alone. They have not only separated the state from the church as an external corporation, but from God as its internal lawgiver, and by so doing have deprived the state of her sacredness, inviolability, or hold on the conscience, scoffed at loyalty as a superstition, and consecrated not civil authority, but what is called "the right of insurrection." Under their teaching the age sympathizes not with authority in its efforts to sustain itself and protect society, but with those who conspire against it—the insurgents, rebels, revolutionists seeking its destruction. The established government that seeks to enforce respect for its legitimate authority and compel obedience to the laws, is held to be despotic, tyrannical, oppressive, and resistance to it to be obedience to God, and a wild howl rings through Christendom against the prince that will not stand still and permit the conspirators to cut his throat. There is hardly a government now in the civilized world that can sustain itself for a moment without an armed force sufficient to overawe or crush the party, or parties in permanent conspiracy against it.

This result is not what was aimed at or desired, but it is the logical or necessary result of the attempt to erect the state on atheistical principles. Unless founded on the divine sovereignty, authority can sustain itself only by force, for political atheism recognizes no right but might. No doubt the politicians have sought an atheistical, or what is the same thing, a purely human, basis for government, in order to secure an open field for human freedom and activity, or individual or social progress. The end aimed at has been good, laudable even, but they forgot that freedom is possible only with authority that protects it against license as well as against despotism, and that there can be no progress where there is nothing that is not progressive. In civil society two things are necessary—stability and movement. The human is the element of movement, for in it are possibilities that can be only successively actualized. But the element of stability can be found only in the divine, in God, in whom there is no unactualized possibility, who, therefore, is immovable, immutable, and eternal. The doctrine that derives authority from God through the people, recognizes in the state both of these elements, and provides alike for stability and progress.

This doctrine is not mere theory; it simply states the real order of things. It is not telling what ought to be, but what is in the real order. It only asserts for civil government the relation to God which nature herself holds to him, which the entire universe holds to the Creator. Nothing in man, in nature, in the universe, is explicable without the creative act of God, for nothing exists without that act. That God "in the beginning created heaven and earth," is the first principle of all science as of all existences, in politics no less than in theology. God and creation comprise all that is or exists, and creation, though distinguishable from God as the act from the actor, is inseparable from him, "for in Him we live and move and have our being." All creatures are joined to him by his creative act, and exist only as through that act they participate of his being. Through that act he is immanent as first cause in all creatures and in every act of every creature. The creature deriving from his creative act can no more continue to exist than it could begin to exist without it. It is as bad philosophy as theology, to suppose that God created the universe, endowed it with certain laws of development or activity, wound it up, gave it a jog, set it a going, and then left it to go of itself. It cannot go of itself, because it does not exist of itself. It did not merely not begin to exist, but it cannot continue to exist, without the creative act. Old Epicurus was a sorry philosopher, or rather, no philosopher at all. Providence is as necessary as creation, or rather, Providence is only continuous creation, the creative act not suspended or discontinued, or not passing over from the creature and returning to God.

Through the creative act man participates of God, and he can continue to exist, act, or live only by participating through it of his divine being. There is, therefore, something of divinity, so to speak, in every creature, and therefore it is that God is worshipped in his works without idolatry. But he creates substantial existences capable of acting as second causes. Hence, in all living things there is in their life a divine element and a natural element; in what is called human life, there are the divine and the human, the divine as first and the human as second cause, precisely what the doctrine of the great Christian theologians assert to be the fact with all legitimate or real government. Government cannot exist without the efficacious presence of God any more than man himself, and men might as well attempt to build up a world as to attempt to found a state without God. A government founded on atheistical principles were less than a castle in the air. It would have nothing to rest on, would not be even so much as "the baseless fabric of a vision," and they who imagine that they really do exclude God from their politics deceive themselves; for they accept and use principles which, though they know it not, are God. What they call abstract principles, or abstract forms of reason, without which there were no logic, are not abstract, but the real, living God himself. Hence government, like man himself, participates of the divine being, and, derived from God through the people, it at the same time participates of human reason and will, thus reconciling authority with freedom, and stability with progress.

The people, holding their authority from God, hold it not as an inherent right, but as a trust from Him, and are accountable to Him for it. It is not their own. If it were their own they might do with it as they pleased, and no one would have any right to call them to an account; but holding it as a trust from God, they are under his law, and bound to exercise it as that law prescribes. Civil rulers, holding their authority from God through the people, are accountable for it both to Him and to them. If they abuse it they are justiciable by the people and punishable by God himself.

Here is the guaranty against tyranny, oppression, or bad government, or what in modern times is called the responsibility of power. At the same time the state is guarantied against sedition, insurrection, rebellion, revolution, by the elevation of the civic virtues to the rank of religious virtues, and making loyalty a matter of conscience. Religion is brought to the aid of the state, not indeed as a foreign auxiliary, but as integral in the political order itself. Religion sustains the state, not because it externally commands us to obey the higher powers, or to be submissive to the powers that be, not because it trains the people to habits of obedience, and teaches them to be resigned and patient under the grossest abuses of power, but because it and the state are in the same order, and inseparable, though distinct, parts of one and the same whole. The church and the state, as corporations or external governing bodies, are indeed separate in their spheres, and the church does not absorb the state, nor does the state the church; but both are from God, and both work to the same end, and when each is rightly understood there is no antithesis or antagonism between them. Men serve God in serving the state as directly as in serving the church. He who dies on the battle-field fighting for his country ranks with him who dies at the stake for his faith. Civic virtues are themselves religious virtues, or at least virtues without which there are no religious virtues, since no man who loves not his brother does or can love God.

The guaranties offered the state or authority are ample, because it has not only conscience, moral sentiment, interest, habit, and the *vis inertia* of the mass, but the whole physical force of the nation, at its command. The individual has, indeed, only moral guaranties against the abuse of power by the sovereign people, which may no doubt sometimes prove insufficient. But moral guaranties are always better than none, and there are none where the people are held to be sovereign in their own native right and might, organized or unorganized, inside or outside of the constitution, as most modern democratic theorists maintain; since, if so, the will of the people, however expressed, is the criterion of right and wrong, just and unjust, true and false, is infallible and impeccable, and no moral right can ever be pleaded against it; they are accountable to nobody, and, let them do what they please, they can do no wrong. This would place the individual at the mercy of the state, and deprive him of all right to complain, however oppressed or cruelly treated. This would establish the absolute despotism of the state, and deny every thing like the natural rights of man, or individual and personal freedom, as has already been shown. Now as men do take part in government, and as men, either individually or collectively, are neither infallible nor impeccable, it is never to be expected, under any possible constitution or form of government, that authority will always be wisely and justly exercised, that wrong will never be done, and the rights of individuals never in any instance be infringed; but with the clear understanding that all power is of God, that the political sovereignty is vested in the people or the collective body, that the civil rulers hold from God through them and are responsible to Him through them, and justiciable by them, there is all the guaranty against the abuse of power by the nation, the political or organic people, that the nature of the case admits. The nation may, indeed, err or do wrong, but in the way supposed you get in the government all the available wisdom and virtue the nation has, and more is never, under any form or constitution of government, practicable or to be expected.

It is a maxim with constitutional statesmen, that "the king reigns, not governs." The people, though sovereign under God, are not the government. The government is in their name and by virtue of authority delegated from God through them, but they are not it, are not their own ministers. It is only when the people forget this and undertake to be their own ministers and to manage their own affairs immediately by themselves instead of selecting agents to do it for them, and holding their agents to a strict account for their management, that they are likely to abuse their power or to sanction injustice. The nation may be misled or deceived for a moment by demagogues, those popular courtiers, but as a rule it is disposed to be just and to respect all natural rights. The wrong is done by individuals who assume to speak in their name, to wield their power, and to be themselves the state. *L'état, c'est moi*, I am the state, said Louis XIV. of France, and while that was conceded the French nation could have in its government no more wisdom or virtue than he possessed, or at least no more than he could appreciate. And under his government France was made responsible for many deeds that the nation would never have sanctioned, if it had been recognized as the depositary of the national sovereignty, or as the French state, and answerable to God for the use it made of political power, or the conduct of its government.

But be this as it may, there evidently can be no physical force in the nation to coerce the nation itself in case it goes wrong, for if the sovereignty vests in the nation, only the nation can rightly command or authorize the employment of force, and all commissions must run in its name. Written constitutions alone will avail little, for they emanate from the people, who can disregard them, if they choose, and alter or revoke them at will. The reliance for the wisdom and justice of the state must after all be on moral guaranties. In the very nature of the case there are and can be no other. But these, placed in a clear light, with an intelligent and religious people, will seldom be found insufficient. Hence the necessity for the protection, not of authority simply or chiefly, but of individual rights and the liberty of religion and intelligence in the nation, of the general understanding that the nation holds its power to govern as a trust from God, and that to God through the people all civil rulers are strictly responsible. Let the mass of the people in any nation lapse into the ignorance and barbarism of atheism, or lose themselves in that supreme sophism called pantheism, the grand error of ancient as well as of modern gentilism, and liberty, social or political, except that wild kind of liberty, and perhaps not even that should be excepted, which obtains among savages, would be lost and irrecoverable.

But after all, this theory does not meet all the difficulties of the case. It derives sovereignty from God, and thus asserts the divine origin of government in the sense that the origin of nature is divine; it derives it from God through the people, collectively, or as society, and therefore concedes it a natural, human, and social element, which distinguishes it from pure theocracy. It, however, does not explain how authority comes from God to the people. The ruler, king, prince, or emperor, holds from God through the people, but how do the people themselves hold from God? Mediately or immediately? If mediately, what is the medium? Surely not the people themselves. The people can no more be the medium than the principle of their own sovereignty. If immediately, then God governs in them as he does in the church, and no man is free to think or act contrary to popular opinion, or in any case to question the wisdom or justice of any of the acts of the state, which is arriving at state absolutism by another process. Besides, this would theoretically exclude all human or natural activity, all human intelligence and free-will from the state, which were to fall into either pantheism or atheism.

VIII. The right of government to govern, or political authority, is derived by the collective people or society, from God through the law of nature. Rulers hold from God through the people or nation, and the people or nation hold from God through the natural law. How nations are founded or constituted, or a particular people becomes a sovereign political people, invested with the rights of society, will be considered in following chapters. Here it suffices to say that supposing a political people or nation, the sovereignty vests in the community, not supernaturally, or by an external supernatural appointment, as the clergy hold their authority, but by the natural law, or law by which God governs the whole moral creation.

They who assert the origin of government in nature are right, so far as they derive it from God through the law of nature, and are wrong only when they understand by the law of nature the physical force or forces of nature, which are not laws in the primary and proper sense of the term. The law of nature is not the order or rule of the divine action in nature which is rightfully called providence, but is, as has been said, law in its proper and primary sense, ordained by the Author of nature, as its sovereign and supreme Lawgiver, and binds all of his creatures who are endowed with reason and free-will, and is called natural, because promulgated through the reason common to all men. Undoubtedly, it was in the first instance, to the first man, supernaturally promulgated, as it is republished and confirmed by Christianity, as an integral part of the Christian code itself. Man needs even yet instruction in relation to matters lying within the range of natural reason, or else secular schools, colleges, and universities would be superfluous, and manifestly the instructor of the first man could have been only the Creator himself.

The knowledge of the natural law has been transmitted from Adam to us through two channels—reason, which is in every man, and in immediate relation with the Creator, and the traditions of the primitive instruction embodied in language and what the Romans call *jus gentium,* or law common to all civilized nations. Under this law, whose prescriptions are promulgated through reason and embodied in universal jurisprudence, nations are providentially constituted, and invested with political sovereignty; and as they are constituted under this law and hold from God through it, it defines their respective rights and powers, their limitation and their extent.

The political sovereignty, under the law of nature, attaches to the people, not individually, but collectively, as civil or political society. It is vested in the political community or nation, not in an individual, or family, or a class, because, under the natural law, all men are equal, as they are under the Christian law, and one man has, in his own right, no authority over another. The family has in the father a natural chief, but political society has no natural chief or chiefs. The authority of the father is domestic, not political, and ceases when his children have attained to majority, have married and become heads of families themselves, or have ceased to make part of the paternal household. The recognition of the authority of the father beyond the limits of his own household, is, if it ever occurs, by virtue of the ordinance, the consent, express or tacit, of the political society. There are no natural-born political chiefs, and wherever we find men claiming or acknowledged to be such, they are either usurpers, what the Greeks called *tyrants*, or they are made such by the will or constitution of the people or the nation.

Both monarchy and aristocracy were, no doubt, historically developed from the authority of the patriarchs, and have unquestionably been sustained by an equally false development of the right of property, especially landed property. The owner of the land, or he who claimed to own it, claimed as an incident of his ownership the right to govern it, and consequently to govern all who occupied it. But however valid may be the landlord's title to the soil, and it is doubtful if man can own any thing in land beyond the usufruct, it can give him under the law of nature no political right. Property, like all natural rights, is entitled by the natural law to protection, but not to govern. Whether it shall be made a basis of political power or not is a question of political prudence, to be determined by the supreme political authority. It was the basis, and almost exclusive basis, in the Middle Ages, under feudalism, and is so still in most states. France and the United States are the principal exceptions in Christendom. Property alone, or coupled with birth, is made elsewhere in some form a basis of political power, and where made so by the sovereign authority, it is legitimate, but not wise nor desirable; for it takes from the weak and gives to the strong. The rich have in their riches advantages enough over the poor, without receiving from the state any additional advantage. An aristocracy, in the sense of families distinguished by birth, noble and patriotic services, wealth, cultivation, refinement, taste, and manners, is desirable in every nation, is a nation's ornament, and also its chief support, but they need and should receive no political recognition. They should form no privileged class in the state or political society.

VII

Constitution of Government

*T*he Constitution is twofold: the constitution of the state or nation, and the constitution of the government. The constitution of the government is, or is held to be, the work of the nation itself; the constitution of the state, or the people of the state, is, in its origin at least, providential, given by God himself, operating through historical events or natural causes. The one originates in law, the other in historical fact. The nation must exist, and exist as a political community, before it can give itself a constitution; and no state, any more than an individual, can exist without a constitution of some sort.

The distinction between the providential constitution of the people and the constitution of the government, is not always made. The illustrious Count de Maistre, one of the ablest political philosophers who wrote in the last century, or the first quarter of the present, in his work on the *Generative Principle of Political Constitutions*, maintains that constitutions are generated, not made, and excludes all human agency from their formation and growth. Disgusted with French Jacobinism, from which he and his king and country had suffered so much, and deeply wedded to monarchy in both church and state, he had the temerity to maintain that God creates expressly royal families for the government of nations, and that it is idle for a nation to expect a good government without a king who has descended from one of those divinely created royal families. It was with some such thought, most likely, that a French journalist, writing home from the United States, congratulated the American people on having a Bonaparte in their army, so that when their democracy failed, as in a few years it was sure to do, they would have a descendant of a royal house to be their king or emperor. Alas! the Bonaparte has left us, and besides, he was not the descendant of a royal house, and was, like the present Emperor of the French, a decided *parvenu*. Still, the Emperor of the French, if only a *parvenu*, bears himself right imperially among sovereigns, and has no peer among any of the descendants of the old royal families of Europe.

There is a truth, however, in De Maistre's doctrine that constitutions are generated, or developed, not created *de novo*, or made all at once. But nothing is more true than that a nation can alter its constitution by its own deliberate and voluntary action, and many nations have done so, and sometimes for the better, as well as for the worse. If the constitution once given is fixed and unalterable, it must be wholly divine, and contain no human element, and the people have and can have no hand in their own government—the fundamental objection to the theocratic constitution of society. To assume it is to transfer to civil society, founded by the ordinary providence of God, the constitution of the church, founded by his gracious or supernatural providence, and to maintain that the divine sovereignty governs in civil society immediately and supernaturally, as in the spiritual society. But such is not the fact. God governs the nation by the nation itself, through its own reason and free-will. De Maistre is right only as to the constitution the nation starts with, and as to the control which that constitution necessarily exerts over the constitutional changes the nation can successfully introduce.

The disciples of Jean Jacques Rousseau recognize no providential constitution, and call the written instrument drawn up by a convention of sovereign individuals the constitution, and the only constitution, both of the people and the government. Prior to its adoption there is no government, no state, no political community or authority. Antecedently to it the people are an inorganic mass, simply individuals, without any political or national solidarity. These individuals, they suppose, come together in their own native right and might, organize themselves into a political community, give themselves a constitution, and draw up and vote rules for their government, as a number of individuals might meet in a public hall and resolve themselves into a temperance society or a debating club. This might do very well if the state were, like the temperance society or debating club, a simple voluntary association, which men are free to join or not as they please, and which they are bound to obey no farther and no longer than suits their convenience. But the state is a power, a sovereignty; speaks to all within its jurisdiction with an imperative voice; commands, and may use physical force to compel obedience, when not voluntarily yielded. Men are born its subjects, and no one can withdraw from it without its express or tacit permission, unless for causes that would justify resistance to its authority. The right of subjects to denationalize or expatriate themselves, except to escape a tyranny or an oppression which would forfeit the rights of power and warrant forcible resistance to it, does not exist, any more than the right of foreigners to become citizens, unless by the consent and authorization of the sovereign; for the citizen or subject belongs to the state, and is bound to it.

The solidarity of the individuals composing the population of a territory or country under one political head is a truth; but "the solidarity of peoples," irrespective of the government or political authority of their respective countries, so eloquently preached a few years since by the Hungarian Kossuth, is not only a falsehood, but a falsehood destructive of all government and of all political organization. Kossuth's doctrine supposes the people, or the populations of all countries, are, irrespective of their governments, bound together *in solido*, each for all and all for each, and therefore not only free, but bound, wherever they find a population struggling nominally for liberty against its government, to rush with arms in their hands to its assistance—a doctrine clearly incompatible with any recognition of political authority or territorial rights. Peoples or nations commune with each other only through the national authorities, and when the state proclaims neutrality or non-intervention, all its subjects are bound to be neutral, and to abstain from all intervention on either side. There may be, and indeed there is, a solidarity, more or less distinctly recognized, of Christian nations, but of the populations with and through their governments, not without them. Still more strict is the solidarity of all the individuals of one and the same nation. These are all bound together, all for each and each for all. The individual is born into society and under the government, and without the authority of the government, which represents all and each, he cannot release himself from his obligations. The state is then by no means a voluntary association. Every one born or adopted into it is bound to it, and cannot without its permission withdraw from it, unless, as just said, it is manifest that he can have under it no protection for his natural rights as a man, more especially for his rights of conscience. This is Vattel's doctrine, and the dictate of common sense.

The constitution drawn up, ordained, and established by a nation for itself is a law—the organic or fundamental law, if you will, but a law, and is and must be the act of the sovereign power. That sovereign power must exist before it can act, and it cannot exist, if vested in the people or nation, without a constitution, or without some sort of political organization of the people or nation. There must, then, be for every state or nation a constitution anterior to the constitution which the nation gives itself, and from which the one it gives itself derives all its vitality and legal force.

Logic and historical facts are here, as elsewhere, coincident, for creation and providence are simply the expression of the Supreme Logic, the Logos, by whom all things are made. Nations have originated in various ways, but history records no instance of a nation existing as an inorganic mass organizing itself into a political community. Every nation, at its first appearance above the horizon, is found to have an organization of some sort. This is evident from the only ways in which history shows us nations originating. These ways are: 1. The union of families in the tribe. 2. The union of tribes in the nation. 3. The migration of families, tribes, or nations in search of new settlements. 4. Colonization, military, agricultural, commercial, industrial, religious, or penal. 5. War and conquest. 6. The revolt, separation, and independence of provinces. 7. The intermingling of the conquerors and conquered, and by amalgamation forming a new people. These are all the ways known to history, and in none of these ways does a people, absolutely destitute of all organization, constitute itself a state, and institute and carry on civil government.

The family, the tribe, the colony are, if incomplete, yet incipient states, or inchoate nations, with an organization, individuality, and a centre of social life of their own. The families and tribes that migrate in search of new settlements carry with them their family and tribal organizations, and retain it for a long time. The Celtic tribes retained it in Gaul till broken up by the Roman conquest, under Cæsar Augustus; in Ireland, till the middle of the seventeenth century; and in Scotland, till the middle of the eighteenth. It subsists still in the *hordes* of Tartary, the Arabs of the Desert, and the Berbers or Kabyles of Africa.

Colonies, of whatever description, have been founded, if not by, at least under, the authority of the mother country, whose political constitution, laws, manners, and customs they carry with them. They receive from the parent state a political organization, which, though subordinate, yet constitutes them embryonic states, with a unity, individuality, and centre of public life in themselves, and which, when they are detached and recognized as independent, render them complete states. War and conquest effect great national changes, but do not, strictly speaking, create new states. They simply extend and consolidate the power of the conquering state.

Provinces revolt and become independent states or nations, but only when they have previously existed as such, and have retained the tradition of their old constitution and independence; or when the administration has erected them into real though dependent political communities. A portion of the people of a state not so erected or organized, that has in no sense had a distinct political existence of its own, has never separated from the national body and formed a new and independent nation. It cannot revolt; it may rise up against the government, and either revolutionize and take possession of the state, or be put down by the government as an insurrection. The amalgamation of the conquering and the conquered forms a new people, and modifies the institutions of both, but does not necessarily form a new nation or political community. The English of to-day are very different from both the Normans and the Saxons, or Dano-Saxons, of the time of Richard Cœur de Lion, but they constitute the same state or political community. England is still England.

The Roman empire, conquered by the Northern barbarians, has been cut up into several separate and independent nations, but because its several provinces had, prior to their conquest by the Roman arms, been independent nations or tribes, and more especially because the conquerors themselves were divided into several distinct nations or confederacies. If the barbarians had been united in a single nation or state, the Roman empire most likely would have changed masters, indeed, but have retained its unity and its constitution, for the Germanic nations that finally seated themselves on its ruins had no wish to destroy its name or nationality, for they were themselves more than half Romanized before conquering Rome. But the new nations into which the empire has been divided have never been, at any moment, without political or governmental organization, continued from the constitution of the conquering tribe or nation, modified more or less by what was retained from the empire.

It is not pretended that the constitutions of states cannot be altered, or that every people starts with a constitution fully developed, as would seem to be the doctrine of De Maistre. The constitution of the family is rather economical than political, and the tribe is far from being a fully developed state. Strictly speaking, the state, the modern equivalent for the city of the Greeks and Romans, was not fully formed till men began to build and live in cities, and became fixed to a national territory. But in the first place, the eldest born of the human race, we are told, built a city, and even in cities we find traces of the family and tribal organization long after their municipal existence—in Athens down to the Macedonian conquest, and in Rome down to the establishment of the Empire; and, in the second place, the pastoral nations, though they have not precisely the city or state organization, yet have a national organization, and obey a national authority. Strictly speaking, no pastoral nation has a civil or political constitution, but they have what in our modern tongues can be expressed by no other term. The feudal *régime*, which was in full vigor even in Europe from the tenth to the close of the fourteenth century, had nothing to do with cities, and really recognized no state proper; yet who hesitates to speak of it as a civil or political system, though a very imperfect one?

The civil order, as it now exists, was not fully developed in the early ages. For a long time the national organizations bore unmistakable traces of having been developed from the patriarchal, and modelled from the family or tribe, as they do still in all the non-Christian world. Religion itself, before the Incarnation, bore traces of the same organization. Even with the Jews, religion was transmitted and diffused, not as under Christianity by conversion, but by natural generation or family adoption. With all the Gentile tribes or nations, it was the same. At first the father was both priest and king, and when the two offices were separated, the priests formed a distinct and hereditary class or caste, rejected by Christianity, which, as we have seen, admits priests only after the order of Melchisedech. The Jews had the synagogue, and preserved the primitive revelation in its purity and integrity; but the Greeks and Romans, more fully than any other ancient nations, preserved or developed the political order that best conforms to the Christian religion; and Christianity, it is worthy of remark, followed in the track of the Roman armies, and it gains a permanent establishment only where was planted, or where it is able to plant, the Græco-Roman civilization. The Græco-Roman republics were hardly less a schoolmaster to bring the world to Christ in the civil order, than the Jewish nation was to bring it to Him in the spiritual order, or in faith and worship. In the Christian order nothing is by hereditary descent, but every thing is by election of grace. The Christian dispensation is teleological, palingenesiac, and the whole order, prior to the Incarnation, was initial, genesiac, and continued by natural generation, as it is still in all nations and tribes outside of Christendom. No non-Christian people is a civilized people, and, indeed, the human race seems not anywhere, prior to the Incarnation, to have attained to its majority: and it is, perhaps, because the race were not prepared for it, that the Word was not sooner incarnated. He came only in the fulness of time, when the world was ready to receive him.

The providential constitution is, in fact, that with which the nation is born, and is, as long as the nation exists, the real living and efficient constitution of the state. It is the source of the vitality of the state, that which controls or governs its action, and determines its destiny. The constitution which a nation is said to give itself, is never the constitution of the state, but is the law ordained by the state for the government instituted under it. Thomas Paine would admit nothing to be the constitution but a written document which he could fold up and put in his pocket, or file away in a pigeon-hole. The Abbé Sieyès pronounced politics a science which he had finished, and he was ready to turn you out constitutions to order, with no other defect than that they had, as Carlyle wittily says, no feet, and could not go. Many in the last century, and some, perhaps, in the present, for folly as well as wisdom has her heirs, confounded the written instrument with the constitution itself. No constitution can be written on paper or engrossed on parchment. What the convention may agree upon, draw up, and the people ratify by their votes, is no constitution, for it is extrinsic to the nation, not inherent and living in it—is, at best, legislative instead of constitutive. The famous Magna Charta drawn up by Cardinal Langton, and wrung from John Lackland by the English barons at Runnymede, was no constitution of England till long after the date of its concession, and even then was no constitution of the state, but a set of restrictions on power. The constitution is the intrinsic or inherent and actual constitution of the people or political community itself; that which makes the nation what it is, and distinguishes it from every other nation, and varies as nations themselves vary from one another.

The constitution of the state is not a theory, nor is it drawn up and established in accordance with any preconceived theory. What is theoretic in a constitution is unreal. The constitutions conceived by philosophers in their closets are constitutions only of Utopia or Dreamland. This world is not governed by abstractions, for abstractions are nullities. Only the concrete is real, and only the real or actual has vitality or force. The French people adopted constitution after constitution of the most approved pattern, and amid bonfires, beating of drums, sound of trumpets, roar of musketry, and thunder of artillery, swore, no doubt, sincerely as well as enthusiastically, to observe them, but all to no effect; for they had no authority for the nation, no hold on its affections, and formed no element of its life. The English are great constitution-mongers—for other nations. They fancy that a constitution fashioned after their own will fit any nation that can be persuaded, wheedled, or bullied into trying it on; but, unhappily, all that have tried it on have found it only an embarrassment or encumbrance. The doctor might as well attempt to give an individual a new constitution, or the constitution of another man, as the statesman to give a nation any other constitution than that which it has, and with which it is born.

The whole history of Europe, since the fall of the Roman empire, proves this thesis. The barbarian conquest of Rome introduced into the nations founded on the site of the empire, a double constitution— the barbaric and the civil—the Germanic and the Roman in the West, and the Tartaric or Turkish and the Græco-Roman in the East. The key to all modern history is in the mutual struggles of these two constitutions and the interests respectively associated with them, which created two societies on the same territory, and, for the most part, under the same national denomination. The barbaric was the constitution of the conquerors; they had the power, the government, rank, wealth, and fashion, were reënforced down to the tenth century by fresh hordes of barbarians, and had even brought the external ecclesiastical society to a very great extent into harmony with itself. The Pope became a feudal sovereign, and the bishops and mitred abbots feudal princes and barons. Yet, after eight hundred years of fierce struggle, the Roman constitution got the upper hand, and the barbaric constitution, as far as it could not be assimilated to the Roman, was eliminated. The original Empire of the West is now as thoroughly

Roman in its constitution, its laws, and its civilization, as it ever was under any of its Christian emperors before the barbarian conquest.

The same process is going on in the East, though it has not advanced so far, having begun there several centuries later, and the Græco-Roman constitution was far feebler there than in the West at the epoch of the conquest. The Germanic tribes that conquered the West had long had close relations with the empire, had served as its allies, and even in its armies, and were partially Romanized. Most of their chiefs had received a Roman culture; and their early conversion to the Christian faith facilitated the revival and permanence of the old Roman constitution. In the East it was different. The conquerors had no touch of Roman civilization, and, followers of the Prophet, they were animated with an intense hatred, which, after the conquest, was changed into a superb contempt, of Christians and Romans. They had their civil constitution in the Koran; and the Koran, in its principles, doctrines, and spirit, is exclusive, and profoundly intolerant. The Græco-Roman constitution was always much weaker in the East, and had far greater obstacles to overcome there than in the West; yet it has survived the shock of the conquest. Throughout the limits of the ancient Empire of the East, the barbaric constitution has received and is daily receiving rude blows, and, but as reënforced by barbarians lying outside of the boundaries of that empire, would be no longer able to sustain itself. The Greek or Christian populations of the empire are no longer in danger of being exterminated or absorbed by the Mohammedan state or population. They are the only living and progressive people of the Ottoman Empire, and their complete success in absorbing or expelling the Turk is only a question of time. They will, in all present probability, reëstablish a Christian and Roman East in much less time from the fall of Constantinople in 1453, than it took the West from the fall of Rome in 476 to put an end to the feudal or barbaric constitution founded by its Germanic invaders.

Indeed, the Roman constitution, laws, and civilization not only gain the mastery in the nations seated within the limits of the old Roman Empire, but extend their power throughout the whole civilized world. The Græco-Roman civilization is, in fact, the only civilization now recognized, and nations are accounted civilized only in proportion as they are Romanized and Christianized. The Roman law, as found in the Institutes, Pandects, and Novellæ of Justinian, or the *Corpus Legis Civilis*, is the basis of the law and jurisprudence of all Christendom. The Græco-Roman civilization, called not improperly Christian civilization, is the only progressive civilization. The old feudal system remains in England little more than an empty name. The king is only the first magistrate of the kingdom, and the House of Lords is only an hereditary senate. Austria is hard at work in the Roman direction, and finds her chief obstacle to success in Hungary, with the Magyars whose feudalism retains almost the full vigor of the Middle Ages. Russia is moving in the same direction; and Prussia and the smaller Germanic states obey the same impulse. Indeed, Rome has survived the conquest—has conquered her conquerors, and now invades every region from which they came. The Roman Empire may be said to be acknowledged and obeyed in lands lying far beyond the farthest limits reached by the Roman eagles, and to be more truly the mistress of the world than under Augustus, Trajan, or the Antonines. Nothing can stand before the Christian and Romanized nations, and all pagandom and Mohammedom combined are too weak to resist their onward march.

All modern European revolutions result only in reviving the Roman Empire, whatever the motives, interests, passions, or theories that initiate them. The French Revolution of the last century and that of the present prove it. France, let people say what they will, stands at the head of the European civilized world, and displays *en grand* all its good and all its bad tendencies. When she moves, Europe moves; when she has a vertigo, all European nations are dizzy; when she recovers her health, her equilibrium, and good sense, others become sedate, steady, and reasonable. She is the head, nay, rather, the heart of Christendom—the head is at Rome—through which circulates the pure and impure blood of the nations. It is in vain Great Britain, Germany, or Russia disputes with her the hegemony of European civilization. They are forced to yield to her at last, to be content to revolve around her as the centre of the political system that masters them. The reason is, France is more completely and sincerely Roman than any other nation. The revolutions that have shaken the world have resulted in eliminating the barbaric elements she had retained, and clearing away all obstacles to the complete triumph of Imperial Rome. Napoleon III. is for France what Augustus was for Rome. The revolutions in Spain and Italy have only swept away the relics of the barbaric constitution, and aided the revival of Roman imperialism. In no country do the revolutionists succeed in establishing their own theories; Cæsar remains master of the field. Even in the United States, a revolution undertaken in favor of the barbaric system has resulted in the destruction of what remained of that system—in sweeping away the last relics of disintegrating feudalism, and in the complete establishment of the Græco-Roman system, with important improvements, in the New World.

The Roman system is republican, in the broad sense of the term, because under it power is never an estate, never the private property of the ruler, but, in whose hands soever vested, is held as a trust to be exercised for the public good. As it existed under the Cæsars, and is revived in modern times, whether under the imperial or the democratic form, it, no doubt, tends to centralism, to the concentration of all the powers and forces of the state in one central government, from which all local authorities and institutions emanate. Wise men oppose it as affording no guaranties to individual liberty against the abuses of power. This it may not do, but the remedy is not in feudalism. The feudal lord holds his authority as an estate, and has over the people under him all the power of Caesar and all the rights of the proprietor. He, indeed, has a guaranty against his liegelord, sometimes a more effective guaranty than his liege-lord has against him; but against his centralized power his vassals and serfs have only the guaranty that a slave has against his owner.

Feudalism is alike hostile to the freedom of public authority and of the people. It is essentially a disintegrating element in the nation. It breaks the unity and individuality of the state, embarrasses the sovereign, and guards against the abuse of public authority by over-powering and suppressing it. Every feudal lord is a more thorough despot in his own domain than Cæsar ever was or could be in the empire; and the monarch, even if strong enough, is yet not competent to intervene between him and his people, any more than the General government in the United States was to intervene between the negro slave and his master. The great vassals of the crown singly, or, if not singly, in combination—and they could always combine in the inter-est of their order—were too strong for the king, or to be brought under any public authority, and could issue from their fortified castles and rob and plunder to their hearts' content, with none to call them to an account. Under the most thoroughly centralized government there is far more liberty for the people, and a far greater security for person and property, except in the case of the feudal nobles themselves, than was even dreamed of while the feudal *régime* was in full vigor. Nobles were themselves free, it is conceded, but not the people. The king was too weak, too restricted in his action by the feudal constitution to reach them, and the higher clergy were *ex officio* sovereigns, princes, barons, or feudal lords, and were led by their private interests to act with the feudal nobility, save when that nobility threatened the tem-poralities of the church. The only reliance, under God, left in feudal times to the poor people was in the lower ranks of the clergy, especially of the regular clergy. All the great German emperors in the twelfth and thirteenth centuries, who saw the evils of feudalism, and attempted to break it up and revive imperial Rome, became involved in quarrels with the chiefs of the religious society, and failed, because the interest of the Popes, as feudal sovereigns and Italian princes, and the interests of the dignified clergy, were for the time bound up with the feudal society, though their Roman culture and civilization made them at heart hostile to it. The student of history, however strong his filial affection towards the visible head of the church, cannot help admiring the grandeur of the political views of Frederic the Second, the greatest and last of the Hohenstaufen, or refrain from dropping a tear over his sad failure. He had great faults as a man, but he had rare genius as a statesman; and it is some consolation to know that he died a Christian death, in charity with all men, after having received the last sacraments of his religion.

The Popes, under the circumstances, were no doubt justified in the policy they pursued, for the Suabian emperors failed to respect the acknowledged rights of the church, and to remember their own incompetency in spirituals; but evidently their political views and aims were liberal, far-reaching, and worthy of admiration. Their success, if it could have been effected without lesion to the church, would have set Europe forward some two or three hundred years, and probably saved it from the schisms of the fourteenth and sixteenth centuries. But it is easy to be wise after the event. The fact is, that during the period when feudalism was in full vigor, the king was merely a shadow; the people found their only consolation in religion, and their chief protectors in the monks, who mingled with them, saw their sufferings, and sympathized with them, consoled them, carried their cause to the castle before the feudal lord and lady, and did, thank God, do something to keep alive religious sentiments and convictions in the bosom

of the feudal society itself. Whatever opinions may be formed of the
monastic orders in relation to the present, this much is certain, that
they were the chief civilizers of Europe, and the chief agents in delivering European society from feudal barbarism.

The aristocracy have been claimed as the natural allies of the
throne, but history proves them to be its natural enemies, whenever it
cannot be used in their service, and kings do not consent to be their
ministers and to do their bidding. A political aristocracy has at heart
only the interests of its order, and pursues no line of policy but the
extension or preservation of its privileges. Having little to gain and
much to lose, it opposes every political change that would either
strengthen the crown or elevate the people. The nobility in the French
Revolution were the first to desert both the king and the kingdom,
and kings have always found their readiest and firmest allies in the
people. The people in Europe have no such bitter feelings towards
royalty as they have towards the feudal nobility—for kings have never
so grievously oppressed them. In Rome the patrician order opposed
alike the emperor and the people, except when they, as chivalric nobles
sometimes will do, turned courtiers or demagogues. They were the
people of Rome and the provinces that sustained the emperors, and
they were the emperors who sustained the people, and gave to the
provincials the privileges of Roman citizens.

Guaranties against excessive centralism are certainly needed, but
the statesman will not seek them in the feudal organization of society—in a political aristocracy, whether founded on birth or private
wealth, nor in a privileged class of any sort. Better trust Cæsar than
Brutus, or even Cato. Nor will he seek them in the antagonism of
interests intended to neutralize or balance each other, as in the English constitution. This was the great error of Mr. Calhoun. No man
saw more clearly than Mr. Calhoun the utter worthlessness of simple
paper constitutions, on which Mr. Jefferson placed such implicit reli-

ance, or that the real constitution is in the state itself, in the manner in which the people themselves are organized; but his reliance was in constituting, as powers in the state, the several popular interests that exist, and pitting them against each other—the famous system of checks and balances of English statesmen. He was led to this, because he distrusted power, and was more intent on guarding against its abuses than on providing for its free, vigorous, and healthy action, going on the principle that "that is the best goverment which governs least." But, if the opposing interests could be made to balance one another perfectly, the result would be an equilibrium, in which power would be brought to a stand-still; and if not, the stronger would succeed and swallow up all the rest. The theory of checks and balances is admirable if the object be to trammel power, and to have as little power in the government as possible; but it is a theory which is born from passions engendered by the struggle against despotism or arbitrary power, not from a calm and philosophical appreciation of government itself. The English have not succeeded in establishing their theory, for, after all, their constitution does not work so well as they pretend. The landed interest controls at one time, and the mercantile and manufacturing interest at another. They do not perfectly balance one another, and it is not difficult to see that the mercantile and manufacturing interest, combined with the moneyed interest, is henceforth to predominate. The aim of the real statesman is to organize all the interests and forces of the state dialectically, so that they shall unite to add to its strength, and work together harmoniously for the common good.

VIII

Constitution of Government
(concluded)

*T*hough the constitution of the people is congenital, like the constitution of an individual, and cannot be radically changed without the destruction of the state, it must not be supposed that it is wholly withdrawn from the action of the reason and free-will of the nation, nor from that of individual statesmen. All created things are subject to the law of development, and may be developed either in a good sense or in a bad; that is, may be either completed or corrupted. All the possibilities of the national constitution are given originally in the birth of the nation, as all the possibilities of mankind were given in the first man. The germ must be given in the original constitution. But in all constitutions there is more than one element, and the several elements may be developed *pari passu*, or unequally, one having the ascendency and suppressing the rest. In the original constitution of Rome the patrician element was dominant, showing that the patriarchal organization of society still retained no little force. The king was only the presiding officer of the senate and the leader of the army in war. His civil functions corresponded very nearly to those of a mayor of the city of New York, where all the effective power is in the aldermen, common council, and heads of departments. Except in name he was little else than a pageant. The kings, no doubt, labored to develop and extend the royal element of the constitution. This was natural; and it was equally natural that they should be resisted by the patricians. Hence when the Tarquins, or Etruscan dynasty, undertook to be kings in fact as well as in name, and seemed likely to succeed, the patricians expelled them, and supplied their place by two consuls annually elected. Here was a modification, but no real change of the constitution. The effective power, as before, remained in the senate.

But there was from early times a plebeian element in the population of the city, though forming at first no part of the political people. Their origin is not very certain, nor their original position in the city. Historians give different accounts of them. But that they should, as they increased in numbers, wealth, and importance, demand admission into the political society, religious or solemn marriage, a voice in the government, and the faculty of holding civil and military offices, was only in the order of regular development. At first the patricians fought them, and, failing to subdue them by force, effected a compromise, and bought up their leaders. The concession which followed of the tribunitial veto was only a further development. By that veto the plebeians gained no initiative, no positive power, indeed, but their tribunes, by interposing it, could stop the proceedings of the government. They could not propose the measures they liked, but they could prevent the legal adoption of measures they disliked—a faculty Mr. Calhoun asserted for the several States of the American Union in his doctrine of nullification, or State veto, as he called it. It was simply an obstructive power.

But from a power to obstruct legislative action to the power to originate or propose it, and force the senate to adopt it through fear of the veto of measures the patricians had at heart, was only a still further development. This gained, the exclusively patrician constitution had disappeared, and Marius, the head of a great plebeian house, could be elected consul and the plebeians in turn threaten to become predominant, which Sylla or Sulla, as dictator, seeing, tried in vain to prevent. The dictator was provided for in the original constitution. Retain the dictatorship for a time, strengthen the plebeian element by ruthless proscriptions of patricians and by recruits from the provinces, unite the tribunitial, pontifical, and military powers in the imperator designated by the army, all elements existing in the constitution from an early day, and already developed in the Roman state, and you have the imperial constitution, which retained to the last the senate and consuls, though with less and less practical power. These changes are very great, but are none of them radical, dating from the recognition of the plebs as pertaining to the Roman people. They are normal developments, not corruptions, and the transition from the consular republic to the imperial was unquestionably a real social and political progress. And yet the Roman people, had they chosen, could have given a different direction to the developments of their constitution. There was Providence in the course of events, but no fatalism.

Sulla was a true patrician, a blind partisan of the past. He sought to arrest the plebeian development led by Marius, and to restore the exclusively patrician government. But it was too late. His proscriptions, confiscations, butcheries, unheard-of cruelties, which anticipated and surpassed those of the French Revolution of 1793, availed nothing. The Marian or plebeian movement, apparently checked for a moment, resumed its march with renewed vigor under Julius, and triumphed at Pharsalia. In vain Cicero, only accidentally associated with the patrician party, which distrusted him—in vain Cicero declaims, Cato scolds, or parades his impractical virtues, Brutus and Cassius seize the assassin's dagger, and strike to the earth "the foremost man of all the world;" the plebeian cause moves on with resistless force, triumphs anew at Philippi, and young Octavius avenges the murder of his uncle, and proves to the world that the assassination of a ruler is a blunder as well as a crime. In vain does Mark Antony desert the movement, rally Egypt and the barbaric East, and seek to transfer the seat of empire from the Tiber to the banks of the Nile or the Orontes; plebeian and imperial Rome wins a final victory at Actium, and definitively secures the empire of the civilized world to the West.

Thus far the developments were normal, and advanced civilization. But Rome still retained the barbaric element of slavery in her bosom, and had conquered more barbaric nations than she had assimilated. These nations she at first governed as tributary states, with their own constitutions and national chiefs; afterwards as Roman provinces, by her own proconsuls and prefects. When the emperors threw open the gates of the city to the provincials, and conceded them the rights and privileges of Roman citizens, they introduced not only a foreign element into the state, destitute of Roman patriotism, but the barbaric and despotic elements retained by the conquered nations as yet only partially assimilated. These elements became germs of anti-republican developments, rather of corruptions, and prepared the down-fall of the empire. Doubtless these corruptions might have been arrested, and would have been, if Roman patriotism had survived the changes effected in the Roman population by the concession of Roman citizenship to provincials; but it did not, and they were favored as time went on by the emperors themselves, and more especially by Dioclesian, a real barbarian, who hated Rome, and by Constantine, surnamed the Great, a real despot, who converted the empire from a republican to a despotic empire. Rome fell from the force of barbarism developed from within, far more than from the force of the barbarians hovering on her frontiers and invading her provinces.

The law of all possible developments is in the providential or congenital constitution; but these possible developments are many and various, and the reason and free-will of the nation as well as of individuals are operative in determining which of them shall be adopted. The nation, under the direction of wise and able statesmen, who understood their age and country, who knew how to discern between normal developments and barbaric corruptions, placed at the head of affairs in season, might have saved Rome from her fate, eliminated the barbaric and assimilated the foreign elements, and preserved Rome as a Christian and republican empire to this day, and saved the civilized world from the ten centuries of barbarism which followed her conquest by the barbarians of the North. But it rarely happens that the real statesmen of a nation are placed at the head of affairs.

Rome did not fall in consequence of the strength of her external enemies, nor through the corruption of private morals and manners, which was never greater than under the first Triumvirate. She fell from the want of true statesmanship in her public men, and patriotism in her people. Private virtues and private vices are of the last consequence to individuals, both here and hereafter; but private virtues never saved, private vices never ruined a nation. Edward the Confessor was a saint, and yet he prepared the way for the Norman conquest of England; and France owes infinitely less to St. Louis than to Louis XI., Richelieu, and Napoleon, who, though no saints, were statesmen. What is specially needed in statesmen is public spirit, intelligence, foresight, broad views, manly feelings, wisdom, energy, resolution; and when statesmen with these qualities are placed at the head of affairs, the state, if not already lost, can, however far gone it may be, be recovered, restored, reinvigorated, advanced, and private vice and corruption disappear in the splendor of public virtue. Providence is always present in the affairs of nations, but not to work miracles to counteract the natural effects of the ignorance, ineptness, short-sightedness, narrow views, public stupidity, and imbecility of rulers, because they are irreproachable and saintly in their private characters and relations, as was Henry VI. of England, or, in some respects, Louis XVI. of France. Providence is God intervening through the laws he by his creative act gives to creatures, not their suspension or abrogation. It was the corruption of the statesmen, in substituting the barbaric element for the proper Roman, to which no one contributed more than Constantine, the first Christian emperor, that was the real cause of the downfall of Rome, and the centuries of barbarism that followed, relieved only by the superhuman zeal and charity of the church to save souls and restore civilization.

But in the constitution of the government, as distinguished from the state, the nation is freer and more truly sovereign. The constitution of the state is that which gives to the people of a given territory political existence, unity, and individuality, and renders it capable of political action. It creates political or national solidarity, in imitation of the solidarity of the race, in which it has its root. It is the providential charter of national existence, and that which gives to each nation its peculiar character, and distinguishes it from every other nation. The constitution of government is the constitution by the sovereign authority of the nation of an agency or ministry for the management of its affairs, and the letter of instructions according to which the agent or minister is to act and conduct the matters intrusted to him. The distinction which the English make between the sovereign and the ministry is analogous to that between the state and the government, only they understand by the sovereign the king or queen, and by the ministry the executive, excluding, or not decidedly including, the legislature and the judiciary. The sovereign is the people as the state or body politic, and as the king holds from God only through the people, he is not properly sovereign, and is to be ranked with the ministry or government. Yet when the state delegates the full or chief governing power to the king, and makes him its sole or principal representative, he may, with sufficient accuracy for ordinary purposes, be called sovereign. Then, understanding by the ministry or government the legislative and judicial, as well as the executive functions, whether united in one or separated into distinct and mutually independent departments, the English distinction will express accurately enough, except for strictly scientific purposes, the distinction between the state and the government.

Still, it is only in despotic states, which are not founded on right, but force, that the king can say, *L'état, c'est moi,* I am the state; and Shakespeare's usage of calling the king of France simply France, and the king of England simply England, smacks of feudalism, under which monarchy is an estate, property, not a public trust. It corresponds to the Scottish usage of calling the proprietor by the name of his estate. It is never to be forgotten that in republican states the king has only a delegated sovereignty, that the people, as well as God, are above him. He holds his power, as the Emperor of the French professes to hold his, by the grace of God and the national will—the only title by which a king or emperor can legitimately hold power.

The king or emperor not being the state, and the government, whatever its form or constitution, being a creature of the state, he can be dethroned, and the whole government even virtually overthrown, without dissolving the state or the political society. Such an event may cause much evil, create much social confusion, and do grave injury to the nation, but the political society *may* survive it; the sovereign remains in the plenitude of his rights, as competent to restore government as he was originally to institute it. When, in 1848, Louis Philippe was dethroned by the Parisian mob, and fled the kingdom, there was in France no legitimate government, for all commissions ran in the king's name; but the organic or territorial people of France, the body politic, remained, and in it remained the sovereign power to organize and appoint a new government. When, on the 2d of December, 1851, the president, by a *coup d'état*, suppressed the legislative assembly and the constitutional government, there was no legitimate government standing, and the power assumed by the president was unquestionably a usurpation; but the nation was competent to condone his usurpation and legalize his power, and by a plebiscitum actually did so. The wisdom or justice of the *coup d'état* is another question, about which men may differ; but when the French nation, by its subsequent act, had condoned it, and formally conferred dictatorial powers on the prince-president, the principal had approved the act of his agent, and given him discretionary powers, and nothing more was to be said. The imperial constitution and the election of the president to be emperor, that followed on December 2d, 1852, were strictly legal, and, whatever men may think of Napoleon III., it must be conceded that there is no legal flaw in his title, and that he holds his power by a title as high and as perfect as there is for any prince or ruler.

But the plebiscitum cannot be legally appealed to or be valid when and where there is a legal government existing and in the full exercise of its constitutional functions, as was decided by the Supreme Court of the United States in a case growing out of what is known as the Dorr rebellion in Rhode Island. A suffrage committee, having no political authority, drew up and presented a new constitution of government to the people, plead a plebiscitum in its favor, and claimed the officers elected under it as the legally elected officers of the state. The court refused to recognize the plebiscitum, and decided that it knew Rhode Island only as represented through the government, which had never ceased to exist. New States in Territories have been organized on the strength of a plebiscitum when the legal Territorial government was in force, and were admitted as States into the Union, which, though irregular and dangerous, could be done without revolution, because Congress, that admitted them, is the power to grant the permission to organize as States and apply for admission. Congress is competent to condone an offence against its own rights. The real danger of the practice is, that it tends to create a conviction that sovereignty inheres in the people individually, or as population, not as the body politic or organic people attached to a sovereign domain; and the people who organize under a plebiscitum are not, till organized and admitted into the Union, an organic or a political people at all. When Louis Napoleon made his appeal to a vote of the French people, he made an appeal to a people existing as a sovereign people, and a sovereign people without a legal government. In his case the plebiscitum was proper and sufficient, even if it be conceded that it was through his own fault that France at the moment was found without a legal government. When a thing is done, though wrongly done, you cannot act as if it were not done, but must accept it as a fact and act accordingly.

The plebiscitum, which is simply an appeal to the people outside of government, is not valid when the government has not lapsed, either by its usurpations or by its dissolution, nor is it valid either in the case of a province, or of a population that has no organic existence as an independent sovereign state. The plebiscitum in France was valid, but in the Grand Duchy of Tuscany, the Duchies of Modena, Parma, and Lucca, and in the Kingdom of the Two Sicilies it was not valid, for their legal governments had not lapsed; nor was it valid in the Æmilian provinces of the Papal States, because they were not a nation or a sovereign people, but only a portion of such nation or people. In the case of the states and provinces—except Lombardy, ceded to France by Austria, and sold to the Sardinian king—annexed to Piedmont to form the new kingdom of Italy, the plebiscitum was invalid, because implying the right of the people to rebel against the legal authority, and to break the unity and individuality of the state of which they form an integral part. The nation is a whole, and no part has the right to secede or separate, and set up a government for itself, or annex itself to another state, without the consent of the whole. The solidarity of the nation is both a fact and a law. The secessionists from the United States defended their action only on the ground that the States of the American Union are severally independent sovereign states, and they only obeyed the authority of their respective states.

The plebiscitum, or irregular appeal to what is called universal suffrage, since adopted by Louis Napoleon in France after the *coup d'état,* is becoming not a little menacing to the stability of governments and the rights and integrity of states, and is not less dangerous to the peace and order of society than "the solidarity of peoples" asserted by Kossuth, the revolutionary ex-governor of Hungary, the last stronghold of feudal barbarism in Christian Europe; for Russia has emancipated her serfs.

The nation, as sovereign, is free to constitute government according to its own judgment, under any form it pleases—monarchial, aristocratic, democratic, or mixed—vest all power in an hereditary monarch, in a class of hereditary nobles, in a king and two houses of parliament, one hereditary, the other elective, or both elective; or it may establish a single, dual, or triple executive, make all officers of government hereditary or all elective, and if elective, elective for a longer or a shorter time, by universal suffrage or a select body of electors. Any of these forms and systems, and many others besides, are or may be legitimate, if established and maintained by the national will. There is nothing in the law of God or of nature, antecedently to the national will, that gives any one of them a right to the exclusion of any one of the others. The imperial system in France is as legitimate as the federative system in the United States. The only form or system that is necessarily illegal is the despotic. That can never be a truly civilized government, nor a legitimate government, for God has given to man no dominion over man. He gave men, as St. Augustine says, and Pope St. Gregory the Great repeats, dominion over the irrational creation, not over the rational, and hence the primitive rulers of men were called pastors or shepherds, not lords. It may be the duty of the people subjected to a despotic government to demean themselves quietly and peaceably towards it, as a matter of prudence, to avoid sedition, and the evils that would necessarily follow an attempted revolution, but not because, founded as it is on mere force, it has itself any right or legality.

All other forms of government are republican in their essential constitution, founded on public right, and held under God from and for the commonwealth, and which of them is wisest and best for the commonwealth is, for the most part, an idle question. "Forms of government," somebody has said, "are like shoes—that is the best form which best fits the feet that are to wear them." Shoes are to be fitted to the feet, not the feet to the shoes, and feet vary in size and conformation. There is, in regard to government, as distinguished from the state, no antecedent right which binds the people, for antecedently to the existence of the government as a fact, the state is free to adopt any form that it finds practicable, or judges the wisest and best for itself. Ordinarily the form of the government practicable for a nation is determined by the peculiar providential constitution of the territorial people, and a form of government that would be practicable and good in one country may be the reverse in another. The English government is no doubt the best practicable in Great Britain, at present at least, but it has proved a failure wherever else it has been attempted. The American system has proved itself, in spite of the recent formidable rebellion to overthrow it, the best and only practicable government for the United States, but it is impracticable everywhere else, and all attempts by any European or other American state to introduce it can end only in disaster: The imperial system apparently works well in France, but though all European states are tending to it, it would not work well at all on the American continent, certainly not until the republic of the United States has ceased to exist. While the United States remain the great American power, that system, or its kindred system, democratic centralism, can never become an American system, as Maximilian's experiment in Mexico is likely to prove.

Political propagandism, except on the Roman plan, that is, by annexation and incorporation, is as impracticable as it is wanting in the respect that one independent people owes to another. The old French Jacobins tried to propagate, even with fire and sword, their system throughout Europe, as the only system compatible with the rights of man. The English, since 1688, have been great political propagandists, and at one time it seemed not unlikely that every European state would try the experiment of a parliamentary-government, composed of an hereditary crown, an hereditary house of lords, and an elective house of commons. The democratic Americans are also great political propagandists, and are ready to sympathize with any rebellion, insurrection, or movement in behalf of democracy in any part of the world, however mean or contemptible, fierce or bloody it may be; but all this is as unstatesmanlike as unjust; unstatesmanlike, for no form of government can bear transplanting, and because every independent nation is the sole judge of what best comports with its own interests, and its judgment is to be respected by the citizens as well as by the governments of other states. Religious propagandism is a right and duty, because religion is catholic, and of universal obligation; and so is the *jus gentium* of the Romans, which is only the application to individuals and nations of the great principles of natural justice; but no political propagandism is ever allowable, because no one form of government is catholic in its nature, or of universal obligation.

Thoughtful Americans are opposed to political propagandism, and respect the right of every nation to choose its own form of government; but they hold that the American system is the best in itself, and that if other nations were as enlightened as the American, they would adopt it. But though the American system, rightly understood, is the best, as they hold, it is not because other nations are less enlightened, which is by no means a fact, that they do not adopt, or cannot bear it, but solely because their providential constitutions do not require or admit it, and an attempt to introduce it in any of them would prove a failure and a grave evil.

Fit your shoes to your feet. The law of the governmental constitution is in that of the nation. The constitution of the government must grow out of the constitution of the state, and accord with the genius, the character, the habits, customs, and wants of the people, or it will not work well, or tend to secure the legitimate ends of government. The constitutions imagined by philosophers are for Utopia, not for any actual, living, breathing people. You must take the state as it is, and develop your governmental constitution from it, and harmonize it with it. Where there is a discrepancy between the two constitutions, the government has no support in the state, in the organic people, or nation, and can sustain itself only by corruption or physical force. A government may be under the necessity of using force to suppress an insurrection or rebellion against the national authority, or the integrity of the national territory, but no government that can sustain itself, not the state, only by physical force or large standing armies, can be a good government, or suited to the nation. It must adopt the most stringent repressive measures, suppress liberty of speech and of conscience, outrage liberty in what it has the most intimate and sacred, and practise the most revolting violence and cruelty, for it can govern only by terror. Such a government is unsuited to the nation.

This is seen in all history: in the attempt of the dictator Sulla to preserve the old patrician government against the plebeian power that time and events had developed in the Roman state, and which was about to gain the supremacy, as we have seen, at Pharsalia, Philippi, and Actium; in the efforts to establish a Jacobinical government in France in 1793; in Rome in 1848, and the government of Victor Emmanuel in Naples in 1860 and 1861. These efforts, proscriptions, confiscations, military executions, assassinations, massacres, are all made in the name of liberty, or in defence of a government supposed to guaranty the well-being of the state and the rights of the people. They are rendered inevitable by the mad attempt to force on a nation a constitution of government foreign to the national constitution, or repugnant to the national tastes, interests, habits, convictions, or whole interior life. The repressive policy, adopted to a certain extent by nearly all European governments, grows out of the madness of a portion of the people of the several states in seeking to force upon the nation an anti-national constitution. The sovereigns may not be very wise, but they are wiser, more national, more patriotic than the mad theorists who seek to revolutionize the state and establish a government that has no hold in the national traditions, the national character, or the national life; and the statesman, the patriot, the true friend of liberty sympathizes with the national authorities, not with the mad theorists and revolutionists.

The right of a nation to change its form of government, and its magistrates or representatives, by whatever name called, is incontestable. Hence the French constitution of 1789, which involved that of 1793, was not illegal, for though accompanied by some irregularities, it was adopted by the manifest will of the nation, and consented to by all orders in the state. Not its legality but its wisdom is to be questioned, together with the false and dangerous theories of government which dictated it. There is no compact or mutual stipulation between the state and the government. The state, under God, is sovereign, and ordains and establishes the government, instead of making a contract, a bargain, or covenant, with it. The common democratic doctrine on this point is right, if by people is understood the organic people attached to a sovereign domain, not the people as individuals or as a floating or nomadic multitude. By people in the political sense, Cicero, and St. Augustine after him, understood the people as the republic, organized in reference to the common or public good. With this understanding, the sovereignty persists in the people, and they retain the supreme authority over the government. The powers delegated are still the powers of the sovereign delegating them, and may be modified, altered, or revoked, as the sovereign judges proper. The nation does not, and cannot abdicate or delegate away its own sovereignty, for sovereign it is, and cannot but be, so long as it remains a nation not subjected to another nation.

By the imperial constitution of the French government, the imperial power is vested in Napoleon III, and made hereditary in his family, in the male line of his legitimate descendants. This is legal, but the nation has not parted with its sovereignty or bound itself by contract forever to a Napoleonic dynasty. Napoleon holds the imperial power "by the grace of God and the will of the nation," which means simply that he holds his authority from God, through the French people, and is bound to exercise it according to the law of God and the national will. The nation is as competent to revoke this constitution as the legislature is to repeal any law it is competent to enact, and in doing so breaks no contract, violates no right, for Napoleon and his descendants hold their right to the imperial throne subject to the national will from which it is derived. In case the nation should revoke the powers delegated, he or they would have no more valid claim to the throne than have the Bourbons, whom the nation has unmistakably dismissed from its service.

The only point here to be observed is, that the change must be by the nation itself, in its sovereign capacity; not by a mob, nor by a part of the nation conspiring, intriguing, or rebelling, without any commission from the nation. The first Napoleon governed by a legal title, but he was never legally dethroned, and the government of the Bourbons, whether of the elder branch or the younger, was never a legal government, for the Bourbons had lost their original rights by the election of the first Napoleon, and never afterwards had the national will in their favor. The republic of 1848 was legal, in the sense that the nation acquiesced in it as a temporary necessity; but hardly anybody believed in it or wanted it, and the nation accepted it as a sort of *locum tenens*, rather than willed or ordained it. Its overthrow by the *coup d'état* may not be legally defensible, but the election of Napoleon III. condoned the illegality, if there was any, and gave the emperor a legal title, that no republican, that none but a despot or a no-government man can dispute. As the will of the nation, in so far as it contravenes not the law of God or the law of nature, binds every individual of the nation, no individual or number of individuals has, or can have, any right to conspire against him, or to labor to oust him from his place, till his escheat has been pronounced by the voice of the nation. The state, in its sovereign capacity, willing it, is the only power competent to revoke or to change the form and constitution of the imperial government. The same must be said of every nation that has a lawful government; and this, while it preserves the national sovereignty, secures freedom of progress, condemns all sedition, conspiracy, rebellion, revolution, as does the Christian law itself.

IX

The United States

Sovereignty, under God, inheres in the organic people, or the people as the republic; and every organic people fixed to the soil, and politically independent of every other people, is a sovereign people, and, in the modern sense, an independent sovereign nation.

Sovereign states may unite in an alliance, league, or confederation, and mutually agree to exercise their sovereign powers or a portion of them in common, through a common organ or agency; but in this agreement they part with none of their sovereignty, and each remains a sovereign state or nation as before. The common organ or agency created by the convention is no state, is no nation, has no inherent sovereignty, and derives all its vitality and force from the persisting sovereignty of the states severally that have united in creating it. The agreement no more affects the sovereignty of the several states entering into it, than does the appointment of an agent affect the rights and powers of the principal. The creature takes nothing from the Creator, exhausts not, lessens not his creative energy, and it is only by his retaining and continuously exerting his creative power that the creature continues to exist.

An independent state or nation may, with or without its consent, lose its sovereignty, but only by being merged in or subjected to another. Independent sovereign states cannot by convention, or mutual agreement, form themselves into a single sovereign state or nation. The compact, or agreement, is made by sovereign states, and binds by virtue of the sovereign power of each of the contracting parties. To destroy that sovereign power would be to annul the compact, and render void the agreement. The agreement can be valid and binding only on condition that each of the contracting parties retains the sovereignty that rendered it competent to enter into the compact, and states that retain severally their sovereignty do not form a single sovereign state or nation. The states in convention cannot become a new and single sovereign state, unless they lose their several sovereignty, and merge it in the new sovereignty; but this they cannot do by agreement, because the moment the parties to the agreement cease to be sovereign, the agreement, on which alone depends the new sovereign state, is vacated, in like manner as a contract is vacated by the death of the contracting parties.

That a nation may voluntarily cede its sovereignty is frankly admitted, but it can cede it only to something or somebody actually existing, for to cede to nothing and not to cede is one and the same thing. They can part with their own sovereignty by merging themselves in another national existence, but not by merging themselves in nothing; and, till they have parted with their own sovereignty, the new sovereign state does not exist. A prince can abdicate his power, because by abdicating he simply gives back to the people the trust he had received from them; but a nation cannot, save by merging itself in another. An independent state not merged in another, or that is not subject to another, cannot cease to be a sovereign nation, even if it would.

That no sovereign state can be formed by agreement or compact has already been shown in the refutation of the theory of the origin of government in convention, or the so-called social compact. Sovereign states are as unable to form themselves into a single sovereign state by mutual compact as are the sovereign individuals imagined by Rousseau. The convention, either of sovereign states or of sovereign individuals, with the best will in the world, can form only a compact or agreement between sovereigns, and an agreement or compact, whatever its terms or conditions, is only an alliance, a league, or a confederation, which no one can pretend is a sovereign state, nation, or republic.

The question, then, whether the United States are a single sovereign state or nation, or a confederacy of independent sovereign states, depends on the question whether the American people originally existed as one people or as several independent states. Mr. Jefferson maintains that before the convention of 1787 they existed as several independent sovereign states, but that since that convention, or the ratification of the constitution it proposed, they exist as one political people in regard to foreign nations, and several sovereign states in regard to their internal and domestic relations. Mr. Webster concedes that originally the States existed as severally sovereign states, but contends that by ratifying the constitution they have been made one sovereign political people, state, or nation, and that the General government is a supreme national government, though with a reservation in favor of State rights. But both are wrong. If the several States of the Union were severally sovereign states when they met in the convention, they are so now; and the constitution is only an agreement or compact between sovereigns, and the United States are, as Mr. Calhoun maintained, only a confederation of sovereign states, and not a single state or one political community.

But if the sovereignty persists in the States severally, any State, saving its faith, may, whenever it chooses to do so, withdraw from the Union, absolve its subjects from all obligation to the Federal authorities, and make it treason in them to adhere to the Federal government. Secession is, then, an incontestable right; not a right held under the constitution or derived from the convention, but a right held prior to it, independently of it, inherent in the State sovereignty, and inseparable from it. The State is bound by the constitution of the Union only while she is in it, and is one of the States united. In ratifying the constitution she did not part with her sovereignty, or with any portion of it, any more than France has parted with her sovereignty, and ceased to be an independent sovereign nation, by vesting the imperial power in Napoleon III. and his legitimate heirs male. The principal parts not with his power to his agent, for the agent is an agent only by virtue of the continued power of the principal. Napoleon is emperor by the will of the French people, and governs only by the authority of the French nation, which is as competent to revoke the powers it has conferred on him, when it judges proper, as it was to confer them. The Union exists and governs, if the States are sovereign, only by the will of the State, and she is as competent to revoke the powers she has delegated as she was to delegate them. The Union, as far as she is concerned, is her creation, and what she is competent to make she is competent to unmake.

In seceding or withdrawing from the Union a State may act very unwisely, very much against her own interests and the interests of the other members of the confederacy; but, if sovereign, she in doing so only exercises her unquestionable right. The other members may regret her action, both for her sake and their own, but they cannot accuse her or her citizens of disloyalty in seceding, nor of rebellion, if in obedience to her authority they defend their independence by force of arms against the Union. Neither she nor they, on the supposition, ever owed allegiance to the Union. Allegiance is due from the citizen to the sovereign state, but never from a sovereign state or from its citizens to any other sovereign state. While the State is in the Union the citizen owes obedience to the United States, but only because his State has, in ratifying the Federal constitution, enacted that it and all laws and treaties made under it shall be law within her territory. The repeal by the State of the act of ratification releases the citizen from the obligation even of obedience, and renders it criminal for him to yield it without her permission.

It avails nothing, on the hypothesis of the sovereignty of the States as distinguished from that of the United States, to appeal to the language or provisions of the Federal constitution. That constitutes the government, not the state or the sovereign. It is ordained by the sovereign, and if the states were severally independent and sovereign states, that sovereign is the States severally, not the States united. The constitution is law for the citizens of a State only so long as the State remains one of the United States. No matter, then, how clear and express the language, or stringent the provisions of the constitution, they bind only the citizens of the States that enact the constitution. The written constitution is simply a compact, and obliges only while the compact is continued by the States, each for itself. The sovereignty of the United States as a single or political people must be established before any thing in the constitution can be adduced as denying the right of secession.

That this doctrine would deprive the General government of all right to enforce the laws of the Union on a State that secedes, or the citizens thereof, is no doubt true; that it would weaken the central power and make the Union a simple voluntary association of states, no better than a rope of sand, is no less true; but what then? It is simply saying that a confederation is inferior to a nation, and that a federal government lacks many of the advantages of a national government. Confederacies are always weak in the centre, always lack unity, and are liable to be dissolved by the influence of local passions, prejudices, and interests. But if the United States are a confederation of states or nations, not a single nation or sovereign state, then there is no remedy.

If the Anglo-American colonies, when their independence of Great Britain was achieved and acknowledged, were severally sovereign states, it has never since been in their power to unite and form a single sovereign state, or to form themselves into one indivisible sovereign nation. They could unite only by mutual agreement, which gives only a confederation, in which each retains its own sovereignty, as two individuals, however closely united, retain each his own individuality. No sovereignty is of conventional origin, and none can emerge from the convention that did not enter it. Either the states are one sovereign people or they are not. If they are not, it is undoubtedly a great disadvantage; but a disadvantage that must be accepted, and submitted to without a murmur.

Whether the United States are one sovereign people or only a confederation is a question of very grave importance. If they are only a confederation of states—and if they ever were severally sovereign states, only a confederation they certainly are—state secession is an inalienable right, and the government has had no right to make war on the secessionists as rebels, or to treat them, when their military power is broken, as traitors, or disloyal persons. The honor of the government, and of the people who have sustained it, is then deeply compromised.

What then is the fact? Are the United States politically one people, nation, state, or republic, or are they simply independent sovereign states united in close and intimate alliance, league, or federation, by a mutual pact or agreement? Were the people of the United States who ordained and established the written constitution one people, or were they not? If they were not before ordaining and establishing the government, they are not now; for the adoption of the constitution did not and could not make them one. Whether they are one or many is then simply a question of fact, to be decided by the facts in the case, not by the theories of American statesmen, the opinion of jurists, or even by constitutional law itself. The old Articles of Confederation and the later Constitution can serve here only as historical documents. Constitutions and laws presuppose the existence of a national sovereign from which they emanate, and that ordains them, for they are the formal expression of a sovereign will. The nation must exist as an historical fact, prior to the possession or exercise of sovereign power, prior to the existence of written constitutions and laws of any kind, and its existence must be established before they can be recognized as having any legal force or vitality.

The existence of any nation, as an independent sovereign nation, is a purely historical fact, for its right to exist as such is in the simple fact that it does so exist. A nation *de facto* is a nation *de jure*, and when we have ascertained the fact, we have ascertained the right. There is no right in the case separate from the fact—only the fact must be really a fact. A people hitherto a part of another people, or subject to another sovereign, is not in fact a nation, because they have declared themselves independent, and have organized a government, and are engaged in what promises to be a successful struggle for independence. The struggle must be practically over; the former sovereign must have practically abandoned the effort to reduce them to submission, or to bring them back under his authority, and if he continues it, does it as a matter of mere form; the postulant must have proved his ability to maintain civil government, and to fulfil within and without the obligations which attach to every civilized nation, before it can be recognized as an independent sovereign nation; because before it is not a fact that it is a sovereign nation. The prior sovereign, when no longer willing or able to vindicate his right, has lost it, and no one is any longer bound to respect it, for humanity demands not martyrs to lost causes.

This doctrine may seem harsh, and untenable even, to those sickly philanthropists who are always weeping over extinct or oppressed nationalities; but nationality in modern civilization is a fact, not a right antecedent to the fact. The repugnance felt to this assertion arises chiefly from using the word *nation* sometimes in a strictly political sense, and sometimes in its original sense of tribe, and understanding by it not simply the body politic, but a certain relation of origin, family, kindred, blood, or race. But God has made of one blood, or race, all the nations of men; and, besides, no political rights are founded by the law of nature on relations of blood, kindred, or family. Under the patriarchal or tribal system, and, to some extent, under feudalism, these relations form the basis of government, but they are economical relations rather than civil or political, and, under Christian and modern civilization, are restricted to the household, are domestic relations, and enter not the state or body politic, except by way of reminiscence or abuse. They are protected by the state, but do not found or constitute it. The vicissitudes of time, the revolutions of states and empires, migration, conquest, and intermixture of families and races, have rendered it impracticable, even if it were desirable, to distribute people into nations according to their relations of blood or descent.

There is no civilized nation now existing that has been developed from a common ancestor this side of Adam, and the most mixed are the most civilized. The nearer a nation approaches to a primitive people of pure unmixed blood, the farther removed it is from civilization. All civilized nations are political nations, and are founded in the fact, not on rights antecedent to the fact. A hundred or more lost nationalities went to form the Roman empire, and who can tell us how many layers of crushed nationalities, superposed one upon another, serve for the foundation of the present French, English, Russian, Austrian, or Spanish nationalities? What other title to independence and sovereignty, than the fact, can you plead in behalf of any European nation? Every one has absorbed and extinguished—no one can say how many—nationalities, that once had as good a right to be as it has, or can have. Whether those nationalities have been justly extinguished or not, is no question for the statesman; it is the secret of Providence. Failure in this world is not always a proof of wrong; nor success, of right. The good is sometimes overborne, and the bad sometimes triumphs; but it it is consoling, and even just, to believe that the good oftener triumphs than the bad.

In the political order, the fact, under God, precedes the law. The nation holds not from the law, but the law holds from the nation. Doubtless the courts of every civilized nation recognize and apply both the law of nature and the law of nations, but only on the ground that they are included, or are presumed to be included, in the national law, or jurisprudence. Doubtless, too, the nation holds from God, under the law of nature, but only by virtue of the fact that it is a nation; and when it is a nation dependent on no other, it holds from God all the rights and powers of any independent sovereign nation. There is no right behind the fact needed to legalize the fact, or to put the nation that is in fact a nation in possession of full national rights. In the case of a new nation, or people, lately an integral part of another people, or subject to another people, the right of the prior sovereign must be extinguished indeed, but the extinction of that right is necessary to complete the fact, which otherwise would be only an initial, inchoate fact, not a *fait accompli*. But that right ceases when its claimant, willingly or unwillingly, formally or virtually, abandons it; and he does so when he practically abandons the struggle, and shows no ability or intention of soon renewing it with any reasonable prospect of success.

The notion of right, independent of the fact as applied to sovereignty, is founded in error. Empty titles to states and kingdoms are of no validity. The sovereignty is, under God, in the nation, and the title and the possession are inseparable. The title of the Palæologi to the Roman Empire of the East, of the king of Sicily, the king of Sardinia,

or the king of Spain—for they are all claimants—to the kingdom of
Jerusalem founded by Godfrey and his crusaders, of the Stuarts to the
thrones of England, Ireland, and Scotland, or of the Bourbons to the
throne of France, are vacated and not worth the parchment on which
they are engrossed. The contrary opinion, so generally entertained,
belongs to barbarism, not to civilization. It is in modern society a relic
of feudalism, which places the state in the government, and makes the
government a private estate—a private, and not a public right—a
right to govern the public, not a right to govern held from or by the
public.

The proprietor may be dispossessed in fact of his estate by violence,
by illegal or unjust means, without losing his right, and another may
usurp it, occupy it, and possess it in fact without acquiring any right or
legal title to it. The man who holds the legal title has the right to oust
him and re-enter upon his estate whenever able to do so. Here, in the
economical order, the fact and the right are distinguishable, and the
actual occupant may be required to show his title-deeds. Holding sovereignty to be a private estate, the feudal lawyers very properly distinguish between governments *de facto* and governments *de jure*, and argue
very logically that violent dispossession of a prince does not invalidate
his title. But sovereignty, it has been shown, is not in the government,
but in the state, and the state is inseparable from the public domain. The
people organized and held by the domain or national territory, are, under God, the sovereign nation, and remain so as long as the nation subsists without subjection to another. The government, as distinguished
from the state or nation, has only a delegated authority, governs only by
a commission from the nation. The revocation of the commission vacates its title and extinguishes its rights. The nation is always sovereign, and every organic people fixed to the soil, and actually independent of every other, is a nation. There can then be no independent nation *de facto* that is not an independent nation *de jure*, nor *de jure* that is

not *de facto*. The moment a people cease to be an independent nation in fact, they cease to be sovereign, and the moment they become in fact an independent nation, they are so of right. Hence in the political order the fact and the right are born and expire together; and when it is proved that a people are in fact an independent nation, there is no question to be asked as to their right to be such nation.

In the case of the United States there is only the question of fact. If they are in fact one people they are so in right, whatever the opinions and theories of statesmen, or even the decisions of courts; for the courts hold from the national authority, and the theories and opinions of statesmen may be erroneous. Certain it is that the States in the American Union have never existed and acted as severally sovereign states. Prior to independence, they were colonies under the sovereignty of Great Britain, and since independence they have existed and acted only as states united. The colonists, before separation and independence, were British subjects, and whatever rights the colonies had they held by charter or concession from the British crown. The colonists never pretended to be other than British subjects, and the alleged ground of their complaint against the mother country was not that she had violated their natural rights as men, but their rights as British subjects—rights, as contended by the colonists, secured by the English constitution to all Englishmen or British subjects. The denial to them of these common rights of Englishmen they called tyranny, and they defended themselves in throwing off their allegiance to George III., on the ground that he had, in their regard, become a tyrant, and the tyranny of the prince absolves the subject from his allegiance.

In the Declaration of Independence they declared themselves independent states indeed, but not severally independent. The declaration was not made by the states severally, but by the states jointly, as the United States. They unitedly declared their independence; they carried on the war for independence, won it, and were acknowledged by foreign powers and by the mother country as the *United* States, not as severally independent sovereign states. Severally they have never exercised the full powers of sovereign states; they have had no flag—symbol of sovereignty—recognized by foreign powers, have made no foreign treaties, held no foreign relations, had no commerce foreign or interstate, coined no money, entered into no alliances or confederacies with foreign states or with one another, and in several respects have been more restricted in their powers in the Union than they were as British colonies.

Colonies are initial or inchoate states, and become complete states by declaring and winning their independence; and if the English colonies, now the United States, had separately declared and won their independence, they would unquestionably have become separately independent states, each invested by the law of nature with all the rights and powers of a sovereign nation. But they did not do this. They declared and won their independence jointly, and have since existed and exercised sovereignty only as states united, or the United States, that is, states sovereign in their union, but not in their separation. This is of itself decisive of the whole question.

But the colonists have not only never exercised the full powers of sovereignty save as citizens of states united, therefore as one people, but they were, so far as a people at all, one people even before independence. The colonies were all erected and endowed with their rights and powers by one and the same national authority, and the colonists were subjects of one and the same national sovereign. Mr. Quincy Adams, who almost alone among our prominent statesmen maintains the unity of the colonial people, adds indeed to their subjection to the same sovereign authority, community of origin, of language, manners, customs, and law. All these, except the last, or common law, may exist without national unity in the modern political sense of the term nation. The English common law was recognized by the colonial courts, and in force in all the colonies, not by virtue of colonial legislation, but by virtue of English authority, as expressed in English jurisprudence. The colonists were under the Common Law, because they were Englishmen, and subjects of the English sovereign. This proves that they were really one people with the English people, though existing in a state of colonial dependence, and not a separate people having nothing politically in common with them but in the accident of having the same royal person for their king. The union with the mother country was national, not personal, as was the union existing between England and Hanover, or that still existing between the empire of Austria, formerly Germany, and the kingdom of Hungary; and hence the British parliament claimed, and not illegally, the right to tax the colonies for the support of the empire, and to bind them in all cases whatsoever—a claim the colonies themselves admitted in principle by recognizing and observing the British navigation laws. The people of the several colonies being really one people before independence, in the sovereignty of the mother country, must be so still, unless they have since, by some valid act, divided themselves or been divided into separate and independent states.

The king, say the jurists, never dies, and the heralds cry, "The king is dead! Live the king!" Sovereignty never lapses, is never in abeyance, and the moment it ceases in one people it is renewed in another. The British sovereignty ceased in the colonies with independence, and the American took its place. Did the sovereignty, which before independence was in Great Britain, pass from Great Britain to the States severally, or to the States united? It might have passed to them severally, but did it? There is no question of law or antecedent right in the case, but a simple question of fact, and the fact is determined by determining who it was that assumed it, exercised it, and has continued to exercise it. As to this there is no doubt. The sovereignty as a fact has been assumed and exercised by the United States, the States united, and never by the

States separately, or severally. Then as a fact the sovereignty that before independence was in Great Britain, passed on independence to the States united, and reappears in all its vigor in the United States, the only successor to Great Britain known to or recognized by the civilized world.

As the colonial people were, though distributed in distinct colonies, still one people, the people of the United States, though distributed into distinct and mutually independent States, are yet one sovereign people, therefore a sovereign state or nation, and not a simple league or confederacy of nations.

There is no doubt that all the powers exercised by the General Government, though embracing all foreign relations and all general interests and relations of all the States, might have been exercised by it under the authority of a mutual compact of the several States, and practically the difference between the compact theory and the national view would be very little, unless in cases like that of secession. On the supposition that the American people are one political people, the government would have the right to treat secession, in the sense in which the seceders understand it, as rebellion, and to suppress it by employing all the physical force at its command; but on the compact theory it would have no such right. But the question now under discussion turns simply on what has been and is the historical fact. Before the States could enter into the compact and delegate sovereign powers to the Union, they must have severally possessed them. It is historically certain that they did not possess them before independence; they did not obtain them by independence, for they did not severally succeed to the British sovereignty, to which they succeeded only as States united. When, then, and by what means did they or could they become severally sovereign States? The United States having succeeded to the British sovereignty in the Anglo-American colonies, they came into possession of full national sovereignty, and have alone held and exercised it ever since independence became a fact. The States severally succeeding only to the colonies, never held, and have never been competent to delegate sovereign powers.

The old Articles of Confederation, it is conceded, were framed on the assumption that the States are severally sovereign; but the several States, at the same time, were regarded as forming one nation, and, though divided into separate States, the people were regarded as one people. The Legislature of New York, as early as 1782, calls for an essential change in the Articles of Confederation, as proved to be inadequate to secure the peace, security, and prosperity of "the nation." All the proceedings that preceded and led to the call of the convention of 1787 were based on the assumption that the people of the United States were one people. The States were called *united*, not confederated States, even in the very Articles of Confederation themselves, and officially the United States were called "the Union." That the united colonies by independence became united States, and formed really one and only one people, was in the thought, the belief, the instinct of the great mass of the people. They acted as they existed through State as they had previously acted through colonial organization, for in throwing off the British authority there was no other organization through which they could act. The States, or people of the States, severally sent their delegates to the Congress of the United States, and these delegates adopted the rule of voting in Congress by States, a rule that might be revived without detriment to national unity. Nothing was more natural, then, than that Congress, composed of delegates elected or appointed by States, should draw up articles of confederation rather than articles of union, in order, if for no other reason, to conciliate the smaller States, and to prevent their jealousy of the larger States such as Virginia, Massachusetts, and Pennsylvania.

Moreover, the Articles of Confederation were drawn up and adopted during the transition from colonial dependence to national independence. Independence was declared in 1776, but it was not a fact till 1782, when the preliminary treaty acknowledging it was signed at Paris. Till then the United States were not an independent nation; they were only a people struggling to become an independent nation. Prior to that preliminary treaty, neither the Union nor the States severally were sovereign. The articles were agreed on in Congress in 1777, but they were not ratified by all the States till May, 1781, and in 1782 the movement was commenced in the Legislature of New York for their amendment. Till the organization under the constitution ordained by the people of the United States in 1787, and which went into operation in 1789, the United States had in reality only a provisional government, and it was not till then that the national government was definitively organized, and the line of demarcation between the General Government and the particular State governments was fixed.

The Confederation was an acknowledged failure, and was rejected by the American people, precisely because it was not in harmony with the unwritten or Providential constitution of the nation; and it was not in harmony with that constitution precisely because it recognized the States as severally sovereign, and substituted confederation for union. The failure of confederation and the success of union are ample proofs of the unity of the American nation. The instinct of unity rejected State sovereignty in 1787 as it did in 1861. The first and the last attempt to establish State sovereignty have failed, and the failure vindicates the fact that the sovereignty is in the States united, not in the States severally.

X

Constitution of the United States

$\mathcal{T}$he constitution of the United States is two-fold, written and un-written, the constitution of the people and the constitution of the government.

The written constitution is simply a law ordained by the nation or people instituting and organizing the government; the unwritten constitution is the real or actual constitution of the people as a state or sovereign community, and constituting them such or such a state. It is Providential, not made by the nation, but born with it. The written constitution is made and ordained by the sovereign power, and presupposes that power as already existing and constituted.

The unwritten or Providential constitution of the United States is peculiar, and difficult to understand, because incapable of being fully explained by analogies borrowed from any other state historically known, or described by political philosophers. It belongs to the Græco-Roman family, and is republican as distinguished from despotic constitutions, but it comes under the head of neither monarchical nor aristocratic, neither democratic nor mixed constitutions, and creates a state which is neither a centralized state nor a confederacy. The difficulty of under-standing it is augmented by the peculiar use under it of the word *state,* which does not in the American system mean a sovereign community or political society complete in itself, like France, Spain, or Prussia, nor yet a political society subordinate to another political society and dependent on it. The American States are all sovereign States united, but, disunited, are no States at all. The rights and powers of the States are not derived from the United States, nor the rights and powers of the United States derived from the States.

The simple fact is, that the political or sovereign people of the United States exists as united States, and only as united States. The Union and the States are coeval, born together, and can exist only together. Separation is dissolution—the death of both. The United States are a state, a single sovereign state; but this single sovereign state consists in the union and solidarity of States instead of individuals. The Union is in each of the States, and each of the States is in the Union.

It is necessary to distinguish in the outset between the United States and the government of the United States, or the so-called Federal government, which the convention refused, contrary to its first intention to call the *national* government. That government is not a supreme national government, representing all the powers of the United States, but a limited government, restricted by its constitution to certain specific relations and interests. The United States are anterior to that government, and the first question to be settled relates to their internal and inherent Providential constitution as one political people or sovereign state. The written constitution, in its preamble, professes to be ordained by "We, the people of the United States." Who are this people? How are they constituted, or what the mode and conditions of their political existence? Are they the people of the States severally? No; for they call themselves the people of the *United* States. Are they a national people, really existing outside and independently of their organization into distinct and mutually independent States? No; for they define themselves to be the people of the United *States*. If they had considered themselves existing as States only, they would have said "We, the States," and if independently of State organization, they would have said "We, the people," do ordain, &c.

The key to the mystery is precisely in this appellation *United States,* which is not the name of the country, for its distinctive name is America, but a name expressive of its political organization. In it there are no sovereign people without States, and no States without union, or that are not *united* States. The term *united* is not part of a proper name, but is simply an adjective qualifying *States,* and has its full and proper sense. Hence while the sovereignty is and must be in the States, it is in the States united, not in the States severally, precisely as we have found the sovereignty of the people is in the people collectively or as society, not in the people individually. The life is in the body, not in the members, though the body could not exist if it had no members; so the sovereignty is in the Union, not in the States severally; but there could be no sovereign union without the States, for there is no union where there is nothing united.

This is not a theory of the constitution, but the constitutional fact itself. It is the simple historical fact that precedes the law and constitutes the law-making power. The people of the United States are one people, as has already been proved: they were one people, as far as a people at all, prior to independence, because under the same Common Law and subject to the same sovereign, and have been so since, for as *united* States they gained their independence and took their place among sovereign nations, and as united States they have possessed and still possess the government. As their existence before independence in distinct colonies did not prevent their unity, so their existence since in distinct States does not hinder them from being one people. The States severally simply continue the colonial organizations, and united they hold the sovereignty that was originally in the mother country. But if one people, they are one people existing in distinct State organizations, as before independence they were one people existing in distinct colonial organizations. This is the original, the unwritten, and Providential constitution of the people of the United States.

This constitution is not conventional, for it existed before the people met or could meet in convention. They have not, as an independent sovereign people, either established their union, or distributed themselves into distinct and mutually independent States. The union and the distribution, the unity and the distinction, are both original in their constitution, and they were born United States, as much and as truly so as the son of a citizen is born a citizen, or as every one born at all is born a member of society, the family, the tribe, or the nation. The Union and the States were born together, are inseparable in their constitution, have lived and grown up together; no serious attempt till the late secession movement has been made to separate them; and the secession movement, to all persons who knew not the real constitution of the United States, appeared sure to succeed, and in fact would have succeeded if, as the secessionists pretended, the Union had been only a confederacy, and the States had been held together only by a conventional compact, and not by a real and living bond of unity. The popular instinct of national unity, which seemed so weak, proved to be strong enough to defeat the secession forces, to trample out the confederacy, and maintain the unity of the nation and the integrity of its domain.

The people can act only as they exist, as they are, not as they are not. Existing originally only as distributed in distinct and mutually independent colonies, they could at first act only through their colonial organizations, and afterward only through their State organizations. The colonial people met in convention, in the person of representatives chosen by colonies, and after independence in the person of representatives chosen by States. Not existing outside of the colonial or State organizations, they could not act outside or independently of them. They chose their representatives or delegates by colonies or States, and called at first their convention a Congress; but by an instinct surer than their deliberate wisdom, they called it not the Congress of the *confederate*, but of the *United* States, asserting constitutional unity as well as constitutional multiplicity. It is true, in their first attempt to organize a general government, they called the constitution they devised Articles of Confederation, but only because they had not attained to full consciousness of themselves; and that they really meant union, not confederation, is evident from their adopting, as the official style of the nation or new power, *united*, not *confederate* States.

That the sovereignty vested in the States united, and was represented in some sort by the Congress, is evident from the fact that the several States, when they wished to adopt State constitutions in place of colonial charters, felt not at liberty to do so without asking and obtaining the permission of Congress, as the elder Adams informs us in his *Diary*, kept at the time; that is, they asked and obtained the equivalent of what has since, in the case of organizing new States, been called an "enabling act." This proves that the States did not regard themselves as sovereign States out of the Union, but as completely sovereign only in it. And this again proves that the Articles of Confederation did not correspond to the real, living constitution of the people. Even then it was felt that the organization and constitution of a State in the Union could be regularly effected only by the permission of Congress; and no Territory can, it is well known, regularly organize itself as a State, and adopt a State constitution, without an enabling act by Congress, or its equivalent.

New States, indeed, have been organized and been admitted into the Union without an enabling act of Congress; but the case of Kansas, if nothing else, proves that the proceeding is irregular, illicit, invalid, and dangerous. Congress, of course, can condone the wrong and validate the act, but it were better that the act should be validly done, and that there should be no wrong to condone. Territories have organized as States, adopted State constitutions, and instituted State governments under what has been called "squatter sovereignty;" but such sovereignty has no existence, because sovereignty is attached to the domain; and the domain is in the United States. It is the offspring of that false view of popular sovereignty which places it in the people personally or generically, irrespective of the domain, which makes sovereignty a purely personal right, not a right fixed to the soil, and is simply a return to the barbaric constitution of power. In all civilized nations, sovereignty is inseparable from the state, and the state is inseparable from the domain. The will of the people, unless they are a state, is no law, has no force, binds nobody, and justifies no act.

The regular process of forming and admitting new States explains admirably the mutual relation of the Union and the several States. The people of a Territory belonging to the United States or included in the public domain not yet erected into a State and admitted into the Union, are subjects of the United States, without any political rights whatever, and, though a part of the population, are no part of the sovereign people of the United States. They become a part of that people, with political rights and franchises, only when they are erected into a State, and admitted into the Union as one of the United States. They may meet in convention, draw up and adopt a constitution declaring or assuming them to be a State, elect State officers, senators, and representatives in the State legislature, and representatives and senators in Congress, but they are not yet a State, and are, as before, under the Territorial government established by the General Government. It does not exist as a State till recognized by Congress and admitted into the Union. The existence of the State, and the rights and powers of the people within the State, depend on their being a State in the Union, or a State united. Hence a State erected on the national domain, but itself outside of the Union, is not an independent foreign State, but simply no State at all, in any sense of the term. As there is no union outside of the States, so is there no State outside of the Union; and to be a citizen either of a State or of the United States, it is necessary to be a citizen of a State, and of a State in the Union. The inhabitants of Territories not yet erected into States are subjects, not citizens—that is, not citizens with political rights. The sovereign people are not the people outside of State organization, nor the people of the States severally, but the distinct people of the several States united, and therefore most appropriately called the people of the United States.

This is the peculiarity of the American constitution, and is substantially the very peculiarity noted and dwelt upon by Mr. Madison in his masterly letter to Edward Everett, published in the "North American Review," October, 1830.

"In order to understand the true character of the constitution of the United States," says Mr. Madison, "the error, not uncommon, must be avoided of viewing it through the medium either of a consolidated government or of a confederated government, whilst it is neither the one nor the other, but a mixture of both. And having, in no model, the similitudes and analogies applicable to other systems of government, it must, more than any other, be its own interpreter, according to its text and *the facts in the case.*

"From these it will be seen that the characteristic peculiarities of the constitution are: 1. The mode of its formation. 2. The division of the supreme powers of government between the States in their united capacity and the States in their individual capacities.

"1. It was formed not by the governments of the component States, as the Federal Government, for which it was substituted, was formed; nor was it formed by a majority of the people of the United States as a single community, in the manner of a consolidated government. It was formed by the States; that is, by the people in each of the States, acting in their highest sovereign capacity, and formed consequently by the same authority which formed the State constitution.

"Being thus derived from the same source as the constitutions of the States, it has within each State the same authority as the constitution of the State, and is as much a constitution in the strict sense of the term, within its prescribed sphere, as the constitutions of the States are within their respective spheres; but with this obvious and essential difference, that, being a compact among the States in their highest capacity, and constituting the people thereof one people for certain purposes, it cannot be altered or annulled at the will of the States individually, as the constitution of a State may be at its individual will.

"2. And that it divides the supreme powers of government between the government of the United States and the governments of the individual States, is stamped on the face of the instrument; the powers of war and of taxation, of commerce and treaties, and other enumerated powers vested in the government of the United States, are of as high and sovereign a character as any of the powers reserved to the State governments."

Mr. Jefferson, Mr. Webster, Chancellor Kent, Judge Story, and nearly all the old Republicans, and even the old Federalists, on the question as to what is the actual constitution of the United States, took substantially the same view; but they all, as well as Mr. Madison himself, speak of the written constitution, which on their theory has and can have only a conventional value. Mr. Madison evidently recognizes no constitution of the people prior to the written constitution, from which the written constitution, or the constitution of the government, derives all its force and vitality. The organization of the American people, which he knew well,—no man better,—and which he so justly characterizes, he supposes to have been deliberately formed by the people themselves, through the convention—not given them by Providence as their original and inherent constitution. But this was merely the effect of the general doctrine which he had adopted, in common with nearly all his contemporaries, of the origin of the state in compact, and may be eliminated from his view of what the constitution actually is, without affecting that view itself.

Mr. Madison lays great stress on the fact that though the constitution of the Union was formed by the States, it was formed, not by the governments, but by the people of the several States; but this makes no essential difference, if the people are the people of the States, and sovereign in their severalty, and not in their union. Had it been formed by the State governments with the acquiescence of the people, it would have rested on as high authority as if formed by the people of the State in convention assembled. The only difference is, that if the State ratified it by the legislature, she could abrogate it by the legislature; if in convention, she could abrogate it only in convention. Mr. Madison, following Mr. Jefferson, supposes the constitution makes the people of the several States one people for certain specific purposes, and leaves it to be supposed that in regard to all other matters, or in all other relations, they are sovereign; and hence he makes the government a mixture of a consolidated government and a confederated government, but neither the one nor the other exclusively. Say the people of the United States were one people in all respects, and under a government which is neither a consolidated nor a confederated government, nor yet a mixture of the two, but a government in which the powers of government are divided between a general government and particular governments, each emanating from the same source, and you will have the simple fact, and precisely what Mr. Madison means, when is eliminated what is derived from his theory of the origin of government in compact. It is this theory of the conventional origin of the constitution, and which excludes the Providential or real constitution of the people, that has misled him and so many other eminent statesmen and constitutional lawyers.

The convention did not create the Union or unite the States, for it was assembled by the authority of the United States who were present in it. The United States or Union existed before the convention, as the convention itself affirms in declaring one of its purposes to be "to provide for a *more perfect union.*" If there had been no union, it could not and would not have spoken of providing for a *more perfect* union, but would have stated its purpose to be to create or form a union. The convention did not form the Union, nor in fact provide for a more perfect union; it simply provided for the more perfect representation or expression in the General government of the Union already existing. The convention, in common with the statesmen at the time, recognized no unwritten or Providential constitution of a people, and regarded the constitution of government as the constitution of the state, and consequently sometimes put the state for the government. In interpreting its language, it is necessary to distinguish between its act and its theory. Its act is law, its theory is not. The convention met, among other things, to organize a government which should more perfectly represent the union of the States than did the government created by the Articles of Confederation.

The convention, certainly, professes to grant or concede powers to the United States, and to prohibit powers to the States; but it simply puts the state for the government. The powers of the United States are, indeed, grants or trusts, but from God through the law of nature, and are grants, trusts, or powers always conceded to every nation or sovereign people. But none of them are grants from the convention. The powers the convention grants or concedes to the United States are powers granted or conceded by the United States to the General government it assembled to organize and establish, which, as it extends over the whole population and territory of the Union, and, as the interests it is charged with relate to all the States in common, or to the people as a whole, is with no great impropriety called the government of the United States, in contradistinction from the State governments, which have each only a local jurisdiction. But the more exact term is, for the one, the general government, and for the others, particular governments, as having charge only of the particular interests of the State; and the two together constitute the government of the United States, or the complete national government; for neither the General government nor the State government is complete in itself. The convention developed a general government, and prescribed its powers, and fixed their limits and extent, as well as the bounds of the powers of the State or particular governments; but they are the United States assembled in convention that do all this, and, therefore, strictly speaking, no powers are conceded to the United States that they did not previously possess. The convention itself, in the constitution it ordained, defines very clearly from whom the General government holds its powers. It holds them, as we have seen, from "We, the people of the United States;" not we, the people of the States severally, but of the States united. If it had meant the States severally, it would have said, We, the States; if it had recognized and meant the population of the country irrespective of its organization into particular States, it would have said simply, We, the people. By saying "We, the people of the United States," it placed the sovereign power where it is, in the people of the States united.

The convention ordains that the powers not conceded to the General government or prohibited to the particular governments, "are reserved to the States respectively, or to the people." But the powers reserved to the States severally are reserved by order of the United States, and the powers not so reserved are reserved to the people. What people? The first thought is that they are the people of the States severally; for the constitution understands by people the state as distinguished from the state government; but if this had been its meaning in this place, it would have said, "are reserved to the States respectively, or to the people" thereof. As it does not say so, and does not define the people it means, it is necessary to understand by them the people called in the preamble "the people of the United States." This is confirmed by the authority reserved to amend the constitution, which certainly is not reserved to the States severally, but necessarily to the power that ordains the constitution—"We, the people of the United States." No power except that which ordains is or can be competent to amend a constitution of government. The particular mode prescribed by the convention in which the constitution of the government may be amended has no bearing on the present argument, because it is prescribed by the States united, not severally, and the power to amend is evidently reserved, not indeed to the General government, but to the United States; for the ratification by any State or Territory not in the Union counts for nothing. The States united, can, in the way prescribed, give more or less power to the General government, and reserve more or less power to the States individually. The so-called reserved powers are really reserved to the people of the United States, who can make such disposition of them as seems to them good.

The conclusion, then, that the General government holds from the States united, not from the States severally, is not invalidated by the fact that its constitution was completed only by the ratification of the States in their individual capacity. The ratification was made necessary by the will of the people in convention assembled; but the convention was competent to complete it and put it in force without that ratification, had it so willed. The general practice under the American system is for the convention to submit the constitution it has agreed on to the people, to be accepted or rejected by a *plebiscitum;* but such submission, though it may be wise and prudent, is not necessary. The convention is held to be the convention of the people, and to be clothed with the full authority of the sovereign people, and it is in this that it differs from the congress or the legislature. It is not a congress of delegates or ministers who are obliged to act under instructions, to report their acts to their respective sovereigns for approval or rejection; it is itself sovereign, and may do whatever the people themselves can do. There is no necessity for it to appeal to a *plebiscitum* to complete its acts. That the convention, on the score of prudence, is wise in doing so, nobody questions; but the convention is always competent, if it chooses, to ordain the constitution without appeal. The power competent to ordain the constitution is always competent to change, modify, or amend it. That amendments to the constitution of the government can be adopted only by being proposed by a convention of all the States in the Union, or by being proposed by a two-thirds vote of both houses of Congress, and ratified by three-fourths of the States, is simply a conventional ordinance, which the convention can change at its pleasure. It proves nothing as it stands but the will of the convention.

The term *ratification* itself, because the term commonly used in reference to treaties between sovereign powers, has been seized on, since sometimes used by the convention, to prove that the constitution emanates from the States severally, and is a treaty or compact between sovereign states, not an organic or fundamental law ordained by a single sovereign will; but this argument is inadmissible, because, as we have just seen, the convention is competent to ordain the constitution without submitting it for ratification, and because the convention uses sometimes the word *adopt* instead of the word *ratify*. That the framers of the constitution held it to be a treaty, compact, or agreement among sovereigns, there is no doubt, for they so held in regard to all constitution of government; and there is just as little doubt that they intended to constitute, and firmly believed that they were constituting a real government. Mr. Madison's authority on this point is conclusive. They unquestionably regarded the States, prior to the ratification of the constitution they proposed, as severally sovereign, as they were declared to be by the old Articles of Confederation, but they also believed that all individuals are sovereign prior to the formation of civil society. Yet very few, if any, of them believed that they remained sovereign after the adoption of the constitution; and we may attribute to their belief in the conventional origin of all government,—the almost universal belief of the time among political philosophers,—the little account which they made of the historical facts that prove that the people of the United States were always one people, and that the States never existed as severally sovereign states.

The political philosophers of the present day do not generally accept the theory held by our fathers, and it has been shown in these pages to be unsound and incompatible with the essential nature of government. The statesmen of the eighteenth century believed that the state is derived from the people individually, and held that sovereignty is created by the people in convention. The rights and powers of the state, they held, were made up of the rights held by individuals under the law of nature, and which the individuals surrendered to civil society on its formation. So they supposed that independent sovereign states might meet in convention, mutually agree to surrender a portion of their rights, organize their surrendered rights into a real government, and leave the convention shorn, at least, of a portion of their sovereignty. This doctrine crops out everywhere in the writings of the elder Adams, and is set forth with rare ability by Mr. Webster, in his great speech in the Senate against the State sovereignty doctrine of General Hayne and Mr. Calhoun, which won for him the honorable title of Expounder of the Constitution—and expound it he, no doubt, did in the sense of its framers. He boldly concedes that prior to the adoption of the constitution, the people of the United States were severally sovereign states, but by the constitution they were made one sovereign political community or people, and that the States, though retaining certain rights, have merged their several sovereignty in the Union.

The subtle mind of Mr. Calhoun, who did not hold that a state can originate in compact, proved to Mr. Webster that his theory could not stand; that, if the States went into the convention sovereign States, they came out of it sovereign States; and that the constitution they formed could from the nature of the case be only a treaty, compact, or agreement between sovereigns. It could create an agency, but not a government. The sovereign States could only delegate the exercise of their sovereign powers, not the sovereign powers themselves. The States could agree to exercise certain specific powers of sovereignty only in common, but the force and vitality of the agreement depended on the States, parties to the agreement, retaining respectively their sovereignty. Hence, he maintained that sovereignty, after as before the convention, vested in the States severally. Hence State sovereignty, and hence his doctrine that in all cases that cannot come properly before the Supreme Court of the United States for decision, each State is free to decide for itself, on which he based the right of nullification, or the State veto of acts of Congress whose constitutionality the State denies. Mr. Calhoun was himself no secessionist, but he laid down the premises from which secession is the logical deduction; and large numbers of young men, among the most open, the most generous, and the most patriotic in the country, adopted his premises, without being aware of this fact any more than he himself was, and who have been behind none in their loyalty to the Union, and in their sacrifices to sustain it, in the late rebellion.

The formidable rebellion which is now happily suppressed, and which attempted to justify itself by the doctrine of State sovereignty, has thrown, in many minds, new light on the subject, and led them to re-examine the historical facts in the case from a different point of view, to see if Mr. Calhoun's theory is not as unfounded as he had proved Mr. Webster's theory to be. The facts in the case really sustain neither, and both failed to see it: Mr. Calhoun because he had purposes to accomplish which demanded State sovereignty, and Mr. Webster because he examined them in the distorting medium of the theory or understanding of the statesmen of the eighteenth century. The civil war has vindicated the Union, and defeated the armed forces of the State sovereignty men; but it has not refuted their doctrine, and as far as it has had any effect, it has strengthened the tendency to consolidation or centralism.

But the philosophy, the theory of government, the understanding of the framers of the constitution, must be considered, if the expression will be allowed, as *obiter dicta*, and be judged on their merits. What binds is the thing done, not the theory on which it was done, or on which the actors explained their work either to themselves or to others. Their political philosophy, or their political theory, may sometimes affect the phraseology they adopt, but forms no rule for interpreting their work. Their work was inspired by and accords with the historical facts in the case, and is authorized and explained by them. The American people were not made one people by the written constitution, as Mr. Jefferson, Mr. Madison, Mr. Webster, and so many others supposed, but were made so by the unwritten constitution, born with and inherent in them.

XI

The Constitution
(continued)

*P*rovidence, or God operating through historical facts, constituted the American people one political or sovereign people, existing and acting in particular communities, organizations, called states. This one people organized as states, meet in convention, frame and ordain the constitution of government, or institute a general government in place of the Continental Congress; and the same people, in their respective State organizations, meet in convention in each State, and frame and ordain a particular government for the State individually, which, in union with the General government, constitutes the complete and supreme government within the States, as the General government, in union with all the particular governments, constitutes the complete and supreme government of the nation or whole country. This is clearly the view taken by Mr. Madison in his letter to Mr. Everett, when freed from his theory of the origin of government in compact.

The constitution of the people as one people, and the distinction at the same time of this one people into particular States, precedes the convention, and is the unwritten constitution, the Providential constitution, of the American people or civil society, as distinguished from the constitution of the government, which, whether general or particular, is the ordination of civil society itself. The unwritten constitution is the creation or constitution of the sovereign, and the sovereign providentially constituted constitutes in turn the government, which is not sovereign, but is clothed with just so much and just so little authority as the sovereign wills or ordains.

The sovereign in the republican order is the organic people, or state, and is with us the United States, for with us the organic people exist only as organized into States united, which in their union form one compact and indissoluble whole. That is to say, the organic American people do not exist as a consolidated people or state; they exist only as organized into distinct but inseparable States. Each State is a living member of the one body, and derives its life from its union with the body, so that the American state is one body with many members; and the members, instead of being simply individuals, are States, or individuals organized into States. The body consists of many members, and is one body, because the members are all members of it, and members one of another. It does not exist as separate or distinct from the members, but exists in their solidarity or membership one of another. There is no sovereign people or existence of the United States distinguishable from the people or existence of the particular States united. The people of the United States, the state called the United States, are the people of the particular States united. The solidarity of the members constitutes the unity of the body. The difference between this view and Mr. Madison's is, that while his view supposes the solidarity to be conventional, originating and existing in compact, or agreement, this supposes it to be real, living, and prior to the convention, as much the work of Providence as the existence in the human body of the living solidarity of its members. One law, one life, circulates through all the members, constituting them a living organism, binding them in living union, all to each and each to all.

Such is the sovereign people, and so far the original unwritten constitution. The sovereign, in order to live and act, must have an organ through which he expresses his will. This organ, under the American system, is primarily the Convention. The convention is the supreme political body, the concrete sovereign authority, and exercises practically the whole sovereign power of the people. The convention persists always, although not in permanent session. It can at any time be convened by the ordinary authority of the government, or, in its failure, by a *plebiscitum.*

Next follows the Government created and constituted by the convention. The government is constituted in such manner, and has such and only such powers, as the convention ordains. The government has, in the strict sense, no political authority under the American system, which separates the government from the convention. All political questions proper, such as the elective franchise, eligibility, the constitution of the several departments of government, as the legislative, the judicial, and the executive, changing, altering, or amending the constitution of government, enlarging or contracting its powers, in a word, all those questions that arise on which it is necessary to take the immediate orders of the sovereign, belong not to the government, but to the convention; and where the will of the sovereign is not sufficiently expressed in the constitution, a new appeal to the convention is necessary, and may always be had.

The constitution of Great Britain makes no distinction between the convention and the government. Theoretically the constitution of Great Britain is feudal, and there is, properly speaking, no British state; there are only the estates, king, lords, and commons, and these three estates constitute the Parliament, which is held to be omnipotent; that is, has the plenitude of political sovereignty. The British Parliament, composed of the three estates, possesses in itself all the powers of the convention in the American constitution, and is at once the convention and the government. The imperial constitution of France recognizes no convention, but clothes the senate with certain political functions, which, in some respects, subjects theoretically the sovereign to his creature. The emperor confessedly holds his power by the grace of God and the will of the nation, which is a clear acknowledgment that the sovereignty vests in the French people as the French state; but the imperial constitution, which is the constitution of the government, not of the state, studies, while acknowledging the sovereignty of the people, to render it nugatory, by transferring it, under various subtle disguises, to the government, and practically to the emperor as chief of the government. The senate, the council of state, the legislative body, and the emperor, are all creatures of the French state, and have properly no political functions, and to give them such functions is to place the sovereign under his own subjects! The real aim of the imperial constitution is to secure despotic power under the guise of republicanism. It leaves and is intended to leave the nation no way of practically asserting its sovereignty but by either a revolution or a *plebiscitum*, and a *plebiscitum* is permissible only where there is no regular government.

The British constitution is consistent with itself, but imposes no restriction on the power of the government. The French imperial constitution is illogical, inconsistent with itself as well as with the free action of the nation. The American constitution has all the advantages of both, and the disadvantages of neither. The convention is not the government like the British Parliament, nor a creature of the state like the French senate, but the sovereign state itself, in a practical form. By means of the convention the government is restricted to its delegated powers, and these, if found in practice either too great or too small, can be enlarged or contracted in a regular, orderly way, without resorting to a revolution or to a *plebiscitum*. Whatever political grievances there may be, there is always present the sovereign convention competent to redress them. The efficiency of power is thus secured without danger to liberty, and freedom without danger to power. The recognition of the convention, the real political sovereign of the country, and its separation from and independence of the ordinary government, is one of the most striking features of the American constitution.

The next thing to be noted, after the convention, is the constitution by the convention of the government. This constitution, as Mr. Madison well observes, divides the powers conceded by the convention to government between the General government and the particular State governments. Strictly speaking, the government is one, and its powers only are divided and exercised by two sets of agents or ministries. This division of the powers of government could never have been established by the convention if the American people had not been providentially constituted one people, existing and acting through particular State organizations. Here the unwritten constitution, or the constitution written in the people themselves, rendered practicable and dictated the written constitution, or constitution ordained by the convention and engrossed on parchment. It only expresses in the government the fact which pre-existed in the national organization and life.

This division of the powers of government is peculiar to the United States, and is an effective safeguard against both feudal disintegration and Roman centralism. Misled by their prejudices and peculiar interests, a portion of the people of the United States, pleading in their justification the theory of State sovereignty, attempted disintegration, secession, and national independence separate from that of the United States, but the central force of the constitution was too strong for them to succeed. The unity of the nation was too strong to be effectually broken. No doubt the reaction against secession and disintegration will strengthen the tendency to centralism, but centralism can succeed no better than disintegration has succeeded, because the General government has no *subsistentia*, no *suppositum*, to borrow a theological term, outside or independent of the States. The particular governments are stronger, if there be any difference, to protect the States against centralism than the General government is to protect the Union against disintegration; and after swinging for a time too far toward one extreme and then too far toward the other, the public mind will recover its equilibrium, and the government move on in its constitutional path.

Republican Rome attempted to guard against excessive centralism by the tribunitial veto, or by the organization of a negative or obstructive power. Mr. Calhoun thought this admirable, and wished to effect the same end here, where it is secured by other, more effective, and less objectionable means, by a State veto on the acts of Congress, by a dual executive, and by substituting concurrent for numerical majorities. Imperial Rome gradually swept away the tribunitial veto, concentrated all power in the hands of the emperor, became completely centralized, and fell. The British constitution seeks the same end by substituting estates for the state, and establishing a mixed government, in which monarchy, aristocracy, and democracy temper, check, or balance each other; but practically the commons estate has become supreme, and the nobility govern not in the house of lords, and can really influence public affairs only through the house of commons. The principle of the British constitution is not the division of the powers of government, but the antagonism of estates, or rather of interests, trusting to the obstructive influence of that antagonism to preserve the government from pure centralism. Hence the study of the British statesman is to manage diverse and antagonistic parties and interests so as to gain the ability to act, which he can do only by intrigue, cajolery, bribery in one form or another, and corruption of every sort. The British government cannot be carried on by fair, honest, and honorable means, any more than could the Roman under the antagonism created by the tribunitial veto. The French tried the English system of organized antagonism in 1789, as a cure for the centralism introduced by Richelieu and Louis XIV., and again under the Restoration and Louis Philippe, and called it the system of constitutional guarantees; but they could never manage it, and they have taken refuge in unmitigated centralism under Napoleon III., who, however well disposed, finds no means in the constitution of the French nation of tempering it. The English system, called the constitutional, and sometimes the parliamentary system, will not work in France, and indeed works really well nowhere.

The American system, sometimes called the Federal system, is not founded on antagonism of classes, estates, or interests, and is in no sense a system of checks and balances. It needs and tolerates no obstructive forces. It does not pit section against section, the States severally against the General government, nor the General government against the State governments, and nothing is more hurtful than the attempt to explain it and work it on the principles of British constitutionalism. The convention created no antagonistic powers; it simply divided the powers of government, and gave neither to the General government nor to the State governments all the powers of government, nor in any instance did it give to the two governments jurisdiction in the same matters. Hence each has its own sphere, in which it can move on without colliding with that of the other. Each is independent and complete in relation to its own work, incomplete and dependent on the other for the complete work of government.

The division of power is not between a *national* government and State governments, but between a *General* government and particular governments. The General government, inasmuch as it extends to matters common to all the States, is usually called the Government of the United States, and sometimes the Federal government, to distinguish it from the particular or State governments, but without strict propriety; for the government of the United States, or the Federal government, means, in strictness, both the General government and the particular governments, since neither is in itself the complete government of the country. The General government has authority within each of the States, and each of the State governments has authority in the Union. The line between the Union and the States severally, is not precisely the line between the General government and the particular governments. As, for instance, the General government lays direct taxes on the people of the States, and collects internal revenue within them; and the citizens of a particular State, and none others, are electors of President and Vice-President of the United States, and representatives in the lower house of Congress, while senators in Congress are elected by the State legislatures themselves.

The line that distinguishes the two governments is that which distinguishes the general relations and interests from the particular relations and interests of the people of the United States. These general relations and interests are placed under the General government, which, because its jurisdiction is coextensive with the Union, is called the Government of the United States; the particular relations and interests are placed under particular governments, which, because their jurisdiction is only coextensive with the States respectively, are called State governments. The General government governs supremely all the people of the United States and Territories belonging to the Union, in all their general relations and interests, or relations and interests common alike to them all; the particular or State government governs supremely the people of a particular State, as Massachusetts, New York, or New Jersey, in all that pertains to their particular or private rights, relations, and interests. The powers of each are equally sovereign, and neither are derived from the other. The State governments are not subordinate to the General government, nor the General government to the State governments. They are co-ordinate governments, each standing on the same level, and deriving its powers from the same sovereign authority. In their respective spheres neither yields to the other. In relation to the matters within its jurisdiction, each gov-

ernment is independent and supreme in regard of the other, and subject only to the convention.

The powers of the General government are the power—

To lay and collect taxes, duties, imposts, and excises, to pay the
debts and provide for the general welfare of the United States; to
borrow money on the credit of the United States; to regulate commerce with foreign nations, among the several States, and with the
Indian tribes; to establish a uniform rule of naturalization, and uniform laws on the subject of bankruptcies throughout the United States;
to coin money and regulate the value thereof, and fix the standard of
weights and measures; to provide for the punishment of counterfeit-
ing the securities and current coin of the United States; to establish
post-offices and post-roads; to promote the progress of science and of
the useful arts, by securing for limited times to authors and inventors
the exclusive right to their respective writings and discoveries; to define and punish piracies and felonies committed on the high seas, and
offences against the law of nations; to declare war, grant letters of
marque and reprisal, and make rules concerning captures on land and
water; to raise and support armies; to provide and maintain a navy; to
make rules for the government of the land and naval forces; to provide for calling forth the militia to execute the laws of the Union,
suppress insurrections, and repel invasions; to provide for organizing,
arming, and disciplining the militia, and of governing such part of
them as may be employed in the service of the United States; to exercise exclusive legislation in all cases whatsoever over such district,
not exceeding ten miles square, as may by cession of particular States
and the acceptance of Congress, become the seat of the government
of the United States, and to exercise a like authority over all places
purchased by the consent of the legislature of the State in which the
same shall be, for the erection of forts, magazines, arsenals, dock-yards,
and other needful buildings; and to make all laws which shall be nec-

essary and proper for carrying into execution the foregoing powers, and all other powers vested by this constitution in the government of the United States, or in any department or office thereof.

In addition to these, the General government is clothed with the treaty-making power, and the whole charge of the foreign relations of the country; with power to admit new States into the Union; to dispose of and make all needful rules and regulations concerning the territory and all other property belonging to the United States; to declare, with certain restrictions, the punishment of treason, the constitution itself defining what is treason against the United States; and to propose, or to call, on the application of the legislatures of two-thirds of all the states, a convention for proposing amendments to this constitution; and is vested with supreme judicial power, original or appellate, in all cases of law and equity arising under this constitution, the laws of the United States, and treaties made or to be made under their authority, in all cases affecting ambassadors, other public ministers, and consuls, in all cases of admiralty and maritime jurisdiction, in all controversies to which the United States shall be a party, all controversies between two or more States, between a State and citizens of another State, between citizens of different States, between citizens of the same State claiming lands under grants of different States, and between a State or the citizens thereof and foreign states, citizens, or subjects.

These, with what is incidental to them, and what is necessary and proper to carry them into effect, are all the positive powers with which the convention vests the General government, or government of the United States, as distinguished from the governments of the particular States; and these, with the exception of what relates to the district in which it has its seat, and places of forts, magazines, &c., are of a general nature, and restricted to the common relations and interests of the people, or at least to interests and relations which extend beyond the limits of a particular State. They are all powers that regard matters which extend beyond not only the individual citizen, but the individual State, and affect alike the relations and interests of all the States, or matters which cannot be disposed of by a State government without the exercise of extra-territorial jurisdiction. They give the government no jurisdiction of questions which affect individuals or citizens only in their private and domestic relations which lie wholly within a particular State. The General government does not legislate concerning private rights, whether of persons or things, the tenure of real estate, marriage, dower, inheritance, wills, the transferrence or transmission of property, real or personal; it can charter no private corporations, out of the District of Columbia, for business, literary, scientific, or eleemosynary purposes, establish no schools, found no colleges or universities, and promote science and the useful arts only by securing to authors and inventors for a time the exclusive right to their writings and discoveries. The United States Bank was manifestly unconstitutional, as probably are the present so-called national banks. The United States Bank was a private or particular corporation, and the present national banks are only corporations of the same sort, though organized under a general law. The pretence that they are established to supply a national currency does not save their constitutionality, for the convention has not given the General government the power nor imposed on it the duty of furnishing a national currency. To coin money, and regulate the value thereof, is something very different from authorizing private companies to issue bank notes, on the basis of the public stocks held as private property, or even on what is called a specie basis. To claim the power under the general welfare clause would be a simple mockery of good sense. It is no more for the general welfare than any other successful private business. The private welfare of each is, no doubt, for the welfare of all, but not therefore is it the "general welfare," for what is private, particular in its nature, is not and cannot be general. To understand by general welfare that which is for the individual welfare of all or the greater number, would be to claim for the General government all the powers of government, and to deny that very division of powers which is the crowning merit of the American system. The general welfare, by the very force of the words themselves, means the common as distinguished from the private or individual welfare. The system of national banks may or may not be a good and desirable system, but it is difficult to understand the constitutional power of the General government to establish it.

On the ground that its powers are general, not particular, the General government has no power to lay a protective tariff. It can lay a tariff for revenue, not for protection of home manufactures or home industry; for the interests fostered, even though indirectly advantageous to the whole people, are in their nature private or particular, not general interests, and chiefly interests of private corporations and capitalists. Their incidental or even consequential effects do not change their direct and essential nature. So with domestic slavery. Slavery comes under the head of private rights, whether regarded on the side of the master or on the side of the slave. The right of a citizen to hold a slave, if a right at all, is the private right of property, and the right of the slave to his freedom is a private and personal right, and neither is placed under the safeguard of the General government, which has nowhere, unless in the District of Columbia and the places over which it has exclusive legislative power in all cases whatsoever, either the right to establish it or to abolish it, except perhaps under the war power, as a military necessity, an indemnity for the past, or a security for the future.

This applies to what are called Territories as well as to the States. The right of the government to govern the Territories in regard to private and particular rights and interests, is derived from no express grant of power, and is held only *ex necessitate*—the United States owning the domain, and there being no other authority competent to govern them. But, as in the case of all powers held *ex necessitate*, the power is restricted to the absolute necessity in the case. What are called Territorial governments, to distinguish them from the State governments, are only provisional governments, and can touch private rights and interests no further than is necessary to preserve order and prepare the way for the organization and installation of a regular State government. Till then the law governing private rights is the law that was in force, if any such there was, when the territory became by purchase, by conquest, or by treaty, attached to the domain of the United States.

Hence the Supreme Court declared unconstitutional the ordinance of 1787, prohibiting slavery in what was called the Territory of the Northwest, and the so-called Missouri Compromise, prohibiting slavery north of the parallel 36° 30¢. The Wilmot proviso was for the same reason unconstitutional. The General government never had and has not any power to exclude slavery from the Territories, any more than to abolish it in the States. But slavery being a local institution, sustained neither by the law of nature nor the law of nations, no citizen migrating from a slave State could carry his slaves with him, and hold them as slaves in the Territory. Rights enacted by local law are rights only in that locality, and slaves carried by their masters into a slave State even, are free, unless the State into which they are carried enacts to the contrary. The only persons that could be held as slaves in a Territory would be those who were slaves or the children of those who were slaves in the Territory when it passed to the United States. The whole controversy on slavery in the Territories, and which culminated in the civil war, was wholly unnecessary, and never could have occurred had the constitution been properly understood and adhered to by both sides. True, Congress could not exclude slavery from the Territory, but neither could citizens migrating to them hold slaves in them; and so really slavery was virtually excluded, for the inhabitants in nearly all of them, not emigrants from the States after the cession to the United States, were too few to be counted.

The General government has power to establish a uniform rule of naturalization, to which all the States must conform, and it was very proper that it should have this power, so as to prevent one State from gaining by its naturalization laws an undue advantage over another; but the General government has itself no power to naturalize a single foreigner, or in any case to say who shall or who shall not be citizens, either of a State or of the United States, or to declare who may or may not be electors even of its own officers. The convention ordains that members of the house of representatives shall be chosen by electors who have the qualifications requisite for electors of the most numerous branch of the State legislature, but the State determines these qualifications, and who do or do not possess them; that the senators shall be chosen by the State legislatures, and that the electors of President and Vice-President shall be appointed in such manner as the respective State legislatures may direct. The whole question of citizenship, what shall or shall not be the qualifications of electors, who shall or shall not be freemen, is reserved to the States, as coming under the head of personal or private rights and franchises. In practice, the exact line of demarcation may not always have been strictly observed either by the General government or by the State governments; but a careful study of the constitution cannot fail to show that the division of powers is the division or distinction between the public and general relations and interests, rights and duties of the people, and their private and particular relations and interests, rights and duties. As these two classes of relations and interests, rights and duties, though distinguishable, are really inseparable in nature, it follows that the two governments are essential to the existence of a complete government, or to the existence of a real government in its plenitude and integrity. Left to either alone, the people would have only an incomplete, an initial, or inchoate government. The General government is the complement of the State governments, and the State governments are the complement of the General government.

The consideration of the powers denied by the convention to the General government and to the State governments respectively, will lead to the same conclusion. To the General government is denied expressly or by necessary implication all jurisdiction in matters of private rights and interests, and to the State government is denied all jurisdiction in rights or interests which extend, as has been said, beyond the boundaries of the State. "No State shall enter into any treaty, alliance, or confederation; grant letters of marque and reprisal; coin money, emit bills of credit, make any thing but gold and silver coin a tender in the payment of debts; pass any bill of attainder, *ex post facto* law, or law impairing the obligation of contracts, or grant any title of nobility. No State shall, without the consent of Congress, lay any imposts or duties on imports or exports, except what may be absolutely necessary for executing its inspection laws, and the net produce of all duties and imposts laid by any State on imports and exports shall be for the use of the treasury of the United States, and all such laws shall be subject to the revision and control of Congress. No State shall, without the consent of Congress, lay any duty of tonnage, keep troops or ships-of-war in time of peace, enter into any agreement or compact with another State or with a foreign power, or engage in war, unless actually invaded, or in such imminent danger as will not admit of delay."

The powers denied to the States in some matters which are rather private and particular, such as bills of attainder, *ex post facto* laws, laws impairing the obligation of contracts, granting titles of nobility, are denied equally to the General government. There is evidently a profound logic in the constitution, and there is not a single provision in it that is arbitrary, or anomalous, or that does not harmonize dialectically with the whole, and with the real constitution of the American people. At first sight the reservation to the State of the appointment of the officers of the militia might seem an anomaly; but as the whole subject of internal police belongs to the State, it should have some military force at its command. The subject of bankruptcies, also, might seem to be more properly within the province of the State, and so it would be if commerce between the several States had not been placed under Congress, or if trade were confined to the citizens of the State and within its boundaries; but as such is not the case, it was necessary to place it under the General government, in order that laws on the subject might be uniform throughout the Union, and that the citizens of all the States, and foreigners trading with them, should be placed on an equal footing, and have the same remedies. The subject follows naturally in the train of commerce, for bankruptcies, as understood at the time, were confined to the mercantile class, bankers, and brokers; and since the regulation of commerce, foreign and inter-state, was to be placed under the sole charge of the General government, it was necessary that bankruptcy should be included. The subject of patents is placed under the General government, though the patent is a private right, because it was the will of the convention that the patent should be good in all the States, as affording more encouragement to science and the useful arts than if good only within a single State, or if the power were left to each State to recognize or not patents granted by another. The right created, though private in its nature, is yet general or common to all the States in its enjoyment or exercise.

The division of the powers of government between a General government and particular governments, rendered possible and practicable by the original constitution of the people themselves, as one people existing and acting through State organizations, is the American method of guarding against the undue centralism to which Roman imperialism inevitably tends; and it is far simpler and more effective than any of the

European systems of mixed governments, which seek their end by organizing an antagonism of interests or classes. The American method demands no such antagonism, no neutralizing of one social force by another, but avails itself of all the forces of society, organizes them dialectically, not antagonistically, and thus protects with equal efficiency both public authority and private rights. The General government can never oppress the people as individuals, or abridge their private rights or personal freedom and independence, because these are not within its jurisdiction, but are placed in charge, within each State, of the State government, which, within its sphere, governs as supremely as the General government: the State governments cannot weaken the public authority of the nation or oppress the people in their general rights and interests, for these are withdrawn from State jurisdiction, and placed under charge of a General government, which, in its sphere, governs as supremely as the State government. There is no resort to a system of checks and balances; there is no restraint on power, and no systematic distrust of power, but simply a division of powers between two co-ordinate governments, distinct but inseparable, moving in distinct spheres, but in the same direction, or to a common end. The system is no invention of man, is no creation of the convention, but is given us by Providence in the living constitution of the American people. The merit of the statesmen of 1787 is that they did not destroy or deface the work of Providence, but accepted it, and organized the government in harmony with the real order, the real elements given them. They suffered themselves in all their positive substantial work to be governed by reality, not by theories and speculations. In this they proved themselves statesmen, and their work survives; and the republic, laugh as sciolists may, is, for the present and future, the model republic—as much so as was Rome in her day; and it is not simply national pride nor American self-conceit that pronounces its establishment the beginning of a new and more advanced order of civilization; such is really the fact.

The only apparently weak point in the system is in the particular States themselves. Feudalism protected the feudal aristocracy effectively for a time against both the king and the people, but left the king and the people without protection against the aristocracy, and hence it fell. It was not adequate to the wants of civil society, did not harmonize all social elements, and protect all social and individual rights and interests, and therefore could not but fail. The General government takes care of public authority and rights; the State protects private rights and personal freedom as against the General government: but what protects the citizens in their private rights, their personal freedom and independence, against the particular State government? Universal suffrage, answers the democrat. Armed with the ballot, more powerful than the sword, each citizen is able to protect himself. But this is theory, not reality. If it were true, the division of the powers of government between two co-ordinate governments would be of no practical importance. Experience does not sustain the theory, and the power of the ballot to protect the individual may be rendered ineffective by the tyranny of party. Experience proves that the ballot is far less effective in securing the freedom and independence of the individual citizen than is commonly pretended. The ballot of an isolated individual counts for nothing. The individual, though armed with the ballot, is as powerless, if he stands alone, as if he had it not. To render it of any avail he must associate himself with a party, and look for his success in the success of his party; and to secure the success of his party, he must give up to it his own private convictions and free will. In practice, individuals are nothing individually, and parties are every thing. Even the suppression of the late rebellion, and the support of the Administration in doing it, was made a party question, and the government found the leaders of the party opposed to the Republican party an obstacle hardly less difficult to surmount than the chiefs of the armies of the so-called Confederate States.

Parties are formed, one hardly knows how, and controlled, no one knows by whom; but usually by demagogues, men who have some private or personal purposes, for which they wish, through party, to use the government. Parties have no conscience, no responsibility, and their very reason of being is, the usurpation and concentration of power. The real practical tendency of universal suffrage is to democratic, instead of an imperial, centralism. What is to guard against this centralism? Not universal suffrage, for that tends to create it; and if the government is left to it, the government becomes practically the will of an evershifting and irresponsible majority. Is the remedy in written or paper constitutions? Party can break through them, and by making the judges elective by party, for short terms, and re-eligible, can do so with impunity. In several of the States, the dominant majority have gained the power to govern at will, without any let or hindrance. Besides, constitutions can be altered, and have been altered, very nearly at the will of the majority. No mere paper constitutions are any protection against the usurpations of party, for party will always grasp all the power it can.

Yet the evil is not so great as it seems, for in most of the States the principle of division of powers is carried into the bosom of the State itself; in some States further than in others, but in all it obtains to some extent. In what are called the New England States, the best-governed portion of the Union, each town is a corporation, having important powers and the charge of all purely local matters—chooses its own officers, manages its own finances, takes charge of its own poor, of its own roads and bridges, and of the education of its own children. Between these corporations and the State government are the counties, that take charge of another class of interests, more general than those under the charge of the town, but less general than those of the State. In the great central and Northwestern States the same system obtains, though less completely carried out. In the Southern and Southwestern States, the town corporations hardly exist, and the rights and interests of the poorer classes of persons have been less well protected in them than in the Northern and Eastern States. But with the abolition of slavery, and the lessening of the influence of the wealthy slaveholding class, with the return of peace and the revival of agricultural, industrial, and commercial prosperity, the New England system, in its main features, is pretty sure to be gradually introduced, or developed, and the division of powers in the State to be as effectively and as systematically carried out as it is between the General government and the particular or State governments. So, though universal suffrage, good as far as it goes, is not alone sufficient, the division of powers affords with it a not inadequate protection.

No government, whose workings are intrusted to men, ever is or can be practically perfect—secure all good, and guard against all evil. In all human governments there will be defects and abuses, and he is no wise man who expects perfection from imperfection. But the American constitution, taken as a whole, and in all its parts, is the least imperfect that has ever existed, and under it individual rights, personal freedom and independence, as well as public authority or society, are better protected than under any other; and as the few barbaric elements retained from the feudal ages are eliminated, the standard of education elevated, and the whole population Americanized, moulded by and to the American system, it will be found to effect all the good, with as little of the evil, as can be reasonably expected from any possible civil government or political constitution of society.

XII

Secession

$\mathscr{T}$he doctrine that a State has a right to secede and carry with it its population and domain, has been effectually put down, and the unity and integrity of the United States as a sovereign nation have been effectively asserted on the battle-field; but the secessionists, though disposed to submit to superior force, and demean themselves henceforth as loyal citizens, most likely hold as firmly to the doctrine as before finding themselves unable to reduce it to practice, and the Union victory will remain incomplete till they are convinced in their understandings that the Union has the better reason as well as the superior military resources. The nation has conquered their bodies, but it is hardly less important for our Statesmen to conquer their minds and win their hearts.

The right of secession is not claimed as a revolutionary right, or even as a conventional right. The secessionists disclaim revolutionary principles, and hold that the right of secession is anterior to the convention, a right which the convention could neither give nor take away, because inherent in the very conception of a sovereign State. Secession is simply the repeal by the State of the act of accession to the Union; and as that act was a free, voluntary act of the State, she must always be free to repeal it. The Union is a copartnership; a State in the Union is simply a member of the firm, and has the right to withdraw when it judges it for its interest to do so. There is no power in a firm to compel a copartner to remain a member any longer than he pleases. He is undoubtedly holden for the obligations contracted by the firm while he remains a member; but for none contracted after he has withdrawn and given due notice thereof.

So of a sovereign State in the Union. The Union itself, apart from the sovereign States that compose it, is a mere abstraction, a nullity, and binds nobody. All its substance and vitality are in the agreement by which the States constitute themselves a firm or copartnership, for certain specific purposes, and for which they open an office and establish an agency under express instructions for the management of the general affairs of the firm. The State is held jointly and severally for all the legal obligations of the Union, contracted while she is in it, but no further; and is free to withdraw when she pleases, precisely as an individual may withdraw from an ordinary business firm. The remaining copartners have no right of compulsion or coercion against the seceding member, for he, saving the obligations already contracted, is as free to withdraw as they are to remain.

The population is fixed to the domain, and goes with it; the domain is attached to the State, and secedes in the secession of the State. Secession, then, carries the entire State, government, people, and domain, out of the Union, and restores *ipso facto* the State to its original position of a sovereign State, foreign to the United States. Being an independent sovereign State, she may enter into a new confederacy, form a new copartnership, or merge herself in some other foreign state, as she judges proper or finds opportunity. The States that seceded formed among themselves a new confederacy, more to their mind than the one formed in 1787, as they had a perfect right to do, and in the war just ended they were not rebels nor revolutionists, but a people fighting for the right of self-government, loyal citizens and true patriots defending the independence and inviolability of their country against foreign invaders. They are to be honored for their loyalty and patriotism, and not branded as rebels and punished as traitors.

This is the secession argument, which rests on no assumption of revolutionary principles or abstract rights of man, and on no allegation of real or imaginary wrongs received from the Union, but simply on the original and inherent rights of the several States as independent sovereign States. The argument is conclusive, and the defence complete, if the Union is only a firm or copartnership, and the sovereignty vests in the States severally. The refutation of the secessionists is in the facts adduced that disprove the theory of State sovereignty, and prove that the sovereignty vests not in the States severally, but in the States united, or that the Union is sovereign, and not the States individually. The Union is not a firm, a copartnership, nor an artificial or conventional union, but a real, living, constitutional union, founded in the original and indissoluble unity of the American people, as one sovereign people. There is, indeed, no such people, if we abstract the States, but there are no States if we abstract this sovereign people or the Union. There is no Union without the States, and there are no States without the Union. The people are born States, and the States are born United States. The Union and the States are simultaneous, born together, and enter alike into the original and essential constitution of the American state. This the facts and reasonings adduced fully establish.

But this one sovereign people that exists only as organized into States, does not necessarily include the whole population or territory included within the jurisdiction of the United States. It is restricted to the people and territory or domain organized into States in the Union, as in ancient Rome the ruling people were restricted to the tenants of the sacred territory, which had been surveyed, and its boundaries marked by the god Terminus, and which by no means included all the territory held by the city, and of which she was both the private proprietor and the public sovereign. The city had vast possessions acquired by confiscation, by purchase, by treaty, or by conquest, and in reference to which her celebrated agrarian laws were enacted, and which have their counterpart in our homestead and kindred laws. In this class of territory, of which the city was the private owner, was the territory of all the Roman provinces, which was held to be only leased to its occupants, who were often dispossessed, and their lands given as a recompense by the consul or imperator to his disbanded legionaries. The provincials were subjects of Rome, but formed no part of the Roman people, and had no share in the political power of the state, till at a late period the privileges of Roman citizens were extended to them, and the Roman people became coextensive with the Roman empire. So the United States have held and still hold large territorial possessions, acquired by the acknowledgment of their independence by Great Britain, the former sovereign, the cession of particular states, and purchase from France, Spain, and Mexico. Till erected into States and admitted into the Union, this territory, with its population, though subject to the United States, makes no part of the political or sovereign territory and people of the United States. It is *under* the Union, not *in* it, as is indicated by the phrase admitting *into* the Union—a legal phrase, since the constitution ordains that "new States may be *admitted* by the Congress *into* this Union."

There can be no secession that separates a State from the national domain, and withdraws it from the territorial sovereignty or jurisdiction of the United States; yet what hinders a State from going out of the Union in the sense that it comes into it, and thus ceasing to belong to the *political* people of the United States?

If the view of the constitution taken in the preceding chapters be correct, and certainly no facts tend to disprove it, the accession of a Territory as a State in the Union is a free act of the territorial people. The Territory cannot organize and apply for admission as a State, without what is called an "enabling act" of Congress or its equivalent; but that act is permissive, not mandatory, and nothing obliges the Territory to organize under it and apply for admission. It may do so or not, as it chooses. What, then, hinders the State once in the Union from going out or returning to its former condition of territory subject to the Union? The original States did not need to come in under an enabling act, for they were born States in the Union, and were never territory outside of the Union and subject to it. But they and the new States, adopted or naturalized States, once in the Union, stand on a footing of perfect equality, and the original States are no more and no less bound than they to remain States in the Union. The ratification of the constitution by the original States was a free act, as much so as the accession of a new State formed from territory subject to the Union is a free act, and a free act is an act which one is free to do or not to do, as he pleases. What a State is free to do or not to do, it is free to undo, if it chooses. There is nothing in either the State constitution or in that of the United States that forbids it.

This is denied. The population and domain are inseparable in the State; and if the State could take itself out of the Union, it would take them out, and be *ipso facto* a sovereign State foreign to the Union. It would take the domain and the population out of the Union, it is conceded and even maintained, but not therefore would it take them out of the jurisdiction of the Union, or would they exist as a State foreign to the Union; for population and territory may coexist, as Dacota, Colorado, or New Mexico, out of the Union, and yet be subject to the Union, or within the jurisdiction of the United States.

But the Union is formed by the surrender by each of the States of its individual sovereignty, and each State by its admission into the Union surrenders its individual sovereignty, or binds itself by a constitutional compact to merge its individual sovereignty in that of the whole. It then cannot cease to be a State in the Union without breach of contract. Having surrendered its sovereignty to the Union, or bound itself by the constitution to exercise its original sovereignty only as one of the United States, it can unmake itself of its state character, only by consent of the United States, or by a successful revolution. It is by virtue of this fact that secession is rebellion against the United States, and that the General government, as representing the Union, has the right and the duty to suppress it by all the forces at its command.

There can be no rebellion where there is no allegiance. The States in the Union cannot owe allegiance to the Union, for they are it, and for any one to go out of it is no more an act of rebellion than it is for a king to abdicate his throne. The Union is not formed by the surrender to it by the several States of their respective individual sovereignty. Such surrender could, as we have seen, form only an alliance, or a confederation, not one sovereign people; and from an alliance, or confederation, the ally or confederate has, saving its faith, the inherent right to secede. The argument assumes that the States were originally each in its individuality a sovereign state, but by the convention which framed the constitution, each surrendered its sovereignty to the whole, and thus several sovereign states became one sovereign political people, governing in general matters through the General government, and in particular matters through particular or State governments. This is Mr. Madison's theory, and also Mr. Webster's; but it has been refuted in the refutation of the theory that makes government originate in compact. A sovereign state can, undoubtedly, surrender its sovereignty, but can surrender it only to something or somebody that really exists; for to surrender to no one or to nothing is, as has been shown, the same thing as not to surrender at all; and the Union, being formed only by the surrender, is nothing prior to it, or till after it is made, and therefore can be no recipient of the surrender.

Besides, the theory is the reverse of the fact. The State does not surrender or part with its sovereignty by coming into the Union, but acquires by it all the rights it holds as a State. Between the original

States and the new States there is a difference of mode by which they become States in the Union, but none in their powers, or the tenure by which they hold them. The process by which new States are actually formed and admitted into the Union, discloses at once what it is that is gained or lost by admission. The domain and population, before the organization of the Territory into one of the United States, are subject to the United States, inseparably attached to the domain of the Union, and under its sovereignty. The Territory so remains, organized or unorganized, under a Territorial government created by Congress. Congress, by an enabling act, permits it to organize as a State, to call a convention to form a State constitution, to elect under it, in such way as the convention ordains, State officers, a State legislature, and, in the way prescribed by the Constitution of the United States, senators and representatives in Congress. Here is a complete organization as a State, yet, though called a State, it is no State at all, and is simply territory, without a single particle of political power. To be a State it must be recognized and admitted by Congress as a State in the Union, and when so recognized and admitted it possesses, in union with the other United States, supreme political sovereignty, jointly in all general matters, and individually in all private and particular matters.

The Territory gives up no sovereign powers by coming into the Union, for before it came into the Union it had no sovereignty, no political rights at all. All the rights and powers it holds are held by the simple fact that it has become a State in the Union. This is as true of the original States as of the new States; for it has been shown in the chapter on *The United States*, that the original British sovereignty under which the colonies were organized and existed passed, on the fact of independence, to the States united, and not to the States severally. Hence if nine States had ratified the constitution, and the other four had stood out, and refused to do it, which was within their competency, they would not have been independent sovereign States, outside of the Union, but Territories under the Union.

Texas forms the only exception to the rule that the States have never been independent of the Union. All the other new States have been formed from territory subject to the Union. This is true of all the States formed out of the Territory of the Northwest, and out of the domain ceded by France, Spain, and Mexico to the United States. All these cessions were held by the United States as territory immediately subject to the Union, before being erected into States; and by far the larger part is so held even yet. But Texas was an independent foreign state, and was annexed as a State without having been first subjected as territory to the United States. It of course lost by annexation its separate sovereignty. But this annexation was held by many to be unconstitutional; it was made when the State sovereignty theory had gained possession of the Government, and was annexed as a State instead of being admitted as a State formed from territory belonging to the United States, for the very purpose of committing the nation to that theory. Its annexation was the prologue, as the Mexican war was the first act in the secession drama, and as the epilogue is the suppression of the rebellion on Texan soil. Texas is an exceptional case, and forms no precedent, and cannot be adduced as invalidating the general rule. Omitting Texas, the simple fact is, the States acquire all their sovereign powers by being States in the Union, instead of losing or surrendering them.

Our American statesmen have overlooked or not duly weighed the facts in the case, because, holding the origin of government in compact, they felt no need of looking back of the constitution to find the basis of that unity of the American people which they assert. Neither Mr. Madison nor Mr. Webster felt any difficulty in asserting it as created by the convention of 1787, or in conceding the sovereignty of the States prior to the Union, and denying its existence after the ratification of the constitution. If it were not that they held that the State originates in convention or the social compact, there would be unpardonable presumption on the part of the present writer in venturing to hazard an assertion contrary to theirs. But, if their theory was unsound, their practical doctrine was not; for they maintained that the American people are one sovereign people, and Mr. Quincy Adams, an authority inferior to neither, maintained that they were always one people, and that the States hold from the Union, not the Union from the States. The States without the Union cease to exist as political communities: the Union without the States ceases to be a Union, and becomes a vast centralized and consolidated state, ready to lapse from a civilized into a barbaric, from a republican to a despotic nation.

The State, under the American system, as distinguished from Territory, is not in the domain and population fixed to it, nor yet in its exterior organization, but solely in the political powers, rights, and franchises which it holds from the United States, or as one of the United States. As these are rights, not obligations, the State may resign or abdicate them and cease to be a State, on the same principle that any man may abdicate or forego his rights. In doing so, the State breaks no oath of allegiance, fails to fulfil no obligation she contracted as a State: she simply forgoes her political rights and franchises. So far, then, secession is possible, feasible, and not unconstitutional or unlawful. But it is, as Mr. Sumner and others have maintained, simply State suicide. Nothing hinders a State from committing suicide, if she chooses, any more than there was something which compelled the Territory to become a State in the Union against its will.

It is objected to this conclusion that the States were, prior to the Union, independent sovereign States, and secession would not destroy the State, but restore it to its original sovereignty and independence, as the secessionists maintain. Certainly, if the States were, prior to the Union, sovereign States; but this is precisely what has been denied and disproved; for prior to the Union there were no States. Secession restores, or reduces, rather, the State to the condition it was in before its admission into the Union; but that condition is that of Territory, or a

Territory subject to the United States, and not that of an independent sovereign state. The State holds all its political rights and powers in the Union from the Union, and has none out of it, or in the condition in which its population and domain were before being a State in the Union.

State suicide, it has been urged, releases its population and territory from their allegiance to the Union, and as there is no rebellion where there is no allegiance, resistance by its population and territory to the Union, even war against the Union, would not be rebellion, but the simple assertion of popular sovereignty. This is only the same objection in another form. The lapse of the State releases the population and territory from no allegiance to the Union; for their allegiance to the Union was not contracted by their becoming a State, and they have never in their State character owed allegiance to the United States. A State owes no allegiance to the United States, for it is one of them, and is jointly sovereign. The relation between the United States and the State is not the relation of suzerain and liegeman or vassal. A State owes no allegiance, for it is not subject to the Union; it is never in their State capacity that its population and territory do or can rebel. Hence, the Government has steadily denied that, in the late rebellion, any State as such rebelled.

But as a State cannot rebel, no State can go out of the Union; and therefore no State in the late rebellion has seceded, and the States that passed secession ordinances are and all along have been States in the Union. No State can rebel, but it does not follow therefrom that no State can secede or cease to exist as a State; it only follows that secession, in the sense of State suicide, or the abdication by the State of its political rights and powers, is not rebellion. Nor does it follow from the fact that no State has rebelled, that no State has ceased to be a State; or that the States that passed secession ordinances have been all along States in the Union.

The secession ordinances were illegal, unconstitutional, not within the competency of the State, and therefore null and void from the beginning. Unconstitutional, illegal, and not within the competency of the State, so far as intended to alienate any portion of the national domain and population thereto annexed, they certainly were, and so far were void and of no effect; but so far as intended to take the State simply as a State out of the Union, they were within the competency of the State, were not illegal or unconstitutional, and therefore not null and void. Acts unconstitutional in some parts and constitutional in others are not wholly void. The unconstitutionality vitiates only the unconstitutional parts; the others are valid, are law, and recognized and enforced as such by the courts.

The secession ordinances are void, because they were never passed by the people of the State, but by a faction that overawed them and usurped the authority of the State. This argument implies that, if a secession ordinance is passed by the people proper of the State, it is valid; which is more than they who urge it against the State suicide doctrine are prepared to concede. But the secession ordinances were in every instance passed by the people of the State in convention legally assembled, therefore by them in their highest State capacity—in the same capacity in which they ordain and ratify the State constitution itself; and in nearly all the States they were in addition ratified and confirmed, if the facts have been correctly reported, by a genuine plebiscitum, or direct vote of the people. In all cases they were adopted by a decided majority of the political people of the State, and after their adoption they were acquiesced in and indeed actively supported by very nearly the whole people. The people of the States adopting the secession ordinances were far more unanimous in supporting secession than the people of the other States were in sustaining the Government in its efforts to suppress the rebellion by coercive measures. It will not do, then, to ascribe the secession ordinances to a faction. The people are never a faction, nor is a faction ever the majority.

There has been a disposition at the North, encouraged by the few Union men at the South, to regard secession as the work of a few ambitious and unprincipled leaders, who, by their threats, their violence, and their overbearing manner, forced the mass of the people of their respective States into secession, against their convictions and their will. No doubt there were leaders at the South, as there are in every great movement at the North; no doubt there were individuals in the seceding States that held secession wrong in principle, and were conscientiously attached to the Union; no doubt, also, there were men who adhered to the Union, not because they disapproved secession, but because they disliked the men at the head of the movement, or because they were keen-sighted enough to see that it could not succeed, that the Union must be the winning side, and that by adhering to it they would become the great and leading men of their respective States, which they certainly could not be under secession. Others sympathized fully with what was called the Southern cause, held firmly the right of secession, and hated cordially the Yankees, but doubted either the practicability or the expediency of secession, and opposed it till resolved on, but, after it was resolved on, yielded to none in their earnest support of it. These last comprised the immense majority of those who voted against secession. Never could those called the Southern leaders have carried the secession ordinances, never could they have carried on the war with the vigor and determination, and with such formidable armies as they collected and armed for four years, making at times the destiny of the Union wellnigh doubtful, if they had not had the Southern heart with them, if they had not been most heartily supported by the overwhelming mass of the people. They led a popular, not a factious movement.

No State, it is said again, has seceded, or could secede. The State is territorial, not personal, and as no State can carry its territory and population out of the Union, no State can secede. Out of the jurisdiction of the Union, or alienate them from the sovereign or national domain, very true; but out of the Union as a State, with rights, powers, or franchises in the Union, not true. Secession is political, not territorial.

But the State holds from the territory or domain. The people are sovereign because attached to a sovereign territory, not the domain because held by a sovereign people, as was established by the analysis of the early Roman constitution. The territory of the States corresponds to the sacred territory of Rome, to which was attached the Roman sovereignty. That territory, once surveyed and consecrated, remained sacred and the ruling territory, and could not be divested of its sacred and governing character. The portions of the territory of the United States once erected into States and consecrated as ruling territory can never be deprived, except by foreign conquest or successful revolution, of its sacred character and inviolable rights.

The State is territorial, not personal, and is constituted by *public*, not by *private* wealth, and is always *respublica* or commonwealth, in distinction from despotism or monarchy in its oriental sense, which is founded on private wealth, or which assumes that the authority to govern, or sovereignty, is the private estate of the sovereign. All power is a domain, but there is no domain without a dominus or lord. In oriental monarchies the dominus is the monarch; in republics it is the public or people fixed to the soil or territory, that is, the people in their territorial, and not in their personal or genealogical relation. The people of the United States are sovereign only within the territory or domain of the United States, and their sovereignty is a state, because fixed, attached, or limited to that specific territory. It is fixed to the soil, not nomadic. In barbaric nations power is nomadic and personal, or genealogical, confined to no locality, but attaches to the chief, and follows wherever he goes. The Gothic chiefs hold their power by a personal title, and have the same authority in their tribes on the Po or the Rhone as on the banks of the Elbe or the Danube. Power migrates with the chief and his people, and may be exercised wherever he and they find themselves, as a Swedish queen held when she ordered the execution of one of her subjects at Paris, without asking permission of the territorial lord. In these nations, power is a personal right, or a private estate, not a state which exists only as attached to the domain, and, as attached to the domain, exists independently of the chief or the government. The distinction is between public domain and private domain.

The American system is republican, and, contrary to what some democratic politicians assert, the American democracy is territorial, not personal; not territorial because the majority of the people are agriculturists or landholders, but because all political rights, powers, or franchises are territorial. The sovereign people of the United States are sovereign only within the territory of the United States. The great body of the freemen have the elective franchise, but no one has it save in his State, his county, his town, his ward, his precinct. Out of the election district in which he is domiciled, a citizen of the United States has no more right to vote than has the citizen or subject of a foreign state. This explains what is meant by the attachment of power to the territory, and the dependence of the state on the domain. The state, in republican states, exists only as inseparably united with the public domain; under feudalism, power was joined to territory or domain, but the domain was held as a private, not as a public domain. All sovereignty rests on domain or proprietorship, and is dominion. The proprietor is the dominus or lord, and in republican states the lord is society, or the public, and the domain is held for the common or public good of all. All political rights are held from society, or the dominus, and therefore it is the elective franchise is held from society, and is a civil right, as distinguished from a natural, or even a purely personal right.

As there is no domain without a lord or dominus, territory alone cannot possess any political rights or franchises, for it is not a domain. In the American system, the dominus or lord is not the particular State, but the United States, and the domain of the whole territory, whether erected into particular States or not, is in the United States alone. The United States do not part with the dominion of that portion of the national domain included within a particular State. The State holds the domain not separately but jointly, as inseparably one of the United States: separated, it has no dominion, is no State, and is no longer a joint sovereign at all, and the territory that it included falls into the condition of any other territory held by the United States not erected into one of the United States.

Lawyers, indeed, tell us that the eminent domain is in the particular State, and that all escheats are to the State, not to the United States. All escheats of private estates, but no public or general escheats. But this has nothing to do with the public domain. The United States are the dominus, but they have, by the constitution, divided the powers of government between a General government and particular State governments, and ordained that all matters of a general nature, common to all the States, should be placed under the supreme control of the former, and all matters of a private or particular character under the supreme control of the latter. The eminent domain of private estates is in the particular State, but the sovereign authority in the particular State is that of the United States expressing itself through the State government. The United States, in the States as well as out of them, is the dominus, as the States respectively would soon find if they were to undertake to alienate any part of their domain to a foreign power, or even to the citizens or subjects of a foreign State, as is also evident from the fact that the United States, in the way prescribed by the constitution, may enlarge or contract at will the rights and powers of the States. The mistake on this point grows out of the habit of restricting the action of the United States to the General government, and not recollecting that the United States govern one class of subjects through the General government and another class through State governments, but that it is one and the same authority that governs in both.

The analogy borrowed from the Roman constitution, as far as applicable, proves the reverse of what is intended. The dominus of the sacred territory was the city, or the Roman state, not the sacred territory itself. The territory received the tenant, and gave him as tenant the right to a seat in the senate; but the right of the territory was derived not from the domain, but from the dominus, that is, the city. But the city could revoke its grant, as it practically did when it conferred the privileges of Roman citizenship on the provincials, and gave to plebeians seats in the senate. Moreover, nothing in Roman history indicates that to the validity of a senatus consultum it was necessary to count the vacant domains of the sacred territory. The particular domain must, under the American system, be counted when it is held by a State, but of itself alone, or even with its population, it is not a State, and therefore as a State domain is vacant and without any political rights or powers whatever.

To argue that the territory and population once a State in the Union must needs always be so, would be well enough if a State in the Union were individually a sovereign state; for territory, with its population not subject to another, is always a sovereign state, even though its government has been subverted. But this is not the fact, for territory with its population does not constitute a State in the Union; and, therefore, when of a State nothing remains but territory and population, the State has evidently disappeared. It will not do then to maintain that State suicide is impossible, and that the States that adopted secession ordinances have never for a moment ceased to be States in the Union, and are free, whenever they choose, to send their representatives and senators to occupy their vacant seats in Congress. They must be reorganized first.

There would also be some embarrassment to the government in holding that the States that passed the secession ordinance remain, notwithstanding, States in the Union. The citizens of a State in the Union cannot be rebels to the United States, unless they are rebels to their State; and rebels to their State they are not, unless they resist its authority and make war on it. The authority of the State in the Union is a legal authority, and the citizen in obeying it is disloyal neither to the State nor to the Union. The citizens in the States that made war on the United States did not resist their State, for they acted by its authority. The only men, on this supposition, in them, who have been traitors or rebels, are precisely the Union men who have refused to go with their respective States, and have resisted, even with armed force, the secession ordinances. The several State governments, under which the so-called rebels carried on the war for the destruction of the Union, if the States are in the Union, were legal and loyal governments of their respective States, for they were legally elected and installed, and conformed to their respective State constitutions. All the acts of these governments have been constitutional. Their entering into a confederacy for attaining a separate nationality has been legal, and the debts contracted by the States individually, or by the confederacy legally formed by them, have been legally contracted, stand good against them, and perhaps against the United States. The war against them has been all wrong, and the confederates killed in battle have been murdered by the United States. The blockade has been illegal, for no nation can blockade its own ports, and the captures and seizures under it, robberies. The Supreme Court has been wrong in declaring the war a territorial civil war, as well as the government in acting accordingly. Now, all these conclusions are manifestly false and absurd, and therefore the assumption that the States in question have all along been States in the Union cannot be sustained.

It is easy to understand the resistance the Government offers to the doctrine that a State may commit suicide, or by its own act abdicate its rights and cease to be a State in the Union. It is admissible on no theory of the constitution that has been widely entertained. It is not admissible on Mr. Calhoun's theory of State sovereignty, for on that theory a State in going out of the Union does not cease to be a State, but simply resumes the powers it had delegated to the General government. It cannot be maintained on Mr. Madison's or Mr. Webster's theory, that the States prior to the Union were severally sovereign, but by the Union were constituted one people; for, if this one people are understood to be a federal people, State secession would not be State suicide, but State independence; and if understood to be one consolidated or centralized people, it would be simply insurrection or rebellion against the national authority, laboring to make itself a revolution. The government seems to have understood Mr. Madison's theory in both senses—in the consolidated sense, in declaring the secessionists insurgents and rebels, and in the federal sense, in maintaining that they have never seceded, and are still States in the Union, in full possession of all their political or State rights. Perhaps, if the government, instead of borrowing from contradictory theories of the constitution which have gained currency, had examined in the light of historical facts the constitution itself, it would have been as constitutional in its doctrine as it has been loyal and patriotic, energetic and successful in its military administration.

Another reason why the doctrine that State secession is State suicide has appeared so offensive to many, is the supposition entertained at one time by some of its friends, that the dissolution of the State vacates all rights and franchises held under it. But this is a mistake. The principle is well known and recognized by the jurisprudence of all civilized nations, that in the transfer of a territory from one territorial sovereign to another, the laws in force under the old sovereign remain in force after the change, till abrogated, or others are enacted in their place by the new sovereign, except such as are necessarily abrogated by the change itself of the sovereign; not, indeed, because the old sovereign retains any authority, but because such is presumed by the courts to be the will of the new sovereign. The principle applies in the case of the death of a State in the Union. The laws of the State are territorial, till abrogated by competent authority, remain the *lex loci*, and are in full force. All that would be vacated would be the public rights of the State, and in no case the private rights of citizens, corporations, or laws affecting them.

But the same conclusion is reached in another way. In the lapse of a State or its return to the condition of a Territory, there is really no change of sovereignty. The sovereignty, both before and after, is the United States. The sovereign authority that governs in the State government, as we have seen, though independent of the General government, is the United States. The United States govern certain matters through a General government, and others through particular State governments. The private rights and interests created, regulated, or protected by the particular State, are created, regulated, or protected by the United States, as much and as plenarily as if done by the General government, and the State laws creating, regulating, or protecting them can be abrogated by no power known to the constitution, but either the State itself, or the United States in convention legally assembled. If this were what is meant by the States that have seceded, or professed to secede, remaining States in the Union, they would, indeed, be States still in the Union, notwithstanding secession, and the government would be right in saying that no State can secede. But this is not what is meant, at least not all that is meant. It is meant not only that the private rights of citizens and corporations remain, but the citizens retain all the public rights of the State, that is, the right to representation in Congress and in the electoral college, and the right to sit in the convention, which is not true.

But the correction of the misapprehension that the private rights and interests are lost by the lapse of the State may remove the graver prejudices against the doctrine of State suicide, and dispose loyal and honest Union men to hear the reasons by which it is supported, and which nobody has refuted or can refute on constitutional grounds. A Territory by coming into the Union becomes a State; a State by going out of the Union becomes a Territory.

XIII

Reconstruction

*T*he question of reconstructing the States that seceded will be practically settled before these pages can see the light, and will therefore be considered here only so far as necessary to complete the view of the constitution of the United States. The manner in which the government proposed to settle, has settled, or will settle the question, proves that both it and the American people have only confused views of the rights and powers of the General government, but imperfectly comprehend the distinction between the legislative and executive departments of that government, and are far more familiar with party tactics than with constitutional law.

It would be difficult to imagine any thing more unconstitutional, more crude, or more glaringly impolitic than the mode of reconstruction indicated by the various executive proclamations that have been issued, bearing on the subject, or even by the bill for guaranteeing the States republican governments, that passed Congress, but which failed to obtain the President's signature. It is, in some measure, characteristic of the American government to understand how things ought to be done only when they are done and it is too late to do them in the right way. Its wisdom comes after action, as if engaged in a series of experiments. But, happily for the nation, few blunders are committed that with our young life and elasticity are irreparable, and that, after all, are greater than are ordinarily committed by older and more experienced nations. They are not of the most fatal character, and are, for the most part, such as are incident to the conceit, the heedlessness, the ardor, and the impatience of youth, and need excite no serious alarm for the future.

There has been no little confusion in the public mind, and in that of the government itself, as to what reconstruction is, who has the power to reconstruct, and how that power is to be exercised. Are the States that seceded States in the Union, with no other disability than that of having no legal governments? or are they Territories subject to the Union? Is their reconstruction their erection into new States, or their restoration as States previously in the Union? Is the power to reconstruct in the States themselves? or is it in the General government? If partly in the people and partly in the General government, is the part in the General government in Congress, or in the Executive? If in Congress, can the Executive, without the authority of Congress, proceed to reconstruct, simply leaving it for Congress to accept or reject the reconstructed State? If the power is partly in the people of the disorganized States, who or what defines that people, decides who may or may not vote in the reorganization? On all these questions there has been much crude, if not erroneous, thinking, and much inconsistent and contradictory action.

The government started with the theory that no State had seceded or could secede, and held that, throughout, the States in rebellion continued to be States in the Union. That is, it held secession to be a purely personal and not a territorial insurrection. Yet it proclaimed eleven States to be in insurrection against the United States, blockaded their ports, and interdicted all trade and intercourse of any kind with them. The Supreme Court, in order to sustain the blockade and interdict as legal, decided the war to be not a war against simply individual or personal insurgents, but "a territorial civil war." This negatived the assumption that the States that took up arms against the United States remained all the while peaceable and loyal States, with all their political rights and powers in the Union. The States in the Union are integral elements of the political sovereignty, for the sovereignty of the American nation vests in the States united; and it is absurd to pretend that the eleven States that made the rebellion and were carrying on a formidable war against the United States, were in the Union, an integral element of that sovereign authority which was carrying on a yet more formidable war against them. Nevertheless, the government still held to its first assumption, that the States in rebellion continued to be States in the Union—loyal States, with all their rights and franchises unimpaired!

That the government should at first have favored or acquiesced in the doctrine that no State had ceased to be a State in the Union, is not to be wondered at. The extent and determination of the secession movement were imperfectly understood, and the belief among the supporters of the government, and, perhaps, of the government itself, was, that it was a spasmodic movement for a temporary purpose, rather than a fixed determination to found an independent separate nationality; that it was and would be sustained by the real majority of the people of none of the States, with perhaps the exception of South Carolina; that the true policy of the government would be to treat the seceders with great forbearance, to avoid all measures likely to exasperate them or to embarrass their loyal fellow citizens, to act simply on the defensive, and to leave the Union men in the several seceding States to gain a political victory at the polls over the secessionists, and to return their States to their normal position in the Union.

The government may not have had much faith in this policy, and Mr. Lincoln's personal authority might be cited to the effect that it had not, but it was urged strongly by the Union men of the Border States. The administration was hardly seated in office, and its members were new men, without administrative experience; the President, who had been legally elected indeed, but without a majority of the popular votes, was far from having the full confidence even of the party that elected him; opinions were divided; party spirit ran high; the excitement was great, the crisis was imminent, the government found itself left by its predecessor without an army or a navy, and almost without arms or ordnance; it knew not how far it could count on popular support, and was hardly aware whom it could trust or should distrust; all was hurry and confusion; and what could the government do but to gain time, keep off active war as long as possible, conciliate all it could, and take ground which at the time seemed likely to rally the largest number of the people to its support? There were men then, warm friends of the administration, and still warmer friends of their country, who believed that a bolder, a less timid, a less cautious policy would have been wiser; that in revolutionary times boldness, what in other times would be rashness, is the highest prudence, on the side of the government as well as on the side of the revolution; that when once it has shown itself, the rebellion that hesitates, deliberates, consults, is defeated—and so is the government. The seceders owed from the first their successes not to their superior organization, to their better preparation, or to the better discipline and appointment of their armies, but to their very rashness, to their audacity even, and the hesitancy, caution, and deliberation of the government. Napoleon owed his successes as general and civilian far more to the air of power he assumed, and the conviction he produced of his invincibility in the minds of his opponents, than to his civil or military strategy and tactics, admirable as they both were.

But the government believed it wisest to adopt a conciliatory, and, in many respects, a temporizing policy, and to rely more on weakening the secessionists in their respective States than on strengthening the hands and hearts of its own stanch and uncompromising supporters. It must strengthen the Union party in the insurrectionary States, and as this party hoped to succeed by political manipulation rather than by military force, the government must rely rather on a show of military power than on gaining any decisive battle. As it hoped, or affected to hope, to suppress the rebellion in the States that seceded through their loyal citizens, it was obliged to assume that secession was the work of a faction, of a few ambitious and disappointed politicians, and that the States were all in the Union, and continued in the loyal portion of their inhabitants. Hence its aid to the loyal Virginians to organize as the State of Virginia, and its subsequent efforts to organize the Union men in Louisiana, Arkansas, and Tennessee, and its disposition to recognize their organization in each of those States as the State itself, though including only a small minority of the territorial people. Had the facts been as assumed, the government might have treated the loyal people of each State as the State itself, without any gross usurpation of power; but, unhappily, the facts assumed were not facts, and it was soon found that the Union party in all the States that seceded, except the western part of Virginia and the eastern section of Tennessee, after secession had been carried by the popular vote, went almost unanimously with the secessionists; for they as well as the secessionists held the doctrine of State sovereignty; and to treat the handful of citizens that remained loyal in each State as the State itself, became ridiculous, and the government should have seen and acknowledged it.

The rebellion being really territorial, and not personal, the State that seceded was no more continued in the loyal than in the disloyal population. While the war lasted, both were public enemies of the United States, and neither had or could have any rights as a State in the Union. The law recognizes a solidarity of all the citizens of a State, and assumes that, when a State is at war, all its citizens are at war, whether approving the war or not. The loyal people in the States that seceded incurred none of the pains and penalties of treason, but they retained none of the political rights of the State in the Union, and, in reorganizing the State after the suppression of the rebellion, they have no more right to take part than the secessionists themselves. They, as well as the secessionists, have followed the territory. It was on this point that the government committed its gravest mistake. As to the reorganization or reconstruction of the State, the whole territorial people stood on the same footing.

Taking the decision of the Supreme Court as conclusive on the subject, the rebellion was territorial, and, therefore, placed all the States as States out of the Union, and retained them only as population and territory under or subject to the Union. The States ceased to exist, that is, as integral elements of the national sovereignty. The question then occurred, are they to be erected into new States, or are they to be reconstructed and restored to the Union as the identical old States that seceded? Shall their identity be revived and preserved, or shall they be new States, regardless of that identity? There can be no question that the work to be done was that of restoration, not of creation; no tribe should perish from Israel, no star be struck from the firmament of the Union. Every inhabitant of the fallen States; and every citizen of the United States must desire them to be revived and continued with their old names and boundaries, and all true Americans wish to continue the constitution as it is, and the Union as it was. Who would see old Virginia, the Virginia of revolutionary fame, of Washington, Jefferson, Madison, of Monroe, the "Old Dominion," once the leading State of the Union, dead without hope of resurrection? or South Carolina, the land of Rutledge, Moultrie, Laurens, Hayne, Sumter, and Marion? There is something grating to him who values State associations, and would encourage State emulation and State pride, in the mutilation of the Old Dominion, and the erection within her borders of the new State called West Virginia. States in the Union are not mere prefectures, or mere dependencies on the General government, created for the convenience of administration. They have an individual, a real existence of their own, as much so as have the individual members of society. They are free members, not of a confederation indeed, but of a higher political community, and reconstruction should restore the identity of their individual life, suspended for a moment by secession, but capable of resuscitation.

These States had become, indeed, for a moment, territory under the Union; but in no instance had they or could they become territory that had never existed as States. The fact that the territory and people had existed as a State, could with regard to none of them be obliterated, and, therefore, they could not be erected into absolutely new States. The process of reconstructing them could not be the same as that of creating new States. In creating a new State, Congress, *ex necessitate*, because there is no other power except the national convention competent to do it, defines the boundaries of the new State, and prescribes the electoral people, or who may take part in the preliminary organization; but in reconstructing States it does neither, for both are done by a law Congress is not competent to abrogate or modify, and which can be done only by the United States in convention assembled, or by the State itself after its restoration. The government has conceded this, and, in part, has acted on it. It preserves, except in Virginia, the old boundaries, and recognizes, or rather professes to recognize the old electoral law, only it claims the right to exclude from the electoral people those who have voluntarily taken part in the rebellion.

The work to be done in States that have seceded is that of reconstruction, not creation; and this work is not and cannot be done exclusively nor chiefly by the General government, either by the Executive or by Congress. That government can appoint military, or even provisional governors, who may designate the time and place of holding the convention of the electoral people of the disorganized State, as also the time and place of holding the elections of delegates to it, and superintend the elections so far as to see the polls are opened, and that none but qualified electors vote, but nothing more. All the rest is the work of the territorial electoral people themselves, for the State within its own sphere must, as one of the United States, be a self-governing community. The General government may concede or withhold permission to the disorganized State to reorganize, as it judges advisable, but it cannot itself reorganize it. If it concedes the permission, it must leave the whole electoral people under the pre-existing electoral law free to take part in the work of reorganization, and to vote according to their own judgment. It has no authority to purge the electoral people, and say who may or may not vote, for the whole question of suffrage and the qualifications of electors is left to the State, and can be settled neither by an act of Congress nor by an Executive proclamation.

If the government theory were admissible, that the disorganized States remain States in the Union, the General government could have nothing to say on the subject, and could no more interfere with elections in any one of them than it could with elections in Massachusetts or New York. But even on the doctrine here defended it can interfere with them only by way of general superintendence. The citizens have, indeed, lost their political rights, but not their private rights. Secession has not dissolved civil society, or abrogated any of the laws of the disorganized State that were in force at the time of secession. The error of the government is not in maintaining that these laws survive the secession ordinances, and remain the territorial law, or *lex loci*, but in maintaining that they do so by will of the State, that has, as a State, really lapsed. They do so by will of the United States, which enacted them through the individual State, and which has not in convention abrogated them, save the law authorizing slavery, and its dependent laws.

This point has already been made, but as it is one of the niceties of the American constitution, it may not be amiss to elaborate it at greater length. The doctrine of Mr. Jefferson, Mr. Madison, and the majority of our jurists, would seem to be that the States, under God, are severally sovereign in all matters not expressly confided to the General government, and therefore that the American sovereignty is divided, and the citizen owes a double allegiance—allegiance to his State, and allegiance to the United States—as if there was a United States distinguishable from the States. Hence Mr. Seward, in an official dispatch to our minister at the court of St. James, says: "The citizen owes allegiance to the State and to the United States." And nearly all who hold allegiance is due to the Union at all, hold that it is also due to the States, only that which is due to the United States is paramount, as that under feudalism due to the overlord. But this is not the case. There is no divided sovereignty, no divided allegiance. Sovereignty is one, and vests not in the General government or in the State government, but in the United States, and allegiance is due to the United States, and to them alone. Treason can be committed only against the United States, and against a State only because against the United States, and is properly cognizable only by the Federal courts. Hence the Union men committed no treason in refusing to submit to the secession ordinances of their respective States, and in sustaining the national arms against secession.

There are two very common mistakes: the one that the States individually possess all the powers not delegated to the General government; and the other that the Union, or United States, have only delegated powers. But the United States possess all the powers of a sovereign state, and the States individually and the General government possess only such powers as the United States in convention delegate to them respectively. The sovereign is neither the General government nor the States severally, but the United States in convention. The United States are the one indivisible sovereign, and this sovereign governs alike general matters in the General government, and particular matters in the several State governments. All legal authority in either emanates from this one indivisible and plenary sovereign, and hence the laws enacted by a State are really enacted by the United States, and derive from

them their force and vitality as laws. Hence, as the United States survive the particular State, the lapse of the State does not abrogate the
State laws, or dissolve civil society within its jurisdiction.

This is evidently so, because civil society in the particular State does
not rest on the State alone, nor on Congress, but on the United States.
Hence all civil rights of every sort created by the individual State are
really held from the United States, and therefore it was that the people
of non-slaveholding States were, as citizens of the United States, responsible for the existence of slavery in the States that seceded. There
is a solidarity of States in the Union as there is of individuals in each of
the States. The political error of the Abolitionists was not in calling
upon the people of the United States to abolish slavery, but in calling
upon them to abolish it through the General government, which had no
jurisdiction in the case; or in their sole capacity as men, on purely humanitarian grounds, which were the abrogation of all government and
civil society itself, instead of calling upon them to do it as the United
States in convention assembled, or by an amendment to the constitution of the United States in the way ordained by that constitution itself.
This understood, the constitution and laws of a defunct State remain in
force by virtue of the will of the United States, till the State is raised
from the dead, restored to life and activity, and repeals or alters them, or
till they are repealed or altered by the United States or the national
convention. But as the defunct State could not, and the convention had
not repealed or altered them, save in the one case mentioned, the General government had no alternative but to treat them and all rights
created by them as the territorial law, and to respect them as such.

What then do the people of the several States that seceded lose by
secession? They lose, besides incurring, so far as disloyal, the pains and
penalties of treason, their political rights, or right, as has just been said,
to be in their own department self-governing communities, with the
right of representation in Congress and the electoral colleges, and to

sit in the national convention, or of being counted in the ratification of amendments to the constitution—precisely what it was shown a Territorial people gain by being admitted as a State into the Union. This is the difference between the constitutional doctrine and that adopted by Mr. Lincoln's and Mr. Johnson's Administrations. But what authority, on this constitutional doctrine, does the General government gain over the people of States that secede, that it has not over others? As to their internal constitution, their private rights of person or property, it gains none. It has over them, till they are reconstructed and restored to the Union, the right to institute for them provisional governments, civil or military, precisely as it has for the people of a territory that is not and has never been one of the United States; but in their reconstruction it has less, for the geographical boundaries and electoral people of each are already defined by a law which does not depend on its will, and which it can neither abrogate nor modify. Here is the difference between the constitutional doctrine and that of the so-called radicals. The State has gone, but its laws remain, so far as the United States in convention does not abrogate them; not because the authority of the State survives, but because the United States so will, or are presumed to will. The United States have by a constitutional amendment abrogated the laws of the several States authorizing slavery, and prohibited slavery forever within the jurisdiction of the Union; and no State can now be reconstructed and be admitted into the Union with a constitution that permits slavery, for that would be repugnant to the constitution of the United States. If the constitutional amendment is not recognized as ratified by the requisite number of States, it is the fault of the government in persisting in counting as States what are no States. Negro suffrage, as white suffrage, is at present a question for the States.

The United States guarantee to such State a republican form of government. And this guarantee, no doubt, authorizes Congress to intervene in the internal constitution of a State so far as to force it to adopt a republican form of government, but not so far as to organize a government for a State, or to compel a territorial people to accept or adopt a State constitution for themselves. If a State attempts to organize a form of government not republican, it can prevent it; and if a Territory adopts an unrepublican form, it can force it to change its constitution to one that is republican, or compel it to remain a Territory under a provisional government. But this gives the General government no authority in the organization or re-organization of States beyond seeing that the form of government adopted by the territorial people is republican. To press it further, to make the constitutional clause a pretext for assuming the entire control of the organization or re-organization of a State, is a manifest abuse—a palpable violation of the constitution and of the whole American system. The authority given by the clause is specific, and is no authority for intervention in the general reconstruction of the lapsed State. It gives authority in no question raised by secession or its consequences, and can give none, except, from within or from without, there is an overt attempt to organize a State in the Union with an unrepublican form of government.

The General government gives permission to the territorial people of the defunct State to re-organize, or it contents itself with suffering them, without special recognition, to reorganize in their own way, and apply to Congress for admission, leaving it to Congress to admit them as a State, or not, according to its own discretion, in like manner as it admits a new State; but the re-organization itself must be the work of the territorial people themselves, under their old electoral law. The power that reconstructs is in the people themselves; the power that admits them, or receives them into the Union, is Congress. The Executive, therefore, has no authority in the matter, beyond that of seeing that the laws are duly complied with; and whatever power he assumes, whether by proclamation or by instructions given to the provisional governors, civil or military, is simply a usurpation of the power of Congress, which it

rests with Congress to condone or not, as it may see fit. Executive proclamations, excluding a larger or a smaller portion of the electoral or
territorial people from the exercise of the elective franchise in re-orga-
nizing the State, and executive efforts to throw the State into the hands
of one political party or another, are an unwarrantable assumption of
power, for the President, in relation to reconstruction, acts only under
the peace powers of the constitution, and simply as the first executive
officer of the Union. His business is to execute the laws, not to make
them. His legislative authority is confined to his qualified veto on the
acts of Congress, and to the recommendation to Congress of such measures as he believes are needed by the country.

In reconstructing a disorganized State, neither Congress nor the
Executive has any power that either has not in time of peace. The Executive, as commander-in-chief of the army, may *ex necessitate* place it
ad interim under a military governor, but he cannot appoint even a provisional civil governor till Congress has created the office and given
him authority to fill it; far less can he legally give instructions to the
civil governor as to the mode or manner of reconstructing the disorganized State, or decide who may or may not vote in the preliminary re-
organization. The Executive could do nothing of the sort, even in regard to a Territory never erected into a State. It belongs to Congress,
not to the Executive, to erect Territorial or provisional governments,
like those of Dacotah, Colorado, Montana, Nebraska, and New Mexico;
and Congress, not the executive, determines the boundaries of the Territory, passes the enabling act, and defines the electoral people, till the
State is organized and able to act herself. Even Congress, in reconstructing and restoring to life and vigor in the Union a disorganized State,
has nothing to say as to its boundaries or its electoral people, nor any
right to interfere between parties in the State, to throw the reconstructed
State into the hands of one or another party. All that Congress can
insist on is, that the territorial people shall reconstruct with a govern-

ment republican in form; that its senators and representatives in Congress, and the members of the State legislature, and all executive and judicial officers of the State shall be bound by oath or affirmation to support and defend the constitution of the United States. In the whole work the President has nothing to do with reconstruction, except to see that peace is preserved and the laws are fully executed.

It may be at least doubted that the Executive has power to proclaim amnesty and pardon to rebels after the civil war has ceased, and ceased it has when the rebels have thrown down their arms and submitted; for his pardoning power is only to pardon after conviction and judgment of the court: it is certain that he has no power to proscribe or punish even traitors, except by due process of law. When the war is over he has only his ordinary peace powers. He cannot then disfranchise any portion of the electoral people of a State that seceded, even though there is no doubt that they have taken part in the rebellion, and may still be suspected of disloyal sentiments. Not even Congress can do it, and no power known to the constitution till the State is reconstructed can do it without due process of law, except the national convention. Should the President do any of the things supposed, he would both abuse the power he has and usurp power that he has not, and render himself liable to impeachment. There are many things very proper, and even necessary to be done, which are high crimes when done by an improper person or agent. The duty of the President, when there are steps to be taken or things to be done which he believes very necessary, but which are not within his competency, is, if Congress is not in session, to call it together at the earliest practicable moment, and submit the matter to its wisdom and discretion.

It must be remembered that the late rebellion was not a merely personal but a territorial rebellion. In such a rebellion, embracing eleven States, and, excluding slaves, a population of at least seven millions, acting under an organized territorial government, preserving internal civil order, supporting an army and navy under regularly commissioned officers, and carrying on war as a sovereign nation—in such a territorial rebellion no one in particular can be accused and punished as a traitor. The rebellion is not the work of a few ambitious or reckless leaders, but of the people, and the responsibility of the crime, whether civil or military, is not individual, but common to the whole territorial people engaged in it; and seven millions, or the half of them, are too many to hang, to exile, or even to disfranchise. Their defeat and the failure of their cause must be their punishment. The interest of the country, as well the sentiment of the civilized world—it might almost be said the law of nations—demands their permission to return to their allegiance, to be treated according to their future merits, as an integral portion of the American people.

The sentiment of the civilized world has much relaxed from its former severity toward political offenders. It regards with horror the savage cruelties of Great Britain to the unfortunate Jacobites, after their defeat under Charles Edward, at Culloden, in 1746, their barbarous treatment of the United Irishmen in 1798, and her brutality to the mutinous Hindoos in 1857-'58; the harshness of Russia toward the insurgent Poles, defeated in their mad attempts to recover their lost nationality; the severity of Austria, under Haynau, toward the defeated Magyars. The liberal press kept up for years, especially in England and the United States, a perpetual howl against the Papal and Neapolitan governments for arresting and imprisoning men who conspired to overthrow them. Louis Kossuth was no less a traitor than Jefferson Davis, and yet the United States solicited his release from a Turkish prison, and sent a national ship to bring him hither as the nation's guest. The people of the United States have held from the first "the right of insurrection," and have given their moral support to every insurrection in the Old or New World they discovered, and for them to treat with severity any portion of the Southern secessionists, who, at the very worst, only acted

on the principles the nation had uniformly avowed and pronounced sacred, would be regarded, and justly, by the civilized world, as little less
than infamous.

Not only the fair fame, but the interest of the Union forbids any
severity toward the people lately in arms against the government. The
interest of the nation demands not the death or the expulsion of the
secessionists, and, least of all, of those classes proscribed by the
President's proclamation of the 29th of May, 1865, nor even their dis-
franchisement, perpetual or temporary; but their restoration to citizenship, and their loyal co-operation with all true-hearted Americans, in
healing the wounds inflicted on the whole country by the civil war. There
need be no fear to trust them. Their cause is lost; they may or may not
regret it, but lost it is, and lost forever. They appealed to the ballot-box,
and were defeated; they appealed from the ballot-box to arms, to war,
and have been again defeated, terribly defeated. They know it and feel it.
There is no further appeal for them; the judgment of the court of last
resort has been rendered, and rendered against them. The cause is finished, the controversy closed, never to be re-opened. Henceforth the
Union is invincible, and it is worse than idle to attempt to renew the
war against it. Henceforth their lot is bound up with that of the nation,
and all their hopes and interests, for themselves and their children, and
their children's children, depend on their being permitted to demean
themselves henceforth as peaceable and loyal American citizens. They
must seek their freedom, greatness, and glory in the freedom, greatness, and glory of the American republic, in which, after all, they can be
far freer, greater, more glorious than in a separate and independent confederacy. All the arguments and considerations urged by Union men
against their secession, come back to them now with redoubled force to
keep them henceforth loyal to the Union.

They cannot afford to lose the nation, and the nation cannot afford
to lose them. To hang or exile them, and depopulate and suffer to run to

waste the lands they had cultivated, were sad thrift, sadder than that of deporting four millions of negroes and colored men. To exchange only those excepted from amnesty and pardon by President Johnson, embracing some two millions or more, the very *pars sanior* of the Southern population, for what would remain or flock in to supply their place, would be only the exchange of Glaucus and Diomed, gold for brass; to disfranchise them, confiscate their estates, and place them under the political control of the freedmen, lately their slaves, and the ignorant and miserable "white trash," would be simply to render rebellion chronic, and to convert seven millions of Americans, willing and anxious to be free, loyal American citizens, into eternal enemies. They have yielded to superior numbers and resources; beaten, but not disgraced, for they have, even in rebellion, proved themselves what they are—real Americans. They are the product of the American soil, the free growth of the American republic, and to disgrace them were to disgrace the whole American character and people.

The wise Romans never allowed a triumph to a Roman general for victories, however brilliant, won over Romans. In civil war, the victory won by the government troops is held to be a victory for the country, in which all parties are victors, and nobody is vanquished. It was as truly for the good of the secessionists to fail, as it was for those who sustained the government to succeed; and the government having forced their submission and vindicated its own authority, it should now leave them to enjoy, with others, the victory which it has won for the common good of all. When war becomes a stern necessity, when it breaks out, and while it lasts, humanity requires it to be waged in earnest, prosecuted with vigor, and made as damaging, as distressful to the enemy as the laws of civilized nations permit. It is the way to bring it to a speedy close, and to save life and property. But when it is over, when the enemy submits, and peace returns, the vanquished should be treated with gentleness and love. No rancor should remain, no vengeance should be sought;

they who met in mortal conflict on the battle-field should be no longer enemies, but embrace as comrades, as friends, as brothers. None but a coward kicks a fallen foe; a brave people is generous, and the victors in the late war can afford to be generous generously. They fought for the Union, and the Union has no longer an enemy; their late enemies are willing and proud to be their countrymen, fellow-citizens, and friends; and they should look to it that small politicians do not rob them in the eyes of the world, by unnecessary and ill-timed severity to the submissive, of the glory of being, as they are, a great, noble, chivalric, generous, and magnanimous people.

The government and the small politicians, who usually are the most influential with all governments, should remember that none of the secessionists, however much in error they have been, have committed the moral crime of treason. They held, with the majority of the American people, the doctrine of State sovereignty, and on that doctrine they had a right to secede, and have committed no treason, been guilty of no rebellion. That was, indeed, no reason why the government should not use all its force, if necessary, to preserve the national unity and the integrity of the national domain; but it is a reason, and a sufficient reason, why no penalty of treason should be inflicted on secessionists or their leaders, after their submission, and recognition of the sovereignty of the United States as that to which they owe allegiance. None of the secessionists have been rebels or traitors, except in outward act, and there can, after the act has ceased, be no just punishment where there has been no criminal intent. Treason is the highest crime, and deserves exemplary punishment; but not where there has been no treasonable intent, where they who committed it did not believe it was treason, and on principles held by the majority of their countrymen, and by the party that had generally held the government, there really was no treason. Concede State sovereignty, and Jefferson Davis was no traitor in the war he made on the United States, for he made none till his State had seceded. He could not then be arraigned for his acts after secession, and at most, only for conspiracy, if at all, before secession.

But, if you permit all to vote in the re-organization of the State who, under the old electoral law, have the elective franchise, you throw the State into the hands of those who have been disloyal to the Union. If so, and you cannot trust them, the remedy is not in disfranchising the majority, but in prohibiting re-organization, and in holding the territorial people still longer under the provisional government, civil or military. The old electoral law disqualifies all who have been convicted of treason either to the State or the United States, and neither Congress nor the Executive can declare any others disqualified on account of disloyalty. But you must throw the State into the hands of those who took part, directly or indirectly, in the rebellion, if you reconstruct the States at all, for they are undeniably the great body of the territorial people in all the States that seceded. These people having submitted, and declared their intention to reconstruct the State as a State in the Union, you must amend the constitution of the United States, unless they are convicted of a disqualifying crime by due process of law, before you can disfranchise them. It is impossible to reconstruct any one of the disorganized States with those alone, or as the dominant party, who have adhered to the Union throughout the fearful struggle, as self-governing States. The State, resting on so small a portion of the people, would have no internal strength, no self-support, and could stand only as upheld by Federal arms, which would greatly impair the free and healthy action of the whole American system.

The government attempted to do it in Virginia, Louisiana, Arkansas, and Tennessee, before the rebellion was suppressed, but without authority and without success. The organizations, effected at great expense, and sustained only by military force, were neither States nor State governments, nor capable of being made so by any executive or congressional action. If the disorganized States, as the government held,

were still States in the Union, these organizations were flagrantly revolutionary, as effected not only without, but in defiance of State authority; if they had seceded and ceased to be States, as was the fact, they
were equally unconstitutional and void of authority, because not created by the free suffrage of the territorial people, who alone are competent to construct or reconstruct a State.

If the Unionists had retained the State organization and government, however small their number, they would have held the State, and
the government would have been bound to recognize and to defend
them as such with all the force of the Union. The rebellion would then
have been personal, not territorial. But such was not the case. The State
organization, the State government, the whole State authority rebelled,
made the rebellion territorial, not personal, and left the Unionists, very
respectable persons assuredly, residing, if they remained at home, in
rebel territory, traitors in the eye of their respective States, and shorn
of all political *status* or rights. Their political *status* was simply that of
the old loyalists, or adherents of the British crown in the American war
for Independence, and it was as absurd to call them the State, as it would
have been for Great Britain to have called the old Tories the colonies.

The theory on which the government attempted to re-organize the
disorganized States rested on two false assumptions: first, that the people
are personally sovereign; and, second, that all the power of the Union
vests in the General government. The first, as we have seen, is the principle of so-called "squatter sovereignty," embodied in the famous Kansas Nebraska Bill, which gave birth, in opposition, to the Republican
party of 1856. The people are sovereign only as the State, and the State
is inseparable from the domain. The Unionists without the State government, without any State organization, could not hold the domain,
which, when the State organization is gone, escheats to the United States,
that is to say, ceases to exist. The American democracy is territorial, not
personal.

The General government, in time of war or rebellion, is indeed invested, for war purposes, with all the power of the Union. This is the war power. But, though apparently unlimited, the war power is yet restricted to war purposes, and expires by natural limitation when peace returns; and peace returns, in a civil war, when the rebels have thrown down their arms and submitted to the national authority, and without any formal declaration. During the war, or while the rebellion lasts, it can suspend the civil courts, the civil laws, the State constitutions, any thing necessary to the success of the war—and of the necessity the military authorities are the judges; but it cannot abolish, abrogate, or reconstitute them. On the return of peace they revive of themselves in all their vigor. The emancipation proclamation of the President, if it emancipated the slaves in certain States and parts of States, and if those whom it emancipated could not be re-enslaved, did not anywhere abolish slavery, or change the laws authorizing it; and if the Government should be sustained by Congress or by the Supreme Court in counting the disorganized States as States in the Union, the legal *status* of slavery throughout the Union, with the exception of Maryland, and perhaps Missouri, is what it was before the war.*

The Government undoubtedly supposed, in the reconstructions it attempted, that it was acting under the war power; but as reconstruction can never be necessary for war purposes, and as it is in its very nature a work of peace, incapable of being effected by military force, since its validity depends entirely on its being the free action of the territorial people to be reconstructed, the General government had and could have, with regard to it, only its ordinary peace powers. Reconstruction is *jure pacis*, not *jure belli*.

Yet such illegal organizations, though they are neither States nor State governments, and incapable of being legalized by any action of the Executive or of Congress, may, nevertheless, be legalized by being

---

*This was the case in August, 1865. It may be quite otherwise before these pages see the light.

indorsed or acquiesced in by the territorial people. They are wrong, as are all usurpations; they are undemocratic, inasmuch as they attempt to give the minority the power to rule the majority; they are dangerous, inasmuch as they place the State in the hands of a party that can stand only as supported by the General government, and thus destroy the proper freedom and independence of the State, and open the door to corruption, tend to keep alive rancor and ill feeling, and to retard the period of complete pacification, which might be effected in three months as well as in three years, or twenty years; yet they can become legal, as other governments illegal in their origin become legal, with time and popular acquiescence. The right way is always the shortest and easiest; but when a government must oftener follow than lead the public, it is not always easy to hit the right way, and still less easy to take it. The general instincts of the people are right as to the end to be gained, but seldom right as to the means of gaining it; and politicians of the Union party, as well as of the late secession party, have an eye in reconstructing, to the future political control of the State when it is reconstructed.

The secessionists, if permitted to retain their franchise, would, even if they accepted abolition, no doubt re-organize their respective States on the basis of white suffrage, and so would the Unionists, if left to themselves. There is no party at the South prepared to adopt negro suffrage, and there would be none at the North if the negroes constituted any considerable portion of the population. As the reconstruction of a State cannot be done under the war power, the General government can no more enfranchise than it can disfranchise any portion of the territorial people, and the question of negro suffrage must be left, where the constitution leaves it—to the States severally, each to dispose of it for itself. Negro suffrage will, no doubt, come in time, as soon as the freedmen are prepared for it, and the danger is that it will be attempted too soon.

It would be a convenience to have the negro vote in the reconstruction of the States disorganized by secession, for it would secure their re-construction with anti-slavery constitutions, and also make sure of the proposed anti-slavery amendment to the Constitution of the United States; but there is no power in Congress to enfranchise the negroes in the States needing reconstruction, and, once assured of their freedom, the freedmen would care little for the Union, of which they understand nothing. They would vote, for the most part, with their former masters, their employers, the wealthier and more intelligent classes, whether loyal or disloyal; for, as a rule, these will treat them with greater personal consideration and kindness than others. The dislike of the negro, and hostility to negro equality, increase as you descend in the social scale. The freedmen, without political instruction or experience, who have had no country, no domicile, understand nothing of loyalty or of disloyalty. They have strong local attachments, but they can have no patriotism. If they adhered to the Union in the rebellion, fought for it, bled for it, it was not from loyalty, but because they knew that their freedom could come only from the success of the Union arms. That freedom secured, they have no longer any interest in the Union, and their local attachments, personal associations, habits, tastes, likes and dislikes, are Southern, not Northern. In any contest between the North and the South, they would take, to a man, the Southern side. After the taunts of the women, the captured soldiers of the Union found, until nearly the last year of the war, nothing harder to bear, when marched as prisoners into Richmond, than the antics and hootings of the negroes. Negro suffrage on the score of loyalty, is at best a matter of indifference to the Union, and as the elective franchise is not a natural right, but a civil trust, the friends of the negro should, for the present, be contented with securing him simply equal rights of person and property.

XIV

Political Tendencies

*T*he most marked political tendency of the American people has been, since 1825, to interpret their government as a pure and simple democracy, and to shift it from a territorial to a purely popular basis, or from the people as the state, inseparably united to the national territory or domain, to the people as simply population, either as individuals or as the race. Their tendency has unconsciously, therefore, been to change their constitution from a republican to a despotic, or from a civilized to a barbaric constitution.

The American constitution is democratic, in the sense that the people are sovereign; that all laws and public acts run in their name; that the rulers are elected by them, and are responsible to them; but they are the people territorially constituted and fixed to the soil, constituting what Mr. Disraeli, with more propriety perhaps than he thinks, calls a "territorial democracy." To this territorial democracy, the real American democracy, stand opposed two other democracies—the one personal and the other humanitarian—each alike hostile to civilization, and tending to destroy the state, and capable of sustaining government only on principles common to all despotisms.

In every man there is a natural craving for personal freedom and unrestrained action—a strong desire to be himself, not another—to be his own master, to go when and where he pleases, to do what he chooses, to take what he wants, wherever he can find it, and to keep what he takes. It is strong in all nomadic tribes, who are at once pastoral and predatory, and is seldom weak in our bold frontier-men, too often real "border ruffians." It takes different forms in different stages of social development, but it everywhere identifies liberty with power. Restricted in its enjoyment to one man, it makes him chief, chief of the family, the tribe, or the nation; extended in its enjoyment to the few, it founds an aristocracy, creates a nobility—for a nobleman meant originally only freeman, as it does still with the Magyars; extended to the many, it founds personal democracy, a simple association of individuals, in which all are equally free and independent, and no restraint is imposed on any one's action, will, or inclination, without his own consent, express or constructive. This is the so-called Jeffersonian democracy, in which government has no powers but such as it derives from the consent of the governed, and is personal democracy or pure individualism—philosophically considered, pure egoism, which says, "I am God." Under this sort of democracy, based on popular, or rather individual sovereignty, expressed by politicians when they call the electoral people, half seriously, half mockingly, "the sovereigns," there obviously can be no state, no social rights or civil authority; there can be only a voluntary association, league, alliance, or confederation, in which individuals may freely act together as long as they find it pleasant, convenient, or useful, but from which they may separate or secede whenever they find it for their interest or their pleasure to do so. State sovereignty and secession are based on the same democratic principle applied to the several States of the Union instead of individuals.

The tendency to this sort of democracy has been strong in large sections of the American people from the first, and has been greatly strengthened by the general acceptance of the theory that government originates in compact. The full realization of this tendency, which, happily, is impracticable save in theory, would be to render every man independent alike of every other man and of society, with full right and power to make his own will prevail. This tendency was strongest in the slaveholding States, and especially, in those States, in the slaveholding class, the American imitation of the feudal nobility of mediæval Europe; and on this side the war just ended was, in its most general expression, a war in defence of personal democracy, or the sovereignty of the people individually, against the humanitarian democracy, represented by the abolitionists, and the territorial democracy, represented by the Government. This personal democracy has been signally defeated in the defeat of the late confederacy, and can hardly again become strong enough to be dangerous.

But the humanitarian democracy, which scorns all geographical lines, effaces all in individualities, and professes to plant itself on humanity alone, has acquired by the war new strength, and is not without menace to our future. The solidarity of the race, which is the condition of all human life, founds, as we have seen, society, and creates what are called social rights, the rights alike of society in regard to individuals and of individuals in regard to society. Territorial divisions or circumscriptions found particular societies, states, or nations; yet as the race is one, and all its members live by communion with God through it and by communion one with another, these particular states or nations are never absolutely independent of each other, but bound together by the solidarity of the race, so that there is a real solidarity of nations as well as of individuals—the truth underlying Kossuth's famous declaration of "the solidarity of peoples."

The solidarity of nations is the basis of international law, binding on every particular nation, and which every civilized nation recognizes, and enforces, on its own subjects or citizens, through its own courts, as an integral part of its own municipal or national law. The personal or individual right is therefore restricted by the rights of society, and the rights of the particular society or nation are limited by international law, or the rights of universal society—the truth the ex-governor of Hungary overlooked. The grand error of Gentilism was in denying the unity and therefore the solidarity of the race, involved in its denial or misconception of the unity of God. It therefore was never able to assign any solid basis to international law, and gave it only a conventional or customary authority, thus leaving the *jus gentium*, which it recognized indeed, without any real foundation in the constitution of things, or authority in the real world. Its real basis is in the solidarity of the race, which has its basis in the unity of God, not the dead or abstract unity asserted by the old Eleatics, the Neo-Platonists, or the modern Unitarians, but the living unity consisting in the threefold relation in the Divine Essence, of Father, Son, and Holy Ghost, as asserted by Christian revelation, and believed, more or less intelligently, by all Christendom.

The tendency in the Southern States has been to overlook the social basis of the state, or the rights of society founded on the solidarity of the race, and to make all rights and powers personal, or individual; and as only the white race has been able to assert and maintain its personal freedom, only men of that race are held to have the right to be free. Hence the people of those States felt no scruple in holding the black or colored race as slaves. Liberty, said they, is the right only of those who have the ability to assert and maintain it. Let the negro prove that he has this ability by asserting and maintaining his freedom, and he will prove his right to be free, and that it is a gross outrage, a manifest injustice, to enslave him; but, till then, let him be my servant, which is best for him and for me. Why ask me to free him? I shall by doing so only change the form of his servitude. Why appeal to *me?* Am I my brother's keeper? Nay, is he my brother? Is this negro, more like an ape or a baboon than a human being, of the same race with myself? I believe it not. But in some instances, at least, my dear slaveholder, your slave is literally your brother, and sometimes even your son, born of your own daughter. The tendency of the Southern democrat was to deny the unity of the race, as well as all obligations of society to protect the weak and helpless, and therefore all true civil society.

At the North there has been, and is even yet, an opposite tendency— a tendency to exaggerate the social element, to overlook the territorial basis of the state, and to disregard the rights of individuals. This tendency has been and is strong in the people called abolitionists. The American abolitionist is so engrossed with the unity that he loses the solidarity of the race, which supposes unity of race and multiplicity of individuals; and fails to see any thing legitimate and authoritative in geographical divisions or territorial circumscriptions. Back of these, back of individuals, he sees humanity, superior to individuals, superior to states, governments, and laws, and holds that he may trample on them all or give them to the winds at the call of humanity or "the higher law." The principle on which he acts is as indefensible as the personal or egoïstical democracy of the slaveholders and their sympathizers. Were his socialistic tendency to become exclusive and realized, it would found in the name of humanity a complete social despotism, which, proving impracticable from its very generality, would break up in anarchy, in which might makes right, as in the slaveholder's democracy.

The abolitionists, in supporting themselves on humanity in its generality, regardless of individual and territorial rights, can recognize no state, no civil authority, and therefore are as much out of the order of civilization, and as much in that of barbarism, as is the slaveholder himself. Wendell Phillips is as far removed from true Christian civilization as was John C. Calhoun, and William Lloyd Garrison is as much of a barbarian and despot in principle and tendency as Jefferson Davis. Hence the great body of the people in the non-slaveholding States, wedded to American democracy as they were and are, could never, as much as they detested slavery, be induced to make common cause with the abolitionists, and their apparent union in the late civil war was accidental, simply owing to the fact that for the time the social democracy and the territorial coincided, or had the same enemy. The great body of the loyal people instinctively felt that pure socialism is as incompatible with American democracy as pure individualism; and the abolitionists are well aware that slavery has been abolished, not for humanitarian or socialistic reasons, but really for reasons of state, in order to save the territorial democracy. The territorial democracy would not unite to eliminate even so barbaric an element as slavery, till the rebellion gave them the constitutional right to abolish it; and even then so scrupulous were they, that they demanded a constitutional amendment, so as to be able to make clean work of it, without any blow to individual or State rights.

The abolitionists were right in opposing slavery, but not in demanding its abolition on humanitarian or socialistic grounds. Slavery is really a barbaric element, and is in direct antagonism to American civilization. The whole force of the national life opposes it, and must finally eliminate it, or become itself extinct; and it is no mean proof of their utter want of sympathy with all the living forces of modern civilization, that the leading men of the South and their prominent friends at the North really persuaded themselves that with cotton, rice, and tobacco, they could effectually resist the anti-slavery movement, and perpetuate their barbaric democracy. They studied the classics, they admired Greece and Rome, and imagined that those nations became great by slavery, instead of being great even in spite of slavery. They failed to take into the account the fact that when Greece and Rome were in the zenith of their glory, all contemporary nations were also slaveholding nations, and that if they were the greatest and most highly civilized nations of their times, they were not fitted to be the greatest and most highly civilized nations of all times. They failed also to perceive that, if the Græco-Roman republic did not include the whole territorial people

in the political people, it yet recognized both the social and the territorial foundation of the state, and never attempted to rest it on pure
individualism; they forgot, too, that Greece and Rome both fell, and
fell precisely through internal weakness caused by the barbarism
within, not through the force of the barbarism beyond their frontiers.
The world has changed since the time when ten thousand of his slaves
were sacrificed as a religious offering to the manes of a single Roman
master. The infusion of the Christian dogma of the unity and solidarity of the race into the belief, the life, the laws, the jurisprudence of all
civilized nations, has doomed slavery and every species of barbarism;
but this our slaveholding countrymen saw not.

It rarely happens that in any controversy, individual or national, the
real issue is distinctly presented, or the precise question in debate is
clearly and distinctly understood by either party. Slavery was only inci-
dentally involved in the late war. The war was occasioned by the colli-
sion of two extreme parties; but it was itself a war between civilization
and barbarism, primarily between the territorial democracy and the
personal democracy, and in reality, on the part of the nation, as much a
war against the socialism of the abolitionist as against the individualism of the slaveholder. Yet the victory, though complete over the former,
is only half won over the latter, for it has left the humanitarian democracy standing, and perhaps for the moment stronger than ever. The
socialistic democracy was enlisted by the territorial, not to strengthen
the government at home, as it imagines, for that it did not do, and could
not do, since the national instinct was even more opposed to it than to
the personal democracy; but under its anti-slavery aspect, to soften the
hostility of foreign powers, and ward off foreign intervention, which
was seriously threatened. The populations of Europe, especially of
France and England, were decidedly anti-slavery, and if the war here
appeared to them a war, not solely for the unity of the nation and the
integrity of its domain, as it really was, in which they took and could

take no interest, but a war for the abolition of slavery, their governments would not venture to intervene. This was the only consideration that weighed with Mr. Lincoln, as he himself assured the author, and induced him to issue his Emancipation Proclamation; and Europe rejoices in our victory over the rebellion only so far as it has liberated the slaves, and honors the late President only as their supposed liberator, not as the preserver of the unity and integrity of the nation. This is natural enough abroad, and proves the wisdom of the anti-slavery policy of the government, which had become absolutely necessary to save the Republic long before it was adopted; yet it is not as the emancipator of some two or three millions of slaves that the American patriot cherishes the memory of Abraham Lincoln, but, aided by the loyal people, generals of rare merit, and troops of unsurpassed bravery and endurance, as the saviour of the American state, and the protector of modern civilization. His anti-slavery policy served this end, and therefore was wise, but he adopted it with the greatest possible reluctance.

There were greater issues in the late war than negro slavery or negro freedom. That was only an incidental issue, as the really great men of the Confederacy felt, who to save their cause were willing themselves at last to free and arm their own negroes, and perhaps were willing to do it even at first. This fact alone proves that they had, or believed they had, a far more important cause than the preservation of negro slavery. They fought for personal democracy, under the form of State sovereignty, against social democracy; for personal freedom and independence against social or humanitarian despotism; and so far their cause was as good as that against which they took up arms; and if they had or could have fought against that, without fighting at the same time against the territorial, the real American, the only civilized democracy, they would have succeeded. It is not socialism nor abolitionism that has won; nor is it the North that has conquered. The Union itself has won no victories over the South, and it is both historically and legally false to say that the South has been subjugated. The Union has preserved itself and American civilization, alike for North and South, East and West. The armies that so often met in the shock of battle were not drawn up respectively by the North and the South, but by two rival democracies, to decide which of the two should rule the future. They were the armies of two mutually antagonistic systems, and neither army was clearly and distinctly conscious of the cause for which it was shedding its blood; each obeyed instinctively a power stronger than itself, and which at best it but dimly discerned. On both sides the cause was broader and deeper than negro slavery, and neither the pro-slavery men nor the abolitionists have won. The territorial democracy alone has won, and won what will prove to be a final victory over the purely personal democracy, which had its chief seat in the Southern States, though by no means confined to them. The danger to American democracy from that quarter is forever removed, and democracy *à la* Rousseau has received a terrible defeat throughout the world, though as yet it is far from being aware of it.

But in this world victories are never complete. The socialistic democracy claims the victory which has been really won by the territorial democracy, as if it had been socialism, not patriotism, that fired the hearts and nerved the arms of the brave men led by McClellan, Grant, and Sherman. The humanitarians are more dangerous in principle than the egoists, for they have the appearance of building on a broader and deeper foundation, of being more Christian, more philosophic, more generous and philanthropic; but Satan is never more successful than under the guise of an angel of light. His favorite guise in modern times is that of philanthropy. He is a genuine humanitarian, and aims to persuade the world that humanitarianism is Christianity, and that man is God; that the soft and charming sentiment of philanthropy is real Christian charity; and he dupes both individuals and nations, and makes them do his work, when they believe they are earnestly and most successfully doing the work of God. Your leading abolitionists are as much affected by satanophany as your leading confederates, nor are they one whit more philosophical or less sophistical. The one loses the race, the other the individual, and neither has learned to apply practically that fundamental truth that there is never the general without the particular, nor the particular without the general, the race without individuals, nor individuals without the race. The whole race was in Adam, and fell in him, as we are taught by the doctrine of original sin, or the sin of the race, and Adam was an individual, as we are taught in the fact that original sin was in him actual or personal sin.

The humanitarian is carried away by a vague generality, and loses men in humanity, sacrifices the rights of men in a vain endeavor to secure the rights of man, as your Calvinist or his brother Jansenist sacrifices the rights of nature in order to secure the freedom of grace. Yesterday he agitated for the abolition of slavery, to-day he agitates for negro suffrage, negro equality, and announces that when he has secured that he will agitate for female suffrage and the equality of the sexes, forgetting or ignorant that the relation of equality subsists only between individuals of the same sex; that God made the man the head of the woman, and the woman for the man, not the man for the woman. Having obliterated all distinction of sex in politics, in social, industrial, and domestic arrangements, he must go farther, and agitate for equality of property. But since property, if recognized at all, will be unequally acquired and distributed, he must go farther still, and agitate for the total abolition of property, as an injustice, a grievous wrong, a theft, with M. Proudhon, or the Englishman Godwin. It is unjust that one should have what another wants, or even more than another. What right have you to ride in your coach or astride your spirited barb while I am forced to trudge on foot? Nor can our humanitarian stop there. Individuals are, and as long as there are individuals will be, unequal:

some are handsomer and some are uglier, some wiser or sillier, more or less gifted, stronger or weaker, taller or shorter, stouter or thinner than others, and therefore some have natural advantages which others have not. There is inequality, therefore injustice, which can be remedied only by the abolition of all individualities, and the reduction of all individuals to the race, or humanity, than in general. He can find no limit to his agitation this side of vague generality, which is no reality, but a pure nullity, for he respects no territorial or individual circumscriptions, and must regard creation itself as a blunder. This is not fancy, for he has gone very nearly as far as it is here shown, if logical, he must go.

The danger now is that the Union victory will, at home and abroad, be interpreted as a victory won in the interest of social or humanitarian democracy. It was because they regarded the war waged on the side of the Union as waged in the interest of this terrible democracy, that our bishops and clergy sympathized so little with the Government in prosecuting it; not, as some imagined, because they were disloyal, hostile to American or territorial democracy, or not heartily in favor of freedom for all men, whatever their race or complexion. They had no wish to see slavery prolonged, the evils of which they, better than any other class of men, knew, and more deeply deplored; none would have regretted more than they to have seen the Union broken up; but they held the socialistic or humanitarian democracy represented by Northern abolitionists as hostile alike to the Church and to civilization. For the same reason that they were backward or reserved in their sympathy, all the humanitarian sects at home and abroad were forward and even ostentatious in theirs. The Catholics feared the war might result in encouraging *La République démocratique et sociale*; the humanitarian sects trusted that it would. If the victory of the Union should turn out to be a victory for the humanitarian democracy, the civilized world will have no reason to applaud it.

That there is some danger that for a time the victory will be taken as a victory for humanitarianism or socialism, it would be idle to deny. It is so taken now, and the humanitarian party throughout the world are in ecstasies over it. The party claim it. The European Socialists and Red Republicans applaud it, and the Mazzinis and the Garibaldis inflict on us the deep humiliation of their congratulations. A cause that can be approved by the revolutionary leaders of European Liberals must be strangely misunderstood, or have in it some infamous element. It is no compliment to a nation to receive the congratulations of men who assert not only people king, but people-God; and those Americans who are delighted with them are worse enemies to the American democracy than ever were Jefferson Davis and his fellow conspirators, and more contemptible, as the swindler is more contemptible than the highwayman.

But it is probable the humanitarians have reckoned without their host. Not they are the real victors. When the smoke of battle has cleared away, the victory, it will be seen, has been won by the Republic, and that that alone has trimuphed. The abolitionists, in so far as they asserted the unity of the race and opposed slavery as a denial of that unity, have also won; but in so far as they denied the reality or authority of territorial and individual circumscriptions, followed a purely socialistic tendency, and sought to dissolve patriotism into a watery sentimentality called philanthropy, have in reality been crushingly defeated, as they will find when the late insurrectionary States are fully reconstructed. The Southern or egoïstical democrats, so far as they denied the unity and solidarity of the race, the rights of society over individuals, and the equal rights of each and every individual in face of the state, or the obligations of society to protect the weak and help the helpless, have been also defeated; but so far as they asserted personal or individual rights which society neither gives nor can take away, and so far as they asserted, not State sovereignty, but State rights, held independently of the General government, and which limit its authority and sphere of action, they share in the victory, as the future will prove.

European Jacobins, revolutionists, conspiring openly or secretly against all legitimate authority, whether in Church or State, have no lot or part in the victory of the American people: not for them nor for men with their nefarious designs or mad dreams, have our brave soldiers fought, suffered, and bled for four years of the most terrible war in modern times, and against troops as brave and as well led as themselves; not for them has the country sacrificed a million of lives, and contracted a debt of four thousand millions of dollars, besides the waste and destruction that it will take years of peaceful industry to repair. They and their barbaric democracy have been defeated, and civilization has won its most brilliant victory in all history. The American democracy has crushed, actually or potentially, every species of barbarism in the New World, asserted victoriously the state, and placed the government definitively on the side of legitimate authority, and made its natural association henceforth with all civilized governments—not with the revolutionary movements to overthrow them. The American people will always be progressive as well as conservative; but they have learned a lesson, which they much needed, against false democracy: civil war has taught them that "the sacred right of insurrection" is as much out of place in a democratic state as in an aristocratic or a monarchical state; and that the government should always be clothed with ample authority to arrest and punish whoever plots its destruction. They must never be delighted again to have their government send a national ship to bring hither a noted traitor to his own sovereign as the nation's guest. The people of the Northern States are hardly less responsible for the late rebellion than the people of the Southern States. Their press had taught them to call every government a tyranny that refused to remain quiet while the traitor was cutting its throat or assassinating the nation, and they had nothing but mad denunciations of the Papal, the

Austrian, and the Neapolitan governments for their severity against conspirators and traitors. But their own government has found it necessary for the public safety to be equally arbitrary, prompt, and severe, and they will most likely require it hereafter to co-operate with the governments of the Old World in advancing civilization, instead of lending all its moral support, as heretofore, to the Jacobins, revolutionists, socialists, and humanitarians, to bring back the reign of barbarism.

The tendency to individualism has been sufficiently checked by the failure of the rebellion, and no danger from the disintegrating element, either in the particular State or in the United States, is henceforth to be apprehended. But the tendency in the opposite direction may give the American state some trouble. The tendency now is, as to the Union, consolidation, and as to the particular state, humanitarianism, socialism, or centralized democracy. Yet this tendency, though it may do much mischief, will hardly become exclusive. The States that seceded, when restored, will always, even in abandoning State sovereignty, resist it, and still assert State rights. When these States are restored to their normal position, they will always be able to protect themselves against any encroachments on their special rights by the General government. The constitution, in the distribution of the powers of government, provides the States severally with ample means to protect their individuality against the centralizing tendency of the General government, however strong it may be.

The war has, no doubt, had a tendency to strengthen the General government, and to cause the people, to a great extent, to look upon it as the supreme and exclusive national government, and to regard the several State governments as subordinate instead of co-ordinate governments. It is not improbable that the Executive, since the outbreak of the rebellion, has proceeded throughout on that supposition, and hence his extraordinary assumptions of power; but when once peace is fully re-established, and the States have all resumed their normal position in the Union, every State will be found prompt enough to resist any attempt to encroach on its constitutional rights. Its instinct of self preservation will lead it to resist, and it will be protected by both its own judiciary and that of the United States.

The danger that the General government will usurp the rights of the States is far less than the danger that the Executive will usurp all the powers of Congress and the judiciary. Congress, during the rebellion, clothed the President, as far as it could, with dictatorial powers, and these powers the Executive continues to exercise even after the rebellion is suppressed. They were given and held under the rights of war, and for war purposes only, and expired by natural limitation when the war ceased; but the Executive forgets this, and, instead of calling Congress together and submitting the work of reconstruction of the States that seceded to its wisdom and authority, undertakes to reconstruct them himself, as if he were an absolute sovereign; and the people seem to like it. He might and should, as commander-in-chief of the army and navy, govern them as military departments, by his lieutenants, till Congress could either create provisional civil governments for them or recognize them as self-governing States in the Union; but he has no right, under the constitution nor under the war power, to appoint civil governors, permanent or provisional; and every act he has done in regard to reconstruction is sheer usurpation, and done without authority and without the slightest plea of necessity. His acts in this respect, even if wise and just in themselves, are inexcusable, because done by one who has no legal right to do them. Yet his usurpation is apparently sustained by public sentiment, and a deep wound is inflicted on the constitution, which will be long in healing.

The danger in this respect is all the greater because it did not originate with the rebellion, but had manifested itself for a long time before. There is a growing disposition on the part of Congress to throw as much of the business of government as possible into the hands of the Executive. The patronage the Executive wields, even in times of peace, is so large that he has indirectly an almost supreme control over the legislative branch of the government. For this, which is, and, if not checked will continue to be, a growing evil, there is no obvious remedy, unless the President is chosen for a longer term of office and made ineligible for a second term, and the mischievous doctrine of rotation in office is rejected as incompatible with the true interests of the public. Here is matter for the consideration of the American statesman. But as to the usurpations of the Executive in these unsettled times, they will be only temporary, and will cease when the States are all restored. They are abuses, but only temporary abuses, and the Southern States, when restored to the Union, will resume their rights in their own sphere, as self-governing communities, and legalize or undo the unwarrantable acts of the Federal Executive.

The socialistic and centralizing tendency in the bosom of the individual States is the most dangerous, but it will not be able to become predominant; for philanthropy, unlike charity, does not begin at home, and is powerless unless it operates at a distance. In the States in which the humanitarian tendency is the strongest, the territorial democracy has its most effective organization. Prior to the outbreak of the rebellion the American people had asserted popular sovereignty, but had never rendered an account to themselves in what sense the people are or are not sovereign. They had never distinguished the three sorts of democracy from one another, asked themselves which of the three is the distinctively American democracy. For them, democracy was democracy, and those who saw dangers ahead sought to avoid them either by exaggerating one or the other of the two exclusive tendencies, or else by restraining democracy itself through restrictions on suffrage. The latter class began to distrust universal suffrage, to lose faith in the people, and to dream of modifying the American constitution so as to make it conform more nearly to the English model. The war has proved that they were wrong, for nothing is more certain than that the people have saved the national unity and integrity almost in spite of their government. The General government either was not disposed or was afraid to take a decided stand against secession, till forced to do it by the people themselves. No wise American can henceforth distrust American democracy. The people may be trusted. So much is settled. But as the two extremes were equally democratic, as the secessionists acted in the name of popular sovereignty, and as the humanitarians were not unwilling to allow separation, and would not and did not engage in the war against secession for the sake of the Union and the integrity of the national domain, the conviction becomes irresistible that it was not democracy in the sense of either of the extremes that made the war and came out of it victorious; and hence the real American democracy must differ from them both, and is neither a personal nor a humanitarian, but a territorial democracy. The true idea of American democracy thus comes out, for the first time, freed from the two extreme democracies which have been identified with it, and henceforth enters into the understandings as well as the hearts of the people. The war has enlightened patriotism, and what was sentiment or instinct becomes reason—a well-defined, and clearly understood constitutional conviction.

In the several States themselves there are many things to prevent the socialistic tendency from becoming exclusive. In the States that seceded socialism has never had a foothold, and will not gain it, for it is resisted by all the sentiments, convictions, and habits of the Southern people, and the Southern people will not be exterminated nor swamped by migrations either from the North or from Europe. They are and always will be an agricultural people, and an agricultural people are and always will be opposed to socialistic dreams, unless unwittingly held for a moment to favor it in pursuit of some special object in which they take a passionate interest. The worst of all policies is that of hanging, exiling, or disfranchising the wealthy landholders of the South, in order to bring up the poor and depressed whites, shadowed forth in the Executive proclamation of the 29th of May, 1865. Of course that policy will not be carried out; and if the negroes are enfranchised, they will always vote with the wealthy landholding class, and aid them in resisting all socialistic tendencies. The humanitarians will fail for the want of a good social grievance against which they can declaim.

In the New England States the humanitarian tendency is strong as a speculation, but only in relation to objects at a distance. It is aided much by the congregational constitution of their religion; yet it is weak at home, and is resisted practically by the territorial division of power. New England means Massachusetts, and nowhere is the subdivision of the powers of government carried further, or the constitution of the territorial democracy more complete, than in that State. Philanthropy seldom works in private against private vices and evils: it is effective only against public grievances, and the farther they are from home and the less its right to interfere with them, the more in earnest and the more effective for evil does it become. Its nature is to mind every one's business but its own. But now that slavery is abolished, there is nowhere in the United States a social grievance of magnitude enough to enlist any considerable number of the people, even of Massachusetts, in a movement to redress it. Negro enfranchisement is a question of which the humanitarians can make something, and they will make the most of it; but as it is a question that each State will soon settle for itself, it will not serve their purpose of prolonged agitation. They could not and never did carry away the nation, even on the question of slavery itself, and abolitionism had comparatively little direct influence in abolishing slavery; and the exclusion of negro suffrage can never be made to appear to the American people as any thing like so great a grievance as was slavery.

Besides, in all the States that did not secede, Catholics are a numerous and an important portion of the population. Their increasing numbers, wealth, and education secure them, as much as the majority may dislike their religion, a constantly increasing influence, and it is idle to leave them out in counting the future of the country. They will, in a very few years, be the best and most thoroughly educated class of the American people; and, aside from their religion, or, rather, in consequence of their religion, the most learned, enlightened, and intelligent portion of the American population; and as much as they have disliked the abolitionists, they have, in the army and elsewhere, contributed their full share to the victory the nation has won. The best things written on the controversy have been written by Catholics, and Catholics are better fitted by their religion to comprehend the real character of the American constitution than any other class of Americans, the moment they study it in the light of their own theology. The American constitution is based on that of natural society, on the solidarity of the race, and the difference between natural society and the church or Christian society is, that the one is initial and the other teleological. The law of both is the same; Catholics, as such, must resist both extremes, because each is exclusive, and whatever is exclusive or one-sided is uncatholic. If they have been backward in their sympathy with the government, it has been through their dislike of the puritanic spirit and the humanitarian or socialistic elements they detected in the Republican party, joined with a prejudice against political and social negro equality. But their church everywhere opposes the socialistic movements of the age, all movements in behalf of barbarism, and they may always be counted on to resist the advance of the socialistic democracy. If the country has had reason to complain of some of them in the late war, it will have, in the future, far stronger reason to be grateful; not to them, indeed, for the citizen owes his life to his country, but to their religion, which has been and is the grand protectress of modern society and civilization.

From the origin of the government there has been a tendency to the extension of suffrage, and to exclude both birth and private property as bases of political rights or franchises. This tendency has often been justified on the ground that the elective franchise is a natural right; which is not true, because the elective franchise is political power, and political power is always a civil trust, never a natural right, and the state judges for itself to whom it will or will not confide the trust; but there can be no doubt that it is a normal tendency, and in strict accordance with the constitution of American civil society, which rests on the unity of the race, and public instead of private property. All political distinctions founded on birth, race, or private wealth are anomalies in the American system, and are necessarily eliminated by its normal developments. To contend that none but property-holders may vote, or none but persons of a particular race may be enfranchised, is unAmerican and contrary to the order of civilization the New World is developing. The only qualification for the elective franchise the American system can logically insist on is that the elector belong to the territorial people—that is, be a natural-born or a naturalized citizen, be a major in full possession of his natural faculties, and unconvicted of any infamous offence. The State is free to naturalize foreigners or not, and under such restrictions as it judges proper; but, having naturalized them, it must treat them as standing on the same footing with natural-born citizens.

The naturalization question is one of great national importance. The migration of foreigners hither has added largely to the national population, and to the national wealth and resources, but less, perhaps, to the development of patriotism, the purity of elections, or the wisdom and integrity of the government. It is impossible that there should be perfect harmony between the national territorial democracy and individuals born, brought up, and formed under a political order in many respects widely different from it; and there is no doubt that the democracy, in its objectionable sense, has been greatly strengthened by the large infusion of naturalized citizens. There can be no question that, if the laboring classes, in whom the national sentiment is usually the strongest, had been composed almost wholly of native Americans, instead of being, as they were, at least in the cities, large towns, and villages, composed almost exclusively of persons foreign born, the Government would have found far less difficulty in filling up the depleted ranks of its armies. But to leave so large a portion of the actual population as the foreign born residing in the country without the rights of citizens, would have been a far graver evil, and would, in the late struggle, have given the victory to secession. There are great national advantages derived from the migration hither of foreign labor, and if the migration be encouraged or permitted, naturalization on easy and liberal terms is the wisest, the best, and only safe policy. The children of foreign-born parents are real Americans.

Emigration has, also, a singular effect in developing the latent powers of the emigrant, and the children of emigrants are usually more active, more energetic than the children of the older inhabitants of the country among whom they settle. Some of our first men in civil life have been sons of foreign-born parents, and so are not a few of our greatest and most successful generals. The most successful of our merchants have been foreign-born. The same thing has been noticed elsewhere, especially in the emigration of the French Huguenots to Holland, Germany, England, and Ireland. The immigration of so many millions from the Old World has, no doubt, given to the American people much of their bold, energetic, and adventurous character, and made them a superior people on the whole to what they would otherwise have been. This has nothing to do with superiority or inferiority of race or blood, but is a natural effect of breaking men away from routine, and throwing them back on their own individual energies and personal resources.

Resistance is offered to negro suffrage, and justly too, till the recently emancipated slaves have served an apprenticeship to freedom; but that resistance cannot long stand before the onward progress of American democracy, which asserts equal rights for all, and not for a race or class only. Some would confine suffrage to landholders, or, at least, to property-holders; but that is inconsistent with the American idea, and is a relic of the barbaric constitution which founds power on private instead of public wealth. Nor are property-owners a whit more likely to vote for the public good than are those who own no property but their own labor. The men of wealth, the business men, manufacturers and merchants, bankers and brokers, are the men who exert the worst influence on government in every country, for they always strive to use it as an instrument of advancing their own private interests. They act on the beautiful maxim, "Let government take care of the rich, and the rich will take care of the poor," instead of the far safer maxim, "Let government take care of the weak, the strong can take care of themselves." Universal suffrage is better than restricted suffrage, but even universal suffrage is too weak to prevent private property from having an undue political influence.

The evils attributed to universal suffrage are not inseparable from it, and, after all, it is doubtful if it elevates men of an inferior class to those elevated by restricted suffrage. The Congress of 1860, or of 1862, was a fair average of the wisdom, the talent, and the virtue of the country, and not inferior to that of 1776, or that of 1789; and the Executive during the rebellion was at least as able and as efficient as it was during the war of 1812, far superior to that of Great Britain, and not inferior to that of France during the Crimean war. The Crimean war developed and placed in high command, either with the English or the French, no generals equal to Halleck, Grant, and Sherman, to say nothing of others. The more aristocratic South proved itself, in both statesmanship and generalship, in no respect superior to the territorial democracy of the North and West.

The great evil the country experiences is not from universal suffrage, but from what may be called rotation in office. The number of political aspirants is so great that, in the Northern and Western States especially, the representatives in Congress are changed every two or four years, and a member, as soon as he has acquired the experience necessary to qualify him for his position, is dropped, not through the fickleness of his constituency, but to give place to another whose aid had been necessary to his first or second election. Employés are "rotated," not because they are incapable or unfaithful, but because there are others who want their places. This is all bad, but it springs not from universal suffrage, but from a wrong public opinion, which might be corrected by the press, but which is mainly formed by it. There is, no doubt, a due share of official corruption, but not more than elsewhere, and that would be much diminished by increasing the salaries of the public servants, especially in the higher offices of the government, both General and State. The pay to the lower officers and employés of the government, and to the privates and non-commissioned officers in the army, is liberal, and, in general, too liberal; but the pay of the higher grades in both the civil and military service is too low, and relatively far lower than it was when the government was first organized.

The worst tendency in the country, and which is not encouraged at all by the territorial democracy, manifests itself in hostility to the military spirit and a standing army. The depreciation of the military spirit comes from the humanitarian or sentimental democracy, which, like all sentimentalisms, defeats itself, and brings about the very evils it seeks to avoid. The hostility to standing armies is inherited from England, and originated in the quarrels between king and parliament, and is a striking evidence of the folly of that bundle of antagonistic forces called the British constitution. In feudal times most of the land was held by military service, and the reliance of government was on the feudal militia; but no real progress was made in eliminating barbarism till the national authority got a regular army at its command, and became able to defend itself against its enemies. It is very doubtful if English civilization has not, upon the whole, lost more than it has gained by substituting parliamentary for royal supremacy, and exchanging the Stuarts for the Guelfs.

No nation is a living, prosperous nation that has lost the military spirit, or in which the profession of the soldier is not held in honor and esteem; and a standing army of reasonable size is public economy. It absorbs in its ranks a class of men who are worth more there than anywhere else; it creates honorable places for gentlemen or the sons of gentlemen without wealth, in which they can serve both themselves and their country. Under a democratic government the most serious embarrassment to the state is its gentlemen, or persons not disposed or not fitted to support themselves by their own hands, more necessary in a democratic government than in any other. The civil service, divinity, law, and medicine, together with literature, science, and art, cannot absorb the whole of this ever-increasing class, and the army and navy would be an economy and a real service to the state were they maintained only for the sake of the rank and position they give to their officers, and the wholesome influence these officers would exert on society and the politics of the country—this even in case there were no wars or apprehension of wars. They supply an element needed in all society, to sustain in it the chivalric and heroic spirit, perpetually endangered by the mercantile and political spirit, which has in it always something low and sordid.

But wars are inevitable, and when a nation has no surrounding nations to fight, it will, as we have just proved, fight itself. When it can have no foreign war, it will get up a domestic war; for the human animal, like all animals, must work off in some way its fighting humor, and the only sure way of maintaining peace is always to be prepared for war. A regular standing army of forty thousand men would have prevented the Mexican war, and an army of fifty thousand well-disciplined and efficient troops at the command of the President on his inauguration in March, 1861, would have prevented the rebellion, or have instantly suppressed it. The cost of maintaining a land army of even a hundred thousand men, and a naval force to correspond, would have been, in simple money value, only a tithe of what the rebellion has cost the nation, to say nothing of the valuable lives that have been sacrificed—for the losses on the rebel side, as well as those on the side of the government, are equally to be counted. The actual losses to the country have been not less than six or eight thousand millions of dollars, or nearly one-half the assessed value of the whole property of the United States according to the census returns of 1860, and which has only been partially cancelled by actual increase of property since. To meet the interest on the debt incurred will require a heavier sum to be raised annually by taxation, twice over, without discharging a cent of the principal, than would have been necessary to maintain an army and navy adequate to the protection of peace and the prevention of the rebellion.

The rebellion is now suppressed, and if the government does not blunder much more in its civil efforts at pacification than it did in its military operations, before 1868 things will settle down into their normal order; but a regular army—not militia or volunteers, who are too expensive—of at least a hundred thousand men of all arms, and a navy nearly as large as that of England or France, will be needed as a peace establishment. The army of a hundred thousand men must form a cadre of an army of three times that number, which will be necessary to place the army on a war footing. Less will answer neither for peace nor war, for the nation has, in spite of herself, to maintain henceforth the rank of a first-class military and maritime power, and take a leading part in political movements of the civilized world, and, to a great extent, hold in her hand the peace of Europe.

Canning boasted that he had raised up the New World to redress the balance of the Old: a vain boast, for he simply weakened Spain and gave the hegemony of Europe to Russia, which the Emperor of the French is trying, by strengthening Italy and Spain, and by a French protectorate in Mexico, to secure to France, both in the Old World and the New—a magnificent dream, but not to be realized. His uncle judged more wisely when he sold Louisiana, left the New World to itself, and sought only to secure to France the hegemony of the Old. But the hegemony of the New World henceforth belongs to the United States, and she will have a potent voice in adjusting the balance of power even in Europe. To maintain this position, which is imperative on her, she must always have a large armed force, either on foot or in reserve, which she can call out and put on a war footing at short notice. The United States must henceforth be a great military and naval power, and the old hostility to a standing army and the old attempt to bring the military into disrepute must be abandoned, and the country yield to its destiny.

Of the several tendencies mentioned, the humanitarian tendency, egoistical at the South, detaching the individual from the race, and socialistic at the North, absorbing the individual in the race, is the most dangerous. The egoistical form is checked, sufficiently weakened by the defeat of the rebels; but the social form believes that it has triumphed, and that individuals are effaced in society, and the States in the Union. Against this, more especially should public opinion and American statesmanship be now directed, and territorial democracy and the division of the powers of government be asserted and vigorously maintained. The danger is that while this socialistic form of democracy is conscious of itself, the territorial democracy has not yet arrived, as the Germans say, at self consciousness—*selbsbewusstseyn*—and operates only instinctively. All the dominant theories and sentimentalities are against it, and it is only Providence that can sustain it.

XV

Destiny—Political & Religious

*I*t has been said in the Introduction to this essay that every living nation receives from Providence a special work or mission in the progress of society, to accomplish which is its destiny, or the end for which it exists; and that the special mission of the United States is to continue and complete in the political order the Græco-Roman civilization.

Of all the states or colonies on this continent, the American Republic alone has a destiny, or the ability to add any thing to the civilization of the race. Canada and the other British Provinces, Mexico and Central America, Columbia and Brazil, and the rest of the South American States, might be absorbed in the United States without being missed by the civilized world. They represent no idea, and the work of civilization could go on without them as well as with them. If they keep up with the progress of civilization, it is all that can be expected of them. France, England, Germany, and Italy might absorb the rest of Europe, and all Asia and Africa, without withdrawing a single laborer from the work of advancing the civilization of the race; and it is doubtful if these nations themselves can severally or jointly advance it much beyond the point reached by the Roman Empire, except in abolishing slavery and including in the political people the whole territorial people. They can only develop and give a general application to the fundamental principles of the Roman constitution. That indeed is much, but it adds no new element nor new combination of pre-existing elements. But nothing of this can be said of the United States.

In the Græco-Roman civilization is found the state proper, and the great principle of the territorial constitution of power, instead of the personal or the genealogical, the patriarchal or the monarchical; and yet with true civil or political principles it mixed up nearly all the elements of the barbaric constitution. The gentile system of Rome recalls the patriarchal, and the relation that subsisted between the patron and his clients has a striking resemblance to that which subsists between the feudal lord and his retainers, and may have had the same origin. The three tribes, Ramnes, Quirites, and Luceres, into which the Roman people were divided before the rise of the plebs, may have been, as Niebuhr contends, local, not genealogical, in their origin, but they were not strictly territorial distinctions, and the division of each tribe into a hundred houses or gentes was not local, but personal, if not, as the name implies, genealogical. No doubt the individuals or families composing the house or gens were not all of kindred blood, for the Oriental custom of adoption, so frequent with our North American Indians, and with all people distributed into tribes, septs, or clans, obtained with the Romans. The adopted member was considered a child of the house, and took its name and inherited its goods. Whether, as Niebuhr maintains, all the free gentiles of the three tribes were called patres or patricians, or whether the term was restricted to the heads of houses, it is certain that the head of the house represented it in the senate, and the vote in the curies was by houses, not by individuals *en masse*. After all, practically the Roman senate was hardly less an estate than the English house of lords, for no one could sit in it unless a landed proprietor and of noble blood. The plebs, though outside of the political people proper, as not being included in the three tribes, when they came to be a power in the republic under the emperors, and the old distinction of plebs and patricians was forgotten, were an estate, and not a local or territorial people.

The republican element was in the fact that the land, which gave the right to participate in political power, was the domain of the state, and the tenant held it from the state. The domain was vested in the state, not in the senator nor the prince, and was therefore *respublica*, not private property—the first grand leap of the human race from barbarism. In all other respects the Roman constitution was no more republican than the feudal. Athens went farther than Rome, and introduced the principle of territorial democracy. The division into demes or wards, whence comes the word *democracy*, was a real territorial division, not personal nor genealogical. And if the equality of all men was not recognized, all who were included in the political class stood on the same footing. Athens and other Greek cities, though conquered by Rome, exerted after their conquest a powerful influence on Roman civilization, which became far more democratic under the emperors than it had been under the patrician senate, which the assassins of Julius Cæsar, and the superannuated conservative party they represented, tried so hard to preserve. The senate and the consulship were opened to the representatives of the great plebeian houses, and the provincials were clothed with the rights of Roman citizens, and uniform laws were established throughout the empire.

The grand error, as has already been said, of the Græco-Roman or gentile civilization, was in its denial or ignorance of the unity of the human race, as well as the Unity of God, and in its including in the state only a particular class of the territorial people, while it held all the rest as slaves, though in different degrees of servitude. It recognized and sustained a privileged class, a ruling order; and if, as subsequently did the Venetian aristocracy, it recognized democratic equality within that order, it held all outside of it to be less than men and without political rights. Practically, power was an attribute of birth and of private wealth. Suffrage was almost universal among freemen, but down almost to the Empire, the people voted by orders, and were counted, not numerically, but by the rank of the order, and the *comitia curiata* could always carry the election over the *comitia centuriata*, and thus power remained always in the hands of the rich and noble few.

The Roman law, as digested by jurists under Justinian in the sixth century, indeed, recognizes the unity of the race, asserts the equality of all men by the natural law, and undertakes to defend slavery on principles not incompatible with that equality. It represents it as a commutation of the punishment of death, which the emperor has the right to inflict on captives taken in war, to perpetual servitude; and as servitude is less severe than death, slavery was really a proof of imperial clemency. But it has never yet been proved that the emperor has the right under the natural law to put captives taken even in a just war to death, and the Roman poet himself bids us "humble the proud, but spare the submissive." In a just war the emperor may kill on the battle-field those in arms against him, but the *jus gentium*, as now interpreted by the jurisprudence of every civilized nation, does not allow him to put them to death after they have ceased resistance, have thrown down their arms, and surrendered. But even if it did, it gives him a right only over the persons captured, not over their innocent children, and therefore no right to establish hereditary slavery, for the child is not punishable for the offences of the parent. The law, indeed, assumed that the captive ceased to exist as a person and treated him as a thing, or mere property of the conqueror; and being property, he could beget only property, which would accrue only to his owner. But there is no power in heaven or earth that can make a person a thing, a mere piece of merchandise, and it is only by a clumsy fiction, or rather by a bare-faced lie, that the law denies the slave his personality and treats him as a thing. If the unity of the race and the brotherhood of all men had been clearly seen and vividly felt, the law would never have attempted to justify perpetual slavery on the ground of its penal character, or indeed on any ground whatever. All men are born under the law of nature with equal rights, and the civil law can justly deprive no man of his liberty, but for a crime, committed by him personally, that justly forfeits his liberty to society.

These defects of the Græco-Roman civilization the European nations have in part remedied, and may completely remedy. They can carry out practically the Christian dogma of the unity of the human race, abolish slavery in every form, make all men equal before the law, and the political people commensurate with the territorial people. Indeed, France has already done it. She has abolished slavery, villenage, serfage, political aristocracy, asserted the equality of all men before the law, vindicated the sovereignty of the people, and established universal suffrage, complete social and territorial democracy. The other nations may do as much, but hardly can any of them do more or advance farther. Yet in France, territorial democracy the most complete results only in establishing the most complete imperial centralism, usually called Cæsarism.

The imperial constitution of France recognizes that the emperor reigns "by the grace of God and the will of the nation," and therefore, that by the grace of God and the will of the nation he may cease to reign; but while he reigns he is supreme, and his will is law. The constitution imposes no real or effective restraint on his power: while he sits upon the throne he is practically France, and the ministers are his clerks; the council of state, the senate, and the legislative body are merely his agents in governing the nation. This may, indeed, be changed, but only to substitute for imperial centralism democratic centralism, which were no improvement, or to go back to the system of antagonisms, checks and balances, called constitutionalism, or parliamentary government, of which Great Britain is the model, and which were a return toward barbarism, or mediæval feudalism.

The human race has its life in God, and tends to realize in all orders the Divine Word or Logos, which is logic itself, and the principle of all conciliation, of the dialectic union of all opposites or extremes. Mankind will be logical; and the worst of all tyrannies is that which forbids them to draw from their principles their last logical consequences, or that prohibits them the free explication and application of the Divine Idea, in which consists their life, their progress. Such tyranny strikes at the very existence of society, and wars against the reality of things. It is supremely sophistical, and its success is death; for the universe in its constitution is supremely logical, and man, individually and socially, is rational. God is the author and type of all created things; and all creatures, each in its order, imitate or copies the Divine Being, who is intrinsically Father, Son, and Holy Ghost, principle, medium, and end. The Son or Word is the medium, which unites the two extremes, whence God is living God—a real, active, living Being—living, concrete, not abstract or dead unity, like the unity of old Xenophanes, Plotinus, and Proclus. In the Holy Trinity is the principle and prototype of all society, and what is called the solidarity of the race is only the outward expression, or copy in the external order, of what theologians term the circumsession of the three Divine Persons of the Godhead.

Now, human society, when it copies the Divine essence and nature either in the distinction of persons alone, or in the unity alone, is sophistical, and wants the principle of all life and reality. It sins against God, and must fail of its end. The English system, which is based on antagonistic elements, on opposites, without the middle term that conciliates them, unites them, and makes them dialectically one, copies the Divine model in its distinctions alone, which, considered alone, are opposites or contraries. It denies, if Englishmen could but see it, the unity of God. The French, or imperial system, which excludes the extremes, instead of uniting them, denies all opposites, instead of conciliating them—denies the distinctions in the model, and copies only the unity, which is the supreme sophism called pantheism. The English constitution has no middle term, and the French no extremes, and each in its way denies the Divine Trinity, the original basis and type of the syllogism. The human race can be contented with neither, for neither allows it free scope for its inherent life and activity. The English system tends to pure individualism; the French to pure socialism or despotism, each endeavoring to suppress an element of the one living and indissoluble TRUTH.

This is not fancy, is not fine-spun speculation, or cold and lifeless abstraction, but the highest theological and philosophical truth, without which there were no reason, no man, no society; for God is the first principle of all being, all existence, all science, all life, and it is in Him that we live and move and have our being. God is at the beginning, in the middle, and at the end of all things—the universal principle, medium, and end; and no truth can be denied without His existence being directly or indirectly impugned. In a deeper sense than is commonly understood is it true that *nisi Dominus ædificaverit domum, in vanum laboraverunt qui ædificant eam.* The English constitution is composed of contradictory elements, incapable of reconciliation, and each element is perpetually struggling with the others for the mastery. For a long time the king labored, intrigued, and fought to free himself from the thraldom in which he was held by the feudal barons; in 1688 the aristocracy and people united and humbled the crown; and now the people are at work seeking to sap both the crown and the nobles. The state is constituted to nobody's satisfaction; and though all may unite in boasting its excellences, all are at work trying to alter or amend it. The work of constituting the state with the English is ever beginning, never ending. Hence the eternal clamor for parliamentary reform.

Great Britain and other European states may sweep away all that remains of feudalism, include the whole territorial people with the equal rights of all in the state or political people, concede to birth and wealth no political rights, but they will by so doing only establish either imperial centralism, as has been done in France, or democratic centralism, clamored for, conspired for, and fought for by the revolutionists of Europe. The special merit of the American system is not in its democracy alone, as too many at home and abroad imagine; but along with its democracy in the division of the powers of government, between a General government and particular State governments, which are not antagonistic governments, for they act on different matters, and neither is nor can be subordinated to the other.

Now, this division of power, which decentralizes the government without creating mutually hostile forces, can hardly be introduced into any European state. There may be a union of states in Great Britain, in Germany, in Italy, perhaps in Spain, and Austria is laboring hard to effect it in her heterogeneous empire; but the union possible in any of them is that of a Bund or confederation, like the Swiss or German Bund, similar to what the secessionists in the United States so recently attempted and have so signally failed to establish. An intelligent Confederate officer remarked that their Confederacy had not been in operation three months before it became evident that the principle on which it was founded, if not rejected, would insure its defeat. It was that principle of State sovereignty, for which the States seceded, more than the superior resources and numbers of the Government, that caused the collapse of the Confederacy. The numbers were relatively about equal, and the military resources of the Confederacy were relatively not much inferior to those of the Government. So at least the Confederate leaders thought, and they knew the material resources of the Government as well as their own, and had calculated them with as much care and accuracy as any men could. Foreign powers also, friendly as well as unfriendly, felt certain that the secessionists would gain their independence, and so did a large part of the people even of the loyal States. The failure is due to the disintegrating principle of State sovereignty, the very principle of the Confederacy. The war has proved that united states are, other things being equal, an overmatch for confederated states.

The European states must unite either as equals or as unequals. As equals, the union can be only a confederacy, a sort of Zollverein, in which each state retains its individual sovereignty; if as unequals, then some one among them will aspire to the hegemony, and you have over again the Athenian Confederation, formed at the conclusion of the Persian war, and its fate. A union like the American cannot be created by a compact, or by the exercise of supreme power. The Emperor of the French cannot erect the several Departments of France into states, and divide the powers of government between them as individual and as united states. They would necessarily hold from the imperial government, which, though it might exercise a large part of its functions through them, would remain, as now, the supreme central government, from which all governmental powers emanate, as our President is apparently attempting, in his reconstruction policy, to make the government of the United States. The elements of a state constituted like the American do not exist in any European nation, nor in the constitution of European society; and the American constitution would have been impracticable even here had not Providence so ordered it that the nation was born with it, and has never known any other.

Rome recognized the necessity of the federal principle, and applied it in the best way she could. At first it was a single tribe or people distributed into distinct gentes or houses; after the Sabine war, a second tribe was added on terms of equality, and the state was dual, composed of two tribes, the Ramnes and the Tities or Quirites, and, afterward, in the time of Tullus Hostilius, were added the Lucertes or Luceres, making the division into three ruling tribes, each divided into one hundred houses or gentes. Each house in each tribe was represented by its chief or decurion in the senate, making the number of senators exactly three hundred, at which number the senate was fixed. Subsequently was added, by Ancus, the plebs, who remained without authority or share in the government of the city of Rome itself, though they might aspire to the first rank in the allied cities. The division into tribes, and the division of the tribes into gentes or houses, and the vote in the state by tribes, and in the tribes by houses, effectually excluded democratic centralism; but the division was not a division of the powers of government between two co-ordinate governments, for the senate had supreme control, like the British parliament, over all matters, general and particular.

The establishment, after the secession of the plebs, of the tribunitial veto, which gave the plebeians a negative power in the state, there was an incipient division of the powers of government; but only a division between the positive and negative powers, not between the general and the particular. The power accorded to the plebs, or commons, as Niebuhr calls them—who is, perhaps, too fond of explaining the early constitution of Rome by analogies borrowed from feudalism, and especially from the constitution of his native Ditmarsch—was simply an obstructive power; and when it, by development, became a positive power, it absorbed all the powers of government, and created the Empire.

There was, indeed, a nearer approach to the division of powers in the American system, between imperial Rome and her allied or confederated municipalities. These municipalities, modelled chiefly after that of Rome, were elective, and had the management of their own local affairs; but their local powers were not co-ordinate in their own sphere with those exercised by the Roman municipality, but subordinate and dependent. The senate had the supreme power over them, and they held their rights subject to its will. They were formally, or virtually, subjugated states, to which the Roman senate, and afterward the Roman emperors, left the form of the state and the mere shadow of freedom. Rome owed much to her affecting to treat them as allies rather than as subjects, and at first these municipal organizations secured the progress of civilization in the provinces; but at a later period, under the emperors, they served only the imperial treasury, and were crushed by the taxes imposed and the contributions levied on them by the fiscal agents of the empire. So heavy were the fiscal burdens imposed on the burgesses, if the term may be used, that it needed an imperial edict to compel them to enter the municipal government; and it became, under the later emperors, no uncommon thing for free citizens to sell themselves into slavery, to escape the fiscal burdens imposed. There are actually imperial edicts extant forbidding freemen to sell themselves as slaves. Thus ended the Roman federative system, and it is difficult to discover in Europe the elements of a federative system that could have a more favorable result.

Now, the political destiny or mission of the United States is, in common with the European nations, to eliminate the barbaric elements retained by the Roman constitution, and specially to realize that philosophical division of the powers of government which distinguish it from both imperial and democratic centralism on the one hand, and, on the other, from the checks and balances or organized antagonisms which seek to preserve liberty by obstructing the exercise of power. No greater problem in statesmanship remains to be solved, and no greater contribution to civilization to be made. Nowhere else than in this New World, and in this New World only in the United States, can this problem be solved, or this contribution be made, and what the Græco-Roman republic began be completed.

But the United States have a religious as well as a political destiny, for religion and politics go together. Church and state, as governments, are separate indeed, but the principles on which the state is founded have their origin and ground in the spiritual order—in the principles revealed or affirmed by religion—and are inseparable from them. There is no state without God, any more than there is a church without Christ or the Incarnation. An atheist may be a politician, but if there were no God there could be no politics. Theological principles are the basis of political principles. The created universe is a dialectic whole, distinct but inseparable from its Creator, and all its parts cohere and are essential to one another. All has its origin and prototype in the Triune God, and throughout expresses unity in triplicity and triplicity in unity, without which there is no real being and no actual or possible life. Every thing has its principle, medium, and end. Natural society is initial, civil government is medial, the church is teleological, but the three are only distinctions in one indissoluble whole.

Man, as we have seen, lives by communion with God through the Divine creative act, and is perfected or completed only through the Incarnation, in Christ, the Word made flesh. True, he communes with God through his kind, and through external nature, society in which he is born and reared, and property through which he derives sustenance for his body; but these are only media of his communion with God, the source of life—not either the beginning or the end of his communion. They have no life in themselves, since their being is in God, and, of themselves, can impart none. They are in the order of second causes, and second causes, without the first cause, are nought. Communion which stops with them, which takes them as the principle and end, instead of media, as they are, is the communion of death, not of life. As religion includes all that relates to communion with God, it must in some form be inseparable from every living act of man, both individually and socially; and, in the long run, men must conform either their politics to their religion or their religion to their politics. Christianity is constantly at work, moulding political society in its own image and likeness, and every political system struggles to harmonize Christianity with itself. If, then, the United States have a political destiny, they have a religious destiny inseparable from it.

The political destiny of the United States is to conform the state to the order of reality, or, so to speak, to the Divine Idea in creation. Their religious destiny is to render practicable and to realize the normal relations between church and state, religion and politics, as concreted in the life of the nation.

In politics, the United States are not realizing a political theory of any sort whatever. They, on the contrary, are successfully refuting all political theories, making away with them, and establishing the state— not on a theory, not on an artificial basis or a foundation laid by human reason or will, but on reality, the eternal and immutable principles in relation to which man is created. They are doing the same in regard to religious theories. Religion is not a theory, a subjective view, an opinion, but is, objectively, at once a principle, a law, and a fact, and, subjectively, it is, by the the aid of God's grace, practical conformity to what is universally true and real. The United States, in fulfilment of their destiny, are making as sad havoc with religious theories as with political theories, and are pressing on with irresistible force to the real or the Divine order which is expressed in the Christian mysteries, which exists independent of man's understanding and will, and which man can neither make nor unmake.

The religious destiny of the United States is not to create a new religion nor to found a new church. All real religion is catholic, and is neither new nor old, but is always and everywhere true. Even our Lord came neither to found a new church nor to create a new religion, but to do the things which had been foretold, and to fulfil in time what had been determined in eternity. God has himself founded the church on catholic principles, or principles always and everywhere real principles. His church is necessarily catholic, because founded on catholic dogmas, and the dogmas are catholic, because they are universal and immutable principles, having their origin and ground in the Divine Being Himself, or in the creative act by which He produces and sustains all things. Founded on universal and immutable principles, the church can never grow old or obsolete, but is the church for all times and places, for all ranks and conditions of men. Man cannot change either the church or the dogmas of faith, for they are founded in the highest reality, which is above him, over him, and independent of him. Religion is above and independent of the state, and the state has nothing to do with the church or her dogmas, but to accept and conform to them as it does to any of the facts or principles of science, to a mathematical truth, or to a physical law.

But while the church, with her essential constitution, and her dogmas are founded in the Divine order, and are catholic and unalterable, the relations between the civil and ecclesiastical authorities may be changed or modified by the changes of time and place. These relations have not been always the same, but have differed in different ages and countries. During the first three centuries of our era the church had no legal *status*, and was either connived at or persecuted by the state. Under the Christian emperors she was recognized by the civil law; her prelates had exclusive jurisdiction in mixed civil and ecclesiastical questions, and were made, in some sense, civil magistrates, and paid as such by the empire. Under feudalism, the prelates received investiture as princes and barons, and formed alone, or in connection with the temporal lords, an estate in the kingdom. The Pope became a temporal prince and suzerain, at one time, of a large part of Europe, and exercised the arbitratorship in all grave questions between Christian sovereigns themselves, and between them and their subjects. Since the downfall of feudalism and the establishment of modern centralized monarchy, the church has been robbed of the greater part of her temporal possessions, and deprived, in most countries, of all civil functions, and treated by the state either as an enemy or as a slave.

In all the sectarian and schismatic states of the Old World, the national church is held in strict subjection to the civil authority, as in Great Britain and Russia, and is the slave of the state; in the other states of Europe, as France, Austria, Spain, and Italy, she is treated with distrust by the civil government, and allowed hardly a shadow of freedom and independence. In France, which has the proud title of eldest daughter of the church, Catholics, as such, are not freer than they are in Turkey.

All religions are said to be free, and all are free, except the religion of the majority of Frenchmen. The emperor, because nominally a Catholic, takes it upon himself to concede the church just as much and just as little freedom in the empire as he judges expedient for his own secular interests. In Italy, Spain, Portugal, Mexico, and the Central and South American states, the policy of the civil authorities is the same, or worse. It may be safely asserted that, except in the United States, the church is either held by the civil power in subjection, or treated as an enemy. The relation is not that of union and harmony, but that of antagonism, to the grave detriment of both religion and civilization.

It is impossible, even if it were desirable, to restore the mixture of civil and ecclesiastical governments which obtained in the Middle Ages; and a total separation of church and state, even as corporations, would, in the present state of men's minds in Europe, be construed, if approved by the church, into a sanction by her of political atheism, or the right of the civil power to govern according to its own will and pleasure in utter disregard of the law of God, the moral order, or the immutable distinctions between right and wrong. It could only favor the absolutism of the state, and put the temporal in the place of the spiritual. Hence, the Holy Father includes the proposition of the entire separation of church and state in the Syllabus of Errors condemned in his Encyclical, dated at Rome, December 8, 1864. Neither the state nor the people, elsewhere than in the United States, can understand practically such separation in any other sense than the complete emancipation of our entire secular life from the law of God, or the Divine order, which is the real order. It is not the union of church and state—that is, the union, or identity rather, of religious and political principles—that it is desirable to get rid of, but the disunion or antagonism of church and state. But this is nowhere possible out of the United States; for nowhere else is the state organized on catholic principles, or capable of acting, when acting from its own constitution, in harmony with a really catholic church, or the religious order really existing, in relation to which all things are created and governed. Nowhere else is it practicable, at present, to maintain between the two powers their normal relations.

But what is not practicable in the Old World is perfectly practicable in the New. The state here being organized in accordance with catholic principles, there can be no antagonism between it and the church. Though operating in different spheres, both are, in their respective spheres, developing and applying to practical life the one and the same Divine Idea. The church can trust the state, and the state can trust the church. Both act from the same principle to one and the same end. Each by its own constitution co-operates with, aids, and completes the other. It is true the church is not formally established as the civil law of the land, nor is it necessary that she should be; because there is nothing in the state that conflicts with her freedom and independence, with her dogmas or her irreformable canons. The need of establishing the church by law, and protecting her by legal pains and penalties, as is still done in most countries, can exist only in a barbarous or semi-barbarous state of society, where the state is not organized on catholic principles, or the civilization is based on false principles, and in its development tends not to the real or Divine order of things. When the state is constituted in harmony with that order, it is carried onward by the force of its own internal constitution in a catholic direction, and a church establishment, or what is called a state religion, would be an anomaly, or a superfluity. The true religion is in the heart of the state, as its informing principle and real interior life. The external establishment, by legal enactment of the church, would afford her no additional protection, add nothing to her power and efficacy, and effect nothing for faith or piety—neither of which can be forced, because both must, from their nature, be free-will offerings to God.

In the United States, false religions are legally as free as the true religion; but all false religions being one-sided, sophistical, and uncatholic, are opposed by the principles of the state, which tend, by their silent but effective workings, to eliminate them. The American state recognizes only the catholic religion. It eschews all sectarianism, and none of the sects have been able to get their peculiarities incorporated into its constitution or its laws. The state conforms to what each holds that is catholic, that is always and everywhere religion; and whatever is not catholic it leaves, as outside of its province, to live or die, according to its own inherent vitality or want of vitality. The state conscience is catholic, not sectarian; hence it is that the utmost freedom can be allowed to all religions, the false as well as the true; for the state, being catholic in its constitution, can never suffer the adherents of the false to oppress the consciences of the adherents of the true. The church being free, and the state harmonizing with her, catholicity has, in the freedom of both, all the protection it needs, all the security it can ask, and all the support it can, in the nature of the case, receive from external institutions, or from social and political organizations.

This freedom may not be universally wise or prudent, for all nations may not be prepared for it: all may not have attained their majority. The church, as well as the state, must deal with men and nations as they are, not as they are not. To deal with a child as with an adult, or with a barbarous nation as with a civilized nation, would be only acting a lie. The church cannot treat men as free men where they are not free men, nor appeal to reason in those in whom reason is undeveloped. She must adapt her discipline to the age, condition, and culture of individuals, and to the greater or less progress of nations in civilization. She herself remains always the same in her constitution, her authority, and her faith; but varies her discipline with the variations of time and place. Many of her canons, very proper and necessary in one age, cease to be so in another, and many which are needed in the Old World would be out of place in the New World. Under the American system, she can deal with the people as free men, and trust them as freemen, because free men they are. The freeman asks, why? and the reason why must be given him, or his obedience fails to be secured. The simple reason that the church commands will rarely satisfy him; he would know why she commands this or that. The full-grown free man revolts at blind obedience, and he regards all obedience as in some measure blind for which he sees only an extrinsic command. Blind obedience even to the authority of the church cannot be expected of the people reared under the American system, not because they are filled with the spirit of disobedience, but because they insist that obedience shall be *rationabile obsequium,* an act of the understanding, not of the will or the affections alone. They are trained to demand a reason for the command given them, to distinguish between the law and the person of the magistrate. They can obey God, but not man, and they must see that the command given has its reason in the Divine order, or the intrinsic catholic reason of things, or they will not yield it a full, entire, and hearty obedience. The reason that suffices for the child does not suffice for the adult, and the reason that suffices for barbarians does not suffice for civilized men, or that suffices for nations in the infancy of their civilization does not suffice for them in its maturity. The appeal to external authority was much less frequent under the Roman Empire than in the barbarous ages that followed its downfall, when the church became mixed up with the state.

This trait of the American character is not uncatholic. An intelligent, free, willing obedience, yielded from personal conviction, after seeing its reasonableness, its justice, its logic, in the Divine order—the obedience of a free man, not of a slave—is far more consonant to the spirit of the church, and far more acceptable to God, than simple, blind obedience; and a people capable of yielding it stand far higher in the scale of civilization than the people that must be governed as children or barbarians. It is possible that the people of the Old World are not prepared for the regimen of freedom in religion any more than they are prepared for freedom in politics; for they have been trained only to obey external authority, and are not accustomed to look on religion as having its reason in the real order, or in the reason of things. They understand no reason for obedience beyond the external command, and do not believe it possible to give or to understand the reason why the command itself is given. They regard the authority of the church as a thing apart, and see no way by which faith and reason can be harmonized. They look upon them as antagonistic forces rather than as integral elements of one and the same whole. Concede them the regimen of freedom, and their religion has no support but in their good-will, their affections, their associations, their habits, and their prejudices. It has no root in their rational convictions, and when they begin to reason they begin to doubt. This is not the state of things that is desirable, but it cannot be remedied under the political *régime* established elsewhere than in the United States. In every state in the world, except the American, the civil constitution is sophistical, and violates, more or less, the logic of things; and, therefore, in no one of them can the people receive a thoroughly dialectic training, or an education in strict conformity to the real order. Hence, in them all, the church is more or less obstructed in her operations, and prevented from carrying out in its fulness her own Divine Idea. She does the best she can in the circumstances and with the materials with which she is supplied, and exerts herself continually to bring individuals and nations into harmony with her Divine law; but still her life in the midst of the nations is a struggle, a warfare.

The United States being dialectically constituted, and founded on real catholic, not sectarian or sophistical principles, presents none of these obstacles, and must, in their progressive development or realization of their political idea, put an end to this warfare, in so far as a warfare between church and state, and leave the church in her normal position in society, in which she can, without let or hindrance, exert her free spirit, and teach and govern men by the Divine law as free men. She may encounter unbelief, misbelief, ignorance, and indifference in few, or in many; but these, deriving no support from the state, which tends constantly to eliminate them, must gradually give way before her invincible logic, her divine charity, the truth and reality of things, and the intelligence, activity, and zeal of her ministers. The American people are, on the surface, sectarians or indifferentists; but they are, in reality, less uncatholic than the people of any other country, because they are, in their intellectual and moral development, nearer to the real order, or, in the higher and broader sense of the word, more truly civilized. The multitude of sects that obtain may excite religious compassion for those who are carried away by them, for men can be saved or attain to their eternal destiny only by truth, or conformity to Him who said, "I am the way, the truth, and the life;" but in relation to the national destiny they need excite no alarm, no uneasiness, for underlying them all is more or less of catholic truth, and the vital forces of the national life repel them, in so far as they are sectarian and not catholic, as substances that cannot be assimilated to the national life. The American state being catholic in its organic principles, as is all real religion, and the church being free, whatever is anti-catholic, or uncatholic, is without any support in either, and having none, either in reality or in itself, it must necessarily fall and gradually disappear.

The sects themselves have a half unavowed conviction that they cannot subsist forever as sects, if unsupported by the civil authority. They are free, but do not feel safe in the United States. They know the real church is catholic, and that they themselves are none of them catholic. The most daring among them even pretends to be no more than a "branch" of the catholic church. They know that only the catholic church can withstand the pressure of events and survive the shocks of time, and hence everywhere their movements to get rid of their sectarianism and to gain a catholic character. They hold conventions of delegates from the whole sectarian world, form "unions," "alliances," and "associations;" but, unhappily for their success, the catholic church does not originate in convention, but is founded by the Word made flesh, and sustained by the indwelling Holy Ghost. The most they can do, even with the best dispositions in the world, is to create a confederation, and confederated sects are something very different from a church inherently one and catholic. It is no more the catholic church than the late Southern Confederacy was the American state. The sectarian combinations may do some harm, may injure many souls, and retard, for a time, the progress of civilization; but in a state organized in accordance with catholic principles, and left to themselves, they are powerless against the national destiny, and must soon wither and die as branches severed from the vine.

Such being the case, no sensible Catholic can imagine that the church needs any physical force against the sects, except to repel actual violence, and protect her in that freedom of speech and possession which is the right of all before the state. What are called religious establishments are needed only where either the state is barbarous or the religion is sectarian. Where the state, in its intrinsic constitution, is in accordance with catholic principles, as in the United States, the church has all she needs or can receive. The state can add nothing more to her power or her security in her moral and spiritual warfare with sectarianism, and any attempt to give her more would only weaken her as against the sects, place her in a false light, partially justify their hostility to her, render effective their declamations against her, mix her up unnecessarily with political changes, interests, and passions, and distract the attention of her ministers from their proper work as churchmen, and impose on them the duties of politicians and statesmen. Where there is nothing in the state hostile to the church, where she is free to act according to her own constitution and laws, and exercise her own discipline on her own spiritual subjects, civil enactments in her favor or against the sects may embarrass or impede her operations, but cannot aid her, for she can advance no farther than she wins the heart and convinces the understanding. A spiritual work can, in the nature of things, be effected only by spiritual means. The church wants freedom in relation to the state—nothing more; for all her power comes immediately from God, without any intervention or mediation of the state.

The United States, constituted in accordance with the real order of things, and founded on principles which have their origin and ground in the principles on which the church herself is founded, can never establish any one of the sects as the religion of the state, for that would violate their political constitution, and array all the other sects, as well as the church herself, against the government. They cannot be called upon to establish the church by law, because she is already in their constitution as far as the state has in itself any relation with religion, and because to establish her in any other sense would be to make her one of the civil institutions of the land, and to bring her under the control of the state, which were equally against her interest and her nature.

The religious mission of the United States is not then to establish the church by external law, or to protect her by legal disabilities, pains, and penalties against the sects, however uncatholic they may be; but to maintain catholic freedom, neither absorbing the state in the church nor the church in the state, but leaving each to move freely, according to its own nature, in the sphere assigned it in the eternal order of things. Their mission separates church and state as external governing bodies, but unites them in the interior principles from which each derives its vitality and force. Their union is in the intrinsic unity of principle, and in the fact that, though moving in different spheres, each obeys one and the same Divine law. With this the Catholic, who knows what Catholicity means, is of course satisfied, for it gives the church all the advantage over the sects of the real over the unreal; and with this the sects have no right to be dissatisfied, for it subjects them to no disadvantage not inherent in sectarianism itself in presence of Catholicity, and without any support from the civil authority.

The effect of this mission of our country fully realized, would be to harmonize church and state, religion and politics, not by absorbing either in the other, or by obliterating the natural distinction between them, but by conforming both to the real or Divine order, which is supreme and immutable. It places the two powers in their normal relation, which has hitherto never been done, because hitherto there never has been a state normally constituted. The nearest approach made to the realization of the proper relations of church and state, prior to the birth of the American Republic, was in the Roman Empire under the Christian emperors; but the state had been perverted by paganism, and the emperors, inheriting the old pontifical power, could never be made to understand their own incompetency in spirituals, and persisted to the last in treating the church as a civil institution under their supervision and control, as does the Emperor of the French in France, even yet. In the Middle Ages the state was so barbarously constituted that the church was obliged to supervise its administration, to mix herself up with the civil government, in order to infuse some intelligence into civil matters, and to preserve her own rightful freedom and independence. When the states broke away from feudalism, they revived the Roman constitution, and claimed the authority in ecclesiastical matters that had been exercised by the Roman Cæsars, and the states that adopted a sectarian religion gave the sect adopted a civil establishment, and subjected it to the civil government, to which the sect not unwillingly consented, on condition that the civil authority excluded the church and all other sects, and made it the exclusive religion of the state, as in England, Scotland, Sweden,

Denmark, Russia, and the states of Northern Germany. Even yet the normal relations of church and state are nowhere practicable in the Old World; for everywhere either the state is more or less barbaric in its constitution, or the religion is sectarian, and the church as well as civilization is obliged to struggle with antagonistic forces, for self-preservation.

There are formidable parties all over Europe at work to introduce what they take to be the American system; but constitutions are generated, not made—Providential, not conventional. Statesmen can only develop what is in the existing constitutions of their respective countries, and no European constitution contains all the elements of the American. European Liberals mistake the American system, and, were they to succeed in their efforts, would not introduce it, but something more hostile to it than the governments and institutions they are warring against. They start from narrow, sectarian, or infidel premises, and seek not freedom of worship, but freedom of denial. They suppress the freedom of religion as the means of securing what they call religious liberty—imagine that they secure freedom of thought by extinguishing the light without which no thought is possible, and advance civilization by undermining its foundation. The condemnation of their views and movements by the Holy Father in the Encyclical, which has excited so much hostility, may seem to superficial and unthinking Americans even, as a condemnation of our American system—indeed, as the condemnation of modern science, intelligence, and civilization itself; but whoever looks below the surface, has some insight into the course of events, understands the propositions and movements censured, and the sense in which they are censured, is well assured that the Holy Father has simply exercised his pastoral and teaching authority to save religion, society, science, and civilization from utter corruption or destruction. The opinions, tendencies, and movements, directly or by implication censured, are the effect of narrow and superficial thinking, of partial and one-sided views, and are sectarian, sophistical, and hostile to all real progress, and tend, as far as they go, to throw society back into the barbarism from which, after centuries of toil and struggle, it is just beginning to emerge. The Holy Father has condemned nothing that real philosophy, real science does not also condemn; nothing, in fact, that is not at war with the American system itself. For the mass of the people, it were desirable that fuller explanations should be given of the sense in which the various propositions censured are condemned, for some of them are not, in every sense, false; but the explanations needed were expected by the Holy Father to be given by the bishops and prelates, to whom, not to the people, save through them, the Encyclical was addressed. Little is to be hoped, and much is to be feared, for liberty, science, and civilization from European Liberalism, which has no real affinity with American territorial democracy and real civil and religious freedom. But God and reality are present in the Old World as well as in the New, and it will never do to restrict their power or freedom.

Whether the American people will prove faithful to their mission, and realize their destiny, or not, is known only to Him from whom nothing is hidden. Providence is free, and leaves always a space for human free-will. The American people can fail, and will fail if they neglect the appointed means and conditions of success; but there is nothing in their present state or in their past history to render their failure probable. They have in their internal constitution what Rome wanted, and they are in no danger of being crushed by exterior barbarism. Their success as feeble colonies of Great Britain in achieving their national independence, and especially in maintaining, unaided, and against the real hostility of Great Britain and France, their national unity and integrity against a rebellion which, probably, no other people could have survived, gives reasonable assurance for their future. The leaders of the rebellion, than whom none better knew or more nicely calculated the strength and resources of the Union, counted with certainty on success, and the ablest, the most experienced, and best-informed statesmen of the Old World felt sure that the Republic was gone, and spoke of it as the *late* United States. Not a few, even in the loyal States, who had no sympathy with the rebellion, believed it idle to think of suppressing it by force, and advised peace on the best terms that could be obtained. But *Ilium fuit* was chanted too soon; the American people were equal to the emergency, and falsified the calculations and predictions of their enemies, and surpassed the expectations of their friends.

The attitude of the real American people during the fearful struggle affords additional confidence in their destiny. With larger armies on foot than Napoleon ever commanded, with their line of battle stretching from ocean to ocean, across the whole breadth of the continent, they never, during four long years of alternate victories and defeats— and both unprecedentedly bloody—for a moment lost their equanimity, or appeared less calm, collected, tranquil, than in the ordinary times of peace. They not for a moment interrupted their ordinary routine of business or pleasure, or seemed conscious of being engaged in any serious struggle which required an effort. There was no hurry, no bustle, no excitement, no fear, no misgiving. They seemed to regard the war as a mere bagatelle, not worth being in earnest about. The on-looker was almost angry with their apparent indifference, apparent insensibility, and doubted if they moved at all. Yet move they did: guided by an un-erring instinct, they moved quietly on with an elemental force, in spite of a timid and hesitating administration, in spite of inexperienced, over-cautious, incompetent, or blundering military commanders, whom they gently brushed aside, and desisted not till their object was gained, and they saw the flag of the Union floating anew in the breeze from the capitol of every State that dared secede. No man could contemplate them without feeling that there was in them a latent power vastly superior to any which they judged it necessary to put forth. Their success proves to all that what, prior to the war, was treated as American arrogance or self-conceit, was only the outspoken confidence in their destiny as a Providential people, conscious that to them is reserved the hegemony of the world.

Count de Maistre predicted early in the century the failure of the United States, because they have no proper name; but his prediction assumed what is not the fact. The United States have a proper name by which all the world knows and calls them. The proper name of the country is America: that of the people is Americans. Speak of Americans simply, and nobody understands you to mean the people of Canada, Mexico, Brazil, Peru, Chile, Paraguay, but everybody understands you to mean the people of the United States. The fact is significant, and foretells for the people of the United States a continental destiny, as is also foreshadowed in the so-called "Monroe doctrine," which France, during our domestic troubles, was permitted, on condition of not intervening in our civil war in favor of the rebellion, to violate.

There was no statesmanship in proclaiming the "Monroe doctrine," for the statesman keeps always, as far as possible, his government free to act according to the exigencies of the case when it comes up, unembarrassed by previous declarations of principles. Yet the doctrine only expresses the destiny of the American people, and which nothing but their own fault can prevent them from realizing in its own good time. Napoleon will not succeed in his Mexican policy, and Mexico will add some fifteen or twenty new States to the American Union as soon as it is clearly for the interests of all parties that it should be done, and it can be done by mutual consent, without war or violence. The Union will fight to maintain the integrity of her domain and the supremacy of her laws within it, but she can never, consistently with her principles or her interests, enter upon a career of war and conquest. Her system is violated, endangered, not extended, by subjugating her neighbors, for subjugation and liberty go not together. Annexation, when it takes place, must be on terms of perfect equality, and by the free act of the state annexed. The Union can admit of no inequality of rights and franchises between the States of which it is composed. The Canadian Provinces and the Mexican and Central American States, when annexed, must be as free as the original States of the Union, sharing alike in the power and the protection of the Republic—alike in its authority, its freedom, its grandeur, and its glory, as one free, independent, self-governing people. They may gain much, but must lose nothing by annexation.

The Emperor Napoleon and his very respectable *protégé*, Maximilian, an able man and a liberal-minded prince, can change nothing in the destiny of the United States, or of Mexico herself; no imperial government can be permanent beside the American Republic, no longer liable, since the abolition of slavery, to be distracted by sectional dissensions. The States that seceded will soon, in some way, be restored to their rights and franchises in the Union, forming not the least patriotic portion of the American people; the negro question will be settled, or settle itself, as is most likely, by the melting away of the negro population before the influx of white laborers; all traces of the late contest in a very few years will be wiped out, the national debt paid, or greatly reduced, and the prosperity and strength of the Republic be greater than ever. Its moral force will sweep away every imperial throne on the continent, without any effort or action on the part of the government. There can be no stable government in Mexico till every trace of the ecclesiastical policy established by the Council of the Indies is obliterated, and the church placed there on the same footing as in the United States; and that can hardly be done without annexation. Maximilian cannot divest the church of her temporal possessions, and place Protestants and Catholics on the same footing, without offending the present church party and deeply injuring religion, and that too without winning the confidence of the republican party. In all Spanish and Portuguese America the relations between the church and state are abnormal, and exceedingly hurtful to both. Religion is in a wretched condition, and politics in a worse condition still. There is no effectual remedy for either but in religious freedom, now impracticable, and to be rendered practicable by no European intervention, for that subjects religion to the state, the very source of the evils that now exist, instead of emancipating it from the state, and leaving it to act according to its own constitution and laws, as under the American system.

But the American people need not trouble themselves about their exterior expansion. That will come of itself as fast as desirable. Let them devote their attention to their internal destiny, to the realization of their mission within, and they will gradually see the whole continent coming under their system, forming one grand nation, a really catholic nation, great, glorious, and free.

Index